W9-AFM-109

The Prose of Life

The Prose of Life

Russian Women Writers from Khrushchev to Putin

Benjamin M. Sutcliffe

THE UNIVERSITY OF WISCONSIN PRESS

Publication of this volume has been made
possible, in part, through support from the
ANDREW W. MELLON FOUNDATION.

The University of Wisconsin Press
1930 Monroe Street, 3rd Floor
Madison, Wisconsin 53711-2059

www.wisc.edu/wisconsinpress/

3 Henrietta Street
London WC2E 8LU, England

5   4   3   2   1

Printed in the United States of America

Library of Congress Cataloging-in-Publication Data
Sutcliffe, Benjamin M.
The prose of life : Russian women writers from Khrushchev to Putin /
Benjamin M. Sutcliffe.
   p.   cm.
Includes bibliographical references and index.
ISBN 978-0-299-23204-7 (pbk.: alk. paper)
ISBN 978-0-299-23203-0 (e-book)
   1. Russian prose literature—Women authors—History and criticism.
2. Women authors, Russian—20th century—Biography.   3. Women authors,
Russian—21st century—Biography.   4. Home in literature.   I. Title.
PG2997.S88   2009
891.78´4408099287—dc22
[B]
2008039543

For

LENA

Contents

Acknowledgments

The idea for this book first arose as a result of my fortuitous meeting with author Marina Kulakova, who was living in Nizhny Novgorod at the time, where I was teaching English. In the cold spring of 1997 Marina's conversations with me sparked my interest in connections between Russian women's writing and the deceptively banal realm of *byt*. The following fall I began my graduate studies at the University of Pittsburgh with a vague yet persistent desire to investigate this topic.

In Pittsburgh Bozenna Goscilo and Chris Metil welcomed me with their hospitality, humor, and humanity. The staff of Hillman Library—in particular Beth Perrier and her colleagues in the interlibrary loan division—made the first phases of this project much easier than it might have been. I am also indebted to Adam Zagelbaum, a good friend since the humid days of 1989, for procuring hard-to-find articles and sending them across two continents. In a similar vein, I salute the untiring efforts of the online Slavic Reference Service at the University of Illinois at Urbana-Champaign. My fellow students in the Department of Slavic Languages and Literatures (1997–2004) provided timely distraction and support. I thank Jerry McCausland for technical expertise and Seth Graham, Tim Schlak, Irina Makoveeva, and Ol'ga Karpushina for many long evenings of stimulating conversation. Matt Bulow—housemate, honorary Slavist, and aficionado of *Apocalypse Now*—helped me keep things in perspective.

This project first took shape as a doctoral dissertation, where I benefited from the conscientious advice of David Birnbaum,

ix

Nancy Condee, and Nancy Glazener. Exemplifying what it means to be a mentor, my advisor, the inimitable Helena Goscilo, supported me both morally and intellectually not only during the dissertation process but throughout my graduate career. In addition to being indebted to her for excellent white wine and square meals, I profited from her practical common sense.

Several trips to Russia contributed to the writing and research for this book. During my 2002–3 dissertation research in Moscow, Georgii Dragunov, Nadia Azhgikhina, Lena Trofimova, Marina Kulakova, Tania Rovenskaia, and Ol'ga Vainshtein helped me with research-related issues and patiently indulged my linguistic shortcomings. I am grateful to the staff of the INION Library, who displayed a high degree of professionalism under difficult conditions. In numerous ways Suzanne Daly-Kupriyanov and Leigh Anderson helped make this year much more pleasant. The staff of the Russian State Library and its Department of Dissertations and Newspapers helped me locate a number of unique scholarly items during my 2005 and 2006 research trips to Moscow.

My colleagues at Miami University were understanding and accommodating as I moved from dissertation to book project. Margaret Ziolkowski, in the Department of German, Russian, and East Asian Languages, was generous with her time and advice. Thanks are also due to Dan Meyers and Steve Sauer for computer help and Indian food. Karen Dawisha, Scott Kenworthy, Gulnaz Sharafutdinova, and Venelin Ganev at the Havighurst Center for Russian and Post-Soviet Studies made the beginning of my career at Miami University memorable, whether in Ohio or while crossing the Chinese-Kyrgyz border. Members of the Dadada Group—Vitaly Chernetsky, Karen Eng, Nicole Thesz, and Mila Ganeva—provided numerous valuable comments on early drafts of the introduction and chapter 1.

Gwen Walker, Michel Hogue, and Sheila Moermond at the University of Wisconsin Press, as well as copyeditor Henry Krawitz, ensured that this project would find a receptive audience. Natasha Kolchevska and Adele Marie Barker made an impressive number of helpful and insightful comments, as did Edith Clowes.

My family provided support and sanity as I meandered from coursework to dissertation to the promised land of the book manuscript. M.J. Sutcliffe in St. Petersburg, Florida, Matt Sutcliffe and Christine Hatcher in Seattle, and Claud Sutcliffe, Leilani and Kukui Sutcliffe, and Brigid Mulloy in Hawai'i (and beyond) have been a source of strength during the many years I have spent investigating Russian women's writing. I am also grateful to Ed Williams and Massey Sutcliffe for help with the rituals of academe. My relatives in Moscow—Elena Iurev'na Khmeleva, Aleksandr Alekseevich Khmelev, and Anton Khmelev—provided me with hot soup and wool socks, and accompanied me on trips to feed the squirrels.

Dissertation research in 2002–3 was made possible thanks to the support of a Foreign Language Area Studies Award (Title VI) and an Andrew W. Mellon Predoctoral Fellowship from the University of Pittsburgh. Portions of this study relating to post-Soviet literature evolved from materials gathered while I was a Research Scholar in 2000 with the American Councils for International Education (Title VIII). Likewise, some of the sources relating to women's prose were collected in 1998 thanks to a grant from the Czechoslovak Nationality Room (Stanley Prostrednik Award). Summer research in Moscow during 2005 and 2006 was funded by Miami University's Summer Research Grant for New Tenure-Track Faculty, College of Arts and Sciences, and the Philip and Elaina Hampton Fund for Faculty International Initiatives. The above organizations and individuals are in no way responsible for any shortcomings in the present book.

Portions of chapters 2 and 3 previously appeared in *Toronto Slavic Quarterly* 3 (winter 2003) and *Soviet and Post-Soviet Review* 33, no. 1 (2005).

This book is dedicated to my wife, Lena, who has given new meaning to our life.

The Prose of Life

Introduction
Engendering *Byt* in Soviet Culture

Opposed to [the] creative urge toward a transformed future is the stabilizing force of an immutable present, overlaid . . . by a stagnating slime, which stifles life in its tight, hard mold. The Russian name for this element is *byt*.

Roman Jakobson

We must remember that for women the closed circle of *byt*, the circle of hell, is also the circle of life, offering a never-ending journey.

Ne pomniashchaia zla (She Who Remembers No Evil)

In 1962, during Nikita Khrushchev's tentative Thaw reforms, two authors sent their manuscripts to Aleksandr Tvardovskii, the daring editor of the liberal journal *Novyi mir*.[1] One had written a scathing fictional depiction of dictator Joseph Stalin's prison system; the other had penned a novel depicting the fate of a Jewish intellectual family in the Soviet Union. Tvardovskii published the account of the labor camps—making Aleksandr Solzhenitsyn famous worldwide—while giving instructions that the manuscript sent by I. Grekova be locked in a safe but that the journal editor should keep in contact with the talented writer. Tvardovskii's decision was not only caused by the novel's scathing depiction of Soviet anti-Semitism. A decade later another female author, Liudmila Petrushevskaia, sent her stories to *Novyi*

3

mir and received a similarly cautious response from Tvardovskii's successor, namely, that although the prose was engaging,
the stories were not publishable.[2] Why did *Novyi mir* believe
these authors' works to be more inflammatory than the first major
exposé of the gulag? Both Grekova and Petrushevskaia focused
on the daily lives of Soviet women. The key to the editors' decisions lies in Russian culture's enduring uneasiness concerning
the everyday and female experiences, and how these two combine in fictional form. While Solzhenitsyn, with the approval of
Khrushchev, revealed the horrific conditions of the vast prison
camp system, Grekova and the young Petrushevskaia had produced more unsettling assessments of Soviet reality by depicting
the quotidian of decidedly apolitical women.

    Gender and *byt* (everyday life) were inherited problems in late
Soviet culture. Functioning as two halves of an equation, they suggested that women are inclined toward domesticity, childcare,
and the endless minutiae needed to support a family, constituting
a major portion of the quotidian.[3] In this book I examine how female prose authors from the 1960s to the 2000s used everyday life
first as an arena for discussing selected problems (1960–84) and
then moved from this tentative description to a more encompassing and damning assessment of how men's and women's lives
differ (1985–91). After 1991 female writers depicted the problems
of women's daily life from a markedly artistic viewpoint. Six
authors exemplify this shift: Natal'ia Baranskaia, I. Grekova (the
pseudonym of mathematician Elena Venttsel'), Liudmila Petrushevskaia, Tat'iana Tolstaia, Svetlana Vasilenko, and Liudmila
Ulitskaia. In the 1990s nine women's anthologies, along with the
writing of Petrushevskaia and Tolstaia, made women's prose an
undeniable yet controversial part of the cultural landscape. Female authors appropriated everyday life as a venue for commenting on often overlooked "women's" issues, even as the nature of
byt itself drastically changed before and after the collapse of the
Soviet Union.

The Gender of Everyday Life in Russian Culture

The everyday is a problematic concept that Russian culture consistently and insistently links to women. *Byt* not only refers to

daily life but also to a corrosive banality threatening the higher aspirations of *bytie* (spiritual or intellectual life)—a quality that distinguishes *byt* from more optimistic Western conceptions of the quotidian. Vladimir Nabokov connects *byt* to *poshlost'*, the soul-killing realm of the material, crass, and insensitive. Female tasks (caring for others, maintaining a household) are a part of *byt*, and the negative adjectives connoting the quotidian echo the alleged attributes of women's lives in Russian culture: petty, small-scale, mundane, exhausting, repetitive.[4]

The myriad problems women confront reappear daily as a new set of crises, effectively erasing previous accomplishments. The resulting ateleological and small-scale struggle sharply differs from traditional "male" activities and *bytie*. Masculine actions often involve sweeping claims to permanent change, whether through philosophical generalizations or the USSR's doomed attempt to build a Marxist utopia. The gender of *byt*, however, is feminine.[5]

Distinctions between masculine and feminine were evident in Soviet iconography, which was dominated by robust builders of communism creating cities or attempting to redirect the flow of rivers—all within the larger project of forging a new civilization. While the male was proactive in culture, the female was assumed to be reactive. Women were relegated either to supporting male-mandated efforts or coping with the effects of state edicts on everyday life.[6]

The implied passivity of reaction exists alongside a problematic corporeality (*telesnost'*). Both Russians and Westerners deem women's activity more physical than mental, unworthy owing to its reduced scale, ephemeral nature, and constricted existence within the home as marked space. Eve Sedgwick has identified a key result of this association: the gendered equation of man/woman as "separate yet equal" becomes the subordination of the female by the male. This inequality was abundantly evident in the Soviet quotidian, which revealed the USSR's much-vaunted gender egalitarianism to be as illusory as its citizens' political freedoms. Even when the state wished to improve the status of women, assumptions that *byt* was female and derivative were impediments.[7]

Russian culture sees the feminine and everyday as secondary yet crucial.[8] The intelligentsia, the group that produced almost all the women authors discussed in this study, envisions *byt* as a conduit to *bytie*, the realm of the spiritual and intellectual. Two trends clarify Russian intellectuals' complicated relations to daily life. First, early in its history the intelligentsia as "bearers of consciousness" became synonymous with the Enlightenment in its metaphorical and historical sense. Bringing the quintessential European culture of rationality to post-medieval Russia was the prerogative and responsibility of the intelligentsia. What resulted was a mandate to educate, which in turn presumed an object neither enlightened nor conscious: the common people (*narod*), typified by the "backward" peasant woman. The more pessimistic intellectuals became over Russia's myriad problems, the further they diverged from the *narod* and its quotidian existence. Before, during, and after the USSR the Russian intelligentsia tried to reconcile *byt* and *bytie*.[9]

It is also important to realize that the intelligentsia existed in a nearly constant state of crisis during the Soviet era. Vera Dunham believes that this uncertainty and change increased demand for domesticity, a key part of *byt*. Sof'ia Petrovna, the title character in Lidiia Chukovskaia's novel (written 1939–40) attempts to preserve a normal home during the Stalinist terror, while several years later state images of heroic mothers characterized women's activities as a humble "second front" contributing to the male military victory over Nazi Germany. In both contexts *byt* is female and marginal yet essential. This subordinate/crucial status was especially pronounced during the Thaw (1953–68) and its emphasis on private life, which built on the government's earlier ambivalent representation of women's efforts in *byt*.[10]

Stalin's successors during the Khrushchev era and more conservative Stagnation (1969–84) periods saw women's quotidian existences as complementing collective-oriented public life. From this viewpoint female success depended on an allegedly innate ability to tend to what Barbara Heldt succinctly terms the "little things" around the home.[11] Men, the dominant Soviet logic continued, were responsible for great events and universalizing pronouncements. Writing about English literature, Sandra Gilbert and Susan Gubar make the analogous contention that the overlapping spaces of home and private life—central to both the quotidian and contemporary conceptions of the individual— delineate woman as man's fallible foil, prone to circular activity, limited in "natural" talents to fornication and procreation. These actions are invisible because of their very ordinariness. Women nevertheless are the prime movers of modernity as they maintain an undervalued yet key domestic arena within which the individual develops.[12] Both female activities and *byt* as their temporal context chronically escape notice: the everyday is omnipresent yet unnoticed. The female writers I examine here found these traits to be both a blessing and a curse when they appropriated the quotidian as a venue for discussing women's lives.

Envisioning the Quotidian: Ambivalence and Apocalypse

Despite the similar gendered nuances that have accrued over the centuries, the Russian conception of *byt* significantly differs from its Western counterparts. The European quotidian is an arena for escape from control (particularly that of the state), where individual choice redeems tedious materiality. For Michel de Certeau decisions in the European everyday are an opportunity for small-scale resistance and transgression, two possibilities important to Russians regardless of gender. Differentiating "strategies" from "tactics," de Certeau perceives the latter as a tool for the less powerful. A "tactic insinuates itself into the other's place, fragmentarily. . . . [A] tactic depends on time—it is always on the watch for opportunities that must be seized 'on the wing.'"[13] The quotidian helps those who can exploit it in their struggles against the more powerful.

The connection between daily life and resistance is not new. For Western modernism daily life had a woman's face, which Andreas Huyssen describes as images of crowded cities, industrialized female workforces, and social unrest. As with de Certeau's description, in this context disorder is more liberating than threatening. Maurice Blanchot elaborates: "The everyday must be thought [of] as the suspect (and the oblique) that always escapes the clear decision of the law, even when the law seeks, by suspicion, to track down every indeterminate manner of being."[14] This formulation, while too dramatic for the French culture to which it referred, fits the Stalinist era (1928–53), which purged personal life (*lichnaia zhizn'*) of its suspect counterpart, individual life (*chastnaia zhizn'*). This strategy of the 1930s and 1940s reflected the tautological reasoning of totalitarianism: the state criminalizes the quotidian, which in turn becomes the locus for future transgression as perceived by the ever-watchful state.[15]

For Western intellectuals everyday life harbored the potential for escape from control. In the 1960s and 1970s the Birmingham School and the advent of cultural studies canonized the contemporary quotidian as a refreshingly interdisciplinary area for study. Beginning in the 1980s, Western scholars of gender, race, and a bevy of related fields saw studies of everyday life as an alternative to the restrictions of normative history.[16]

Unlike in the West, Russian scholarship binding *byt* to any type of resistance dates from the 1990s. Soviet political strictures only partially explain this divergence. More fundamentally, the intelligentsia saw—and continues to see—the everyday as a barrier to *bytie*. This line of reasoning, which authors such as Ulitskaia have challenged, assumes that the quotidian frustrates meaningful human endeavors: either agency is abandoned to a force beyond the individual's control (war, political repression) or petty problems hinder higher aspirations.

According to this logic, daily life cannot promote independence; at best it is a physical counterpart to the world of ideas (*bytie*). Iurii Lotman's key definition of *byt* upholds this reasoning and yields a series of interesting suppositions. "*Byt* is the ordinary flow of life in its real and practical forms. It is the things that surround us, our habits and everyday behavior. *Byt* surrounds us like air and, like air, is only noticed when it is spoiled or in short supply. We notice the peculiarities of others' *byt*, but our own escapes us—we are inclined to consider it 'just life,' the natural norm of practical existence [*bytie*]. *Byt* is thus always located in the realm of practice; it is above all the world of things."[17]

Byt is the world of the mundane made invisible by unimportance, omnipresence, and its subordination to the symbolic cosmos of *bytie*. The gap between *byt* and *bytie* reiterates the Eastern Orthodox separation of body and soul and their gendered equivalents, female and male. This dichotomy is analogous to the modernist distinction between masculine high and female mass culture, a division that Huyssen attacks.[18] The parallel conceptions of modernism and theology underscore the twentieth century's dependence on the same conservative thinking it tried to evade: polarization as worldview shaped modernism, Orthodoxy, and the Soviet scientific atheism that attempted to replace it.

The quotidian is defined by what is not, namely, the spiritual and intellectual realm. For Stephen Hutchings this juxtaposition distinguishes Russia's "cultural *binarism*" from European "philosophical *dualism*." Because Russian culture is built on binaries, it cannot contain a neutral space, which would be the equivalent of a moral vacuum.[19] Unlike in the West, daily life cannot be impartial. There is no middle ground, whether between *bytie* and *byt*, male and female, or good and evil. Indeed, the conception of neutrality as a threat guided critical assessments of women authors' depictions of *byt*, as attacks on the "amoral" everyday in Baranskaia's and Grekova's prose showed.

As Hutchings and Huyssen argue, the early twentieth century provided some of the most serious attacks on the everyday. Roman Jakobson, never doubting that *byt* is the enemy of civilization, makes explicit those concerns embedded in Lotman's later and more balanced assessment of the quotidian. Discussing the failure of the futurist and acmeist poets to remake Russian culture, Jakobson identifies their foe as the "stabilizing force of an immutable present, overlaid, as this present is, by a stagnating slime, which stifles life in its tight, hard mold. The Russian name for this element is *byt*." Only slightly overstating this concept's etymological and cultural uniqueness, he claims that "in the European collective consciousness there is no concept of such a force as might oppose and break down the established norms of life."[20] Equating *byt* with immobility and a threat to meaning takes on additional significance when one remembers that the quotidian is the realm of women, needed to continue Russian civilization yet hindering *bytie* and the "established norms of life."

Jakobson's dire formulation negates the utopian rebelliousness implicit in Blanchot's axiom that everyday life invigorates through chaos. *Byt*, to use a key Stalinist verb, wrecks organized efforts to change existence and even sabotages previous progress. Both conceptions, however, assume that everyday life is what a culture deems commonplace. This shared basis raises a key problem, namely, typicality (*tipichnost'*) as the quotidian's ability to point to its own essence. Often typicality is an image or character symbolizing the ethos of an era irrespective of whether the image is actually "average" in a statistical sense. Such a conception continues a pattern central to nineteenth-century Russian realism, when the "superfluous man" was an ideological type who critiqued the educated Russians' inability to change society. This type mutated during Stalinist socialist realism, producing the messianic positive hero. Like his predecessor, this (usually male) character supposedly reflects the "typical" essence of his age. The positive hero, however, must safeguard the radiant future, not perpetuate the doubt and ennui of his negative counterpart in critical realism.[21]

Despite holding diametrically opposing views, Soviet dissident Andrei Siniavskii and nineteenth-century radical Nikolai Dobroliubov both mined the quotidian for ideological meaning. Digging beneath the literary image of *byt,* they tried to identify and transform the typical as the essence of Russian culture. Siniavskii critiqued the immorality he espied in Soviet *byt,* an everydayness whose principles were shaped by Dobroliubov and the earlier critic's own disgust at the corrupting apathy of the tsarist quotidian. Siniavskii and Dobroliubov exemplify their respective centuries' attempts to read literature as social consciousness, implying a depiction of the quotidian that first diagnoses and then cures social ills. Not surprisingly, these efforts failed. By its very nature the quotidian frustrates final answers, theoretical generalizations, and universalizing prescriptions endorsed by those intellectuals Gary Saul Morson sardonically labels "semiotic totalitarians."[22] *Byt* resists attempts to identity its essence. This intractability complicates appropriation by women authors, some of whom perpetuated the failed efforts of Siniavskii and Dobroliubov but (as I explain in chapter 1) with a different agenda.

The derivative connotations of female and quotidian in Russian culture complement each other. Long considered devoid of serious talent, women are consigned to *byt* as an ontological dead zone where materiality has vanquished the reason and consciousness the intelligentsia deifies. Because the female purportedly lacks great mental potential, critics assume her to be particularly vulnerable to the twin phantoms haunting literary representations of *byt*: *poshlost'* and *grafomanstvo* (bad writing).[23]

Echoing Nabokov, Svetlana Boym describes *poshlost'* as "the

Russian version of banality, with a characteristic national flavoring of metaphysics and high morality, and a peculiar conjunction of the sexual and spiritual."[24] In her view, combining opposites threatens the sound esthetic judgment traditionally claimed by the intelligentsia. *Grafomanstvo*, a compulsive desire to express oneself in (low-quality) writing, is to literature what *poshlost'* is to the intelligentsia's sense of taste: an anti-esthetic potentially contaminating its antipode. Both labels often mask other intentions. The critic's explicit attack may employ a phrase (e.g., *obyvatel'*) conflating suspect morality and dubious taste, but the signified transgression is not using literature as moral instruction.

This hostility derives from worries over threats to high culture: *poshlost'* and *grafomanstvo*, critics surmise, can reduce art to unintended farce as the ethical force of the written word degenerates into meaningless scribbling. What results is the victory of *telesnost'* (the physical, *byt*) over *ideinost'* (the ideational, *bytie*). *Poshlost'* and *grafomanstvo* are anathema to the intelligentsia's maxim that the mental/spiritual triumphs over adverse material conditions. This belief is paramount in the post-Soviet era precisely because intellectuals have discovered their redundancy in the new era of commercialization and "low" genres.

Given this long-standing hostility to daily life, Lotman's investigations of *byt* in general and its neutrality in particular were truly groundbreaking. Due to his own intellectual interests and Soviet censorship, however, Lotman's work examined the already distant quotidian of the eighteenth and early nineteenth centuries: this everydayness was less a living force than a collection of museum pieces. Lotman and his colleagues at the Tartu School nonetheless created a valuable precedent for Russian studies of private life, the quotidian, and gender in the 1980s and 1990s. Subsequent investigators focused on the Soviet period, itself now doomed to the "enormous condescension" E. P. Thompson laments in history's treatment of events.[25] In the first post-Soviet decades, translations of Western theorists such as Michel Foucault and an upsurge in Russian interdisciplinary research made cultural studies (and analysis of the everyday) more familiar to academics in the former USSR.

Beginning in the 1980s Western Slavists turned their attention to *byt*. Their new interest arose from the expanding field of cultural studies and a desire to move beyond Cold War investigations with their "top-down" analyses of the *nomenklatura*. This move often entailed revisionist critiques of the Soviet state's previously posited monolithic character. Indeed, scholars showed how everyday life made distinctions between the personal and political counterproductive and often impossible. The shift in analysis from policy to the quotidian likewise helped bring women's experiences out from under the long shadow of Kremlinology, where they had been "hidden in plain view."[26]

These new studies envisioned *byt* less as a neutral space than as a network of signs indicating how the everyday reflects and perpetuates cultural anxieties and the sociopolitical factors creating them. The ordinariness that Nabokov scorns and Jakobson fears led to myriad discoveries for scholars, where each detail within the quotidian hints at the *bytie* Russian culture prizes. Reevaluating *byt* brings forth its own problems, as Morson suggests in critiquing the urge of "semiotic totalitarians" to construct cultural coherence from the everyday's scattered parts. The recent upsurge of interest in everyday life has scholars negotiating a careful path between the Scylla of neglect and the Charybdis of totalizing interpretation. The present study is indebted to both recent and pioneering discussions of everyday life, whose precedents now permit an investigation of how women's prose developed around *byt*.

Gender and Everyday Life in Soviet Culture

Daily life's banal facade hides a host of cultural complexities. As Joan Scott suggests, one of the most important of these is how the everyday acts as the arena within which men and women experience gender. This is especially true in Russia, with its tendency to use female experience as shorthand for the nation's perceived backwardness and alterity in the face of European modernity.[27] Women's lives symbolized the antithesis of Western progress and, later, the Marxist-Leninist script for history.

Soviet policy had a paradoxical and unfulfilling relationship with *byt*. Following the lead of the prerevolutionary intelligentsia, the victorious Bolsheviks despised the everyday as a petty frustration foiling ideational attempts to create a new society. The government, however, also recognized daily life as the key battlefield of what Sheila Fitzpatrick has famously termed the "cultural front."[28] The quotidian was an irksome indication of the revolution's unfinished agenda. Bolshevik attempts to create communal living and radical poet Vladimir Maiakovskii's 1920s polemic against *poshlost'* signaled the fact that daily life imperiled the Soviet project as much as the Whites did. *Byt* also reflected more elemental struggles with materiality—famine, a decaying infrastructure, shortages of goods—hindering the march toward communism. However, unlike the Civil War or a Five-Year Plan, by its very nature the everyday contained what Mikhail Bakhtin deems a chronic "inconclusiveness" that denies closure or any attempt to declare victory over *byt*.[29]

The Bolsheviks feared that *byt* contaminated female citizens, leading to a politicized association of "backward" females with an equally unenlightened quotidian. The decade after 1917 emphasized the liberation of women from the old *byt*. Although Stalinism for its part promoted women's industrial labor, it supported the patriarchal family as the basic unit of society by limiting divorce and criminalizing abortion. At the same time, the state literally and figuratively policed the private sphere to secure a quotidian that, not properly subdued during the 1920s, now needed to be purged. While *byt* was still far from being a priority, it fell under the state's panoptic gaze. This sort of attempt to watch over the everyday recalls Blanchot's protests against the state's relation to a quotidian it distrusts in terms of an "inexhaustible, irrecusable, always unfinished daily that always escapes forms or structures (particularly those of political society: bureaucracy, the wheels of government, parties)."[30] The most successful Soviet attempt to break down the boundaries between public and private was the communal apartment (*kommunalka*), with its ubiquitous and inquisitive neighbors. This pragmatic approach to managing (but never solving) the enduring Soviet housing crisis looms large in the fiction of women writers well into the 1990s.

After the Soviet defeat of Nazi Germany in 1945, attempts to harness women and their meddlesome *byt* to the cause of postwar recovery coexisted with the validation of female citizens as a "body politic" that literally and figuratively sustained Soviet culture.[31] Film and fiction imagined personal life as a cozy, feminized version of the masculine-dominated public sphere. The era lauded visible heroines, yet their primary function was to stand at the side of even more noble male heroes (including the Father of the Peoples himself). In an ironic revision of base-superstructure theory, the Stalinist woman supported the more visible edifice of male civilization as well as physically and symbolically reproducing it.

Such an arrangement did not promote the sexual equality ideologues and enthusiasts ascribed to the building of communism. Postwar society emphasized the quotidian as deserved comfort for the victorious male veteran, a nest feathered by an attentive housewife. This Soviet myth operated against a reality of continued shortages of goods and widespread hunger, which meant that work was a large part of most women's identity, as the state reluctantly acknowledged when lauding the achievements of the USSR's numerous single mothers and widows.[32]

Stalinist recognition of women's efforts in industrialization and defeating the Nazis created a crucial precedent for extending this attention to their personal lives as well. However, during the Thaw such works as Vera Panova's "Mal'chik i devochka" (A Boy and a Girl, 1960), as well as the early stories of Baranskaia and Grekova, revealed *byt* to be far less glorious than the Stalinist world of epic deeds. Although the previous era had assumed harmonious relations between the conjoined opposites public/private and man/woman, Alexander Prokhorov and Josephine Woll suggest that the Thaw's increased scrutiny of private life discarded this assumption as one more instance of socialist realist varnishing.[33]

The state had not lost interest in managing private life. Oleg Kharkhordin and Susan Reid chart a Foucauldian shift from Stalinist direct intervention (purges and forced collectivization) to subtler control (advice manuals; more advertisements targeting women). Such a move is clear in publications such as the admonitory brochure *Ne veselo byt' meshchaninom!* (It's No Fun Being a Philistine!, 1965), where "the . . . writer hotly and passionately exposes [*oblichaet*] philistinism and philistines, their pitiful little joys and their sad lives."[34] The presence of a preeminent verb of the Stalinist purges ("exposes") and publication by the Political Literature Publishing House imply that the private still concerned the state.

The 1960s prose of Grekova and Baranskaia both benefited and suffered from its focus on the quotidian.[35] Depictions of *byt* and its discontents often coincided with national campaigns against alcoholism and other vices, a happenstance that increased the likelihood of publishing such "trifling" subject matter. These authors employed literature as a venue for critiquing social ills while also establishing *byt* as a serious issue.[36] However, until the late 1980s authorities had to carefully control such discussions, as Grekova and Petrushevskaia discovered when *Novyi mir* reluctantly refused to publish them.

Postwar expectations for material comfort, plus the Thaw's somewhat wider possibilities for critiquing *byt*'s shortcomings, provoked a reevaluation of the everyday yet reaffirmed its status as a female realm. It is inaccurate to suggest that the era rehabilitated *byt*. As Dunham indicates, Stalinism never condemned the everyday per se, but it did proscribe discussion of darker aspects of the female quotidian, such as rape, adultery, and depression.[37] The Thaw culture's reinvestment in private life was guarded and circumscribed, sometimes revealing just as much by silence as by description (e.g., the non-topic of domestic violence in Baranskaia's prose). Women writers imitated and influenced a tendency selectively to document *byt*, dividing the post-Stalinist everyday into varying layers of accessibility and acceptability. For instance, Baranskaia's discussion of male alcoholism was permissible, but a description of its female counterpart was not.[38]

Focusing on the private also narrowed the angle through which Russians saw their culture. Moving from the Stalinist panorama to the Thaw's close-up revealed the cracks in the previously posited monolithic unity of everyday life. As Bakhtin has demonstrated, proximity to the subject of representation profanes the sacred, exposes humorous flaws, and promotes fearlessness. This new scrutiny, however, was less comic than weary and somber: much post-Stalinist attention to the everyday dealt with reconstituting families shattered by war.[39]

Mothers and wives were urged to rationalize daily life, which could involve a new, "modern" look for the apartment or better time management for housework. Outside the home, decreased female university enrollment from 1950 to 1963 meant that more women found themselves occupying lower-paying positions. During the three decades after Stalinism, some columnists argued that women brought upon themselves the "double burden" of job and housework by futilely attempting to move from the domestic to the social sphere. This retrograde notion implied that such an essentially "unnatural" shift, alongside the incorrigibly weak male character, caused women to overextend themselves. At the same time, as Lynne Attwood points out, women rarely entered management and, owing to the high number of unskilled female laborers, received salaries less than two thirds those of men.[40]

During Stagnation sociologists, journalists, and authors warned of demographic trends threatening to make ethnic Russians a minority in the USSR. Within the racist overtones of this discussion, Baranskaia's novella *Nedelia kak nedelia* (A Week Like Any Other, 1969) alluded to the reasons educated urban women had only one child, which included lack of meaningful state support, irresponsible husbands, and the stresses of *byt*. Female citizens had little access to reliable reproductive information or sex education materials despite the connections between lack of sexual knowledge and the divorces hindering birthrates.[41]

Unsurprisingly, the vicissitudes of women's daily lives were more often ascribed to the citizen-mother than to the government allegedly supporting her. In addition to falling birthrates, critics maintained, single mothers and female-dominated school staff were mollycoddling (male) children.[42] This threat to gender stability, along with smaller ethnic Russian families, augured a change in the literal and metaphorical makeup of Soviet society. A backlash against the perceived blurring of male/female roles shows the close connection between gender and stability in Russian culture and its Soviet incarnation. These axiomatic distinctions formed a set of fundamental binary oppositions, with Marxist-Leninist rhetoric (and its claim to gender equality) a superficial afterthought. While surface ideologies changed during and after de-Stalinization, a conservative deep structure prescribed rigid and enduring gender differences.[43]

The 1968 invasion of Czechoslovakia, which shattered the illusions of the liberal intelligentsia, ended the Thaw in Russian culture. After this watershed, domesticity implied opposition to an official realm marred by cynicism and the inertia that would later give the era of Stagnation its name. Public life became synonymous with corruption and opportunism, while the intelligentsia perpetuated the myth of a private world divorced from such spiritual corrosion. Intellectuals viewed the home and one's community of friends as a safe zone suitable for expressing thoughts and emotions contrary to those promoted by the state.[44] Women, however, had little time for reflection. The much-maligned lines, primitive consumer technology, and shortages of goods—especially outside Moscow and Leningrad—continued to make maintaining a home difficult. Another problem involving the Russian males' notorious distaste for housework was frequently debated in the media and on the pages of women's fiction.[45]

With the onset of perestroika (1985–91) authors as dissimilar as the conservative village writer Valentin Rasputin and ironic feminist Nina Gorlanova warned that *byt* was changing from noisome wasteland to landscape of apocalypse. After the onset of Mikhail Gorbachev's unpopular economic reforms, Soviets wearied by exacerbated shortages of goods, job losses, and increasing disenchantment with politics found little respite in the private sphere. Glasnost films such as Vasilii Pichul's *Malen'kaia Vera* (Little Vera, 1988) envisioned *byt* as a cesspool of sex, drinking, and despair.

While Thaw and Stagnation established the private and the everyday as a legitimate topic for representation, perestroika displayed the frequently horrific nature of *byt* to a shocked public. Petrushevskaia proved to be the author most adept at dismantling the distinctions between the hidden and the exposed in the self's interactions with others.[46] With a maniacal obsession rivaling that of her characters, she exposed *byt*'s seamy side and shattered the sacrosanct myth of the noble intellectual.

Previous decades had pointed to the possibility of private life's corruption by exposure to the morally bankrupt public arena. Now, however, women authors such as Elena Tarasova and Marina Karpova illuminated the darkest recesses of *lichnaia* and *chastnaia zhizn'* even as the press highlighted the excesses of the political sphere during Stalinism, Thaw, and Stagnation. Little escaped the vigilance of the public gaze; perestroika searched for meaning through exposure, scandal, and polemic.

This newly liberated opinion restricted the image of the female, partially in response to Gorbachev urging women to return to the home. At the same time pornography, marketed along Western lines, flooded into the USSR, objectifying women. Retrograde gender roles replaced an increasingly unappealing Marxism-Leninism, a shift in allegiances Tat'iana Klimenkova links to women's gradual exclusion from public life.[47] As was the case during the Thaw, a return to conservative norms for female citizens was one response to massive cultural changes.

Beginning in the late 1980s the West—particularly the United States—saturated Russia with new consumer goods. Beth Holmgren accurately notes that the subsequent backlash against imported products and ideas extended to Russians' negative conception of feminism, which had gained a tentative foothold in academic circles during the early 1990s.[48] Theory had little impact on everyday life and popular culture. From the standpoint of gender, perestroika was less a step forward than a quick leap backward to polarized images of women as either mistress or wife. The era's vaunted openness and restructuring produced few positive gains for female Soviet citizens.

Post-Soviet culture continued to link *byt* with both women and catastrophic change. Troped as either Mother Russia or a demanding Western-style consumer, woman as symbol was once again abstracted as state and advertisers removed her from everyday problems. This split image suggested that the female, the purported bedrock of Russian culture, was in fact a mutable entity that could produce clichéd images of the chaste Russian maiden or the scandalmongers dominating talk shows. For female citizens the double burden of career and household worsened due to high prices, reduced social services, and increased unemployment disproportionately affecting women and the intelligentsia. Post-Soviet mores encouraged women's return to the home, while economic hardship made it impossible for them to remain without work. Apart from a set of undesirable images (e.g., woman as sexual plaything), the female was now virtually invisible in public discourse.[49]

The transition to a market economy radically altered the position of both female and male authors. Beginning in the early 1990s, a fundamental shift from high/elite to low/popular literature signaled the lowered priority of intellectual culture. *Byt*— Lotman's cosmos of common objects—now appeared in advertisements, mystery novels, and talk shows targeting a broader spectrum of the population. This marketing of the quotidian did not focus increased attention on women's issues. The search for a new national identity, which emphasized such large-scale issues as economic collapse and the wars in Chechnya, elided women's everyday concerns.

The success of Ulitskaia, Vasilenko, and other writers, however, made women's prose a recognized part of intellectual culture even as female authors (e.g., Aleksandra Marinina, Dar'ia Dontsova, and Tat'iana Ustinova) dominated the booming mystery genre. The rich variety of styles and content in post-Soviet women's writing justifies the hope that a broadened concept of women in literature may become an enduring part of Russian culture.[50] The popularity of women's prose suggested that its humanistic image of *byt* resonated with readers and that everyday life continued to preoccupy the Russian consciousness.

Documentation, *Byt*, and Literature: The Allure of the Real

In the 1960s an old tendency in Russian literature reemerged under a new label: documentation. This amorphous continuum, variously known in the West as "life writing" or historical fiction, encompasses autobiography at one end and truth-oriented fiction at the other. In Russian culture literary documentation has had several pseudonyms: "historicism," "documentalism," and "literature of fact." As Jane Harris indicates in her fine essay on Russian autobiography, Soviet critics saw this trend toward documentation as a healthy culture admiring its reassuring reflection in literary form. However, even a cursory glance at *byt*, gender, or twentieth-century history reveals this attitude to be incorrect and its manifestation in writing to be no less problematic.

Critics nevertheless united behind the appeal of fact to contemporary prose, espying this motivation in authors as diverse
as the ambivalent novelist Iurii Trifonov and the multitude of
writers lauding Soviet industrialization. Both contemporary reality and key historical events (particularly the Civil War and the
defeat of the Nazis) were favorite topics. While some argued for
"documentalism" as the purview of traditional nonfiction (autobiography, memoirs), others extended it to fiction, poetry, and
drama. (One extremely naive or cynical critic devoted several
documentary works to Lenin, the most mythologized figure in
Soviet culture.)[51]

Documentation is crucial to examining women's writing as a
fictional representation of *byt*. This tendency encouraged authors
to use narrative strategies to create an aura of authenticity, a
ploy they were quite willing to adopt. The inherent contradic-
tions and tensions within the nebulous documentary impulse are
oddly appropriate for addressing the unstable everyday that had
long bedeviled the Russian intelligentsia and its literary efforts.

It is no coincidence that documentation, familiar to Russian
readers through the 1920s "literature of fact," resurfaced during
the Thaw.[52] The decline of the Stalinist novel created niches for a
plethora of themes and genres. However, the same patterns that
Katerina Clark observed in socialist realism continued in documentary literature, with its presumably better grounding in reality. What was original about documentation, supporters averred,
was how it analyzed the facts coming from a reality that demanded rational examination. This claim was hardly novel in the
context of scientific communism or, for that matter, nineteenth-
century realism. What made documentation new in the post-
1953 context was its apparent moving away from the varnished
optimism of socialist realism into the world of facts, expressed as
a result of the era's new desire for sincerity. Citing Lidiia Ginzburg, critic Nina Dikushina saw no contradiction between objectivity and literature. Indeed, she optimistically argues that the
readers' love for documentary literature showed society's attraction to objectivity, trust, and verifiable information.[53] Dikushina
blithely ignored how this imagined union between the bound-
less optimism of Soviet "reality" and its flawless reflection in
belles lettres recalled the same Stalinist hypocrisy that Ginzburg

decried. Only one critic (writing in more liberal Czechoslovakia) revealed the referent behind this trend: documentation is literary de-Stalinization, where the "literature of fact" tries to overcome the legacy of the cult of personality.[54] This prescient assessment appeared in 1965, three years before Soviet-led forces put an end to Czechoslovakia's errant attempt to escape the lingering effects of Stalinism.

There is likewise no hint from critics that the Brezhnev era's omnipresent irony complicated the documentary drive to seamlessly join life and literature. On the contrary, this writing, its supporters assure us, is the transparent result of art depicting reality. The future of this reality is likewise not in doubt. Documentation shows how the present follows the narrow yet unswerving path stretching toward the radiant future of communism. Such reasoning is fundamentally flawed. Drawing on what it misconstrues as the easily legible truths of history, documentary literature reflects how the past has molded the present and, more important, how the present is already shaping the future.[55] As with Dikushina's wishful marriage of fiction and fact, this conception of literature as mirroring history in its revolutionary development parrots the utopian phrases of socialist realism. The latter was, for its part, only the most odious manifestation of Russian culture's centuries-old desiderata for literature: didacticism, transparency, and allegiance (whether to the state or its morally righteous opponents).

Documentation's imagined relationship between reality and its fictional representation is built on another underlying pattern of Russian intellectual culture: transforming the raw into the finished. At first glance this goal appears to be a function of genre, where documentary prose is the result of journalistic writing (*publitsistika*) reworked in artistic form. Within this schema the artist refines factual writing, producing a work firmly based in reality yet linked to the best traditions of Russian fiction. Dikushina describes an analogous transformation, which helps us to understand how women's writing appropriated the rhetoric of the documentary genre. Skillful authors, she declares, use documentation to sift through characters' traits and reveal what is typical within them. By linking characters to history, the wellspring of Russian literature, the creative process makes documents into art.[56] The movement from the commonplace to the profound, from the prosaic to the artistic, reiterates the intelligentsia's eternal urge to escape from *byt* to *bytie*. From this stance the relationship between documentation and the reality it describes is less an interaction between equals than the condescending appreciation the colonizer shows the colonized. When female authors strayed from this precept, opponents accused them of engaging in journalism instead of literature.

Documentation shaped the development of women's prose in the sense that this drive toward objectivity's most important effect—the allure of the real—guided how critics viewed the image of *byt* in literature. Tzvetan Todorov notes that the mimetic narrative—a fictional work depicting reality—persuades readers that its imagined world conforms to fact and not to fiction. Verisimilitude is thus not an a priori truth but a mistake of the naive reader, who identifies the world depicted within the literary work as "consistent with reality."[57] To assume an unmediated relationship between reality and literature (documentary or otherwise) is to mistake the manufactured result for the initial material.

Bakhtin provides two analogous caveats. He first notes that one should not confuse reality with its counterpart in literature. Readers should likewise not conflate the "author-as-creator" with the human author, a seemingly commonplace warning that nevertheless challenges both the Soviet drive for transparent authorial intent and the traditional Russian penchant for assuming authors' works to be an outgrowth of their personal lives.[58] As with the preceding discussion of documentation and de-Stalinization, Bakhtin's warnings were in tune with the times: his comments on differentiating fiction and reality were written in 1937–38, at the height of the Stalinist purges of imagined political enemies.

Since the 1960s (and particularly after 1991) Russian women's prose has received much critical attention of an increasingly diverse and sophisticated nature. As a rule these analyses have either focused on one or two authors or emphasized a single chronological slice of Russian culture, unwittingly neglecting the everyday as a common cultural heritage.

It is difficult to consider the development of women authors such as Baranskaia or Ulitskaia without understanding how and why their adaptation of a changing quotidian influenced theme, style, and the extent to which they adopted previous portrayals of *byt*. When critics note how Tolstaia's writing appears to be several generations removed from more staid earlier authors, they reveal the need to examine literary depictions of daily life as a factor unifying this chronologically dispersed group of authors.[59] Women's writing initially appropriated a stringent adherence to verisimilitude. This mode of representation and the proclivity for documentary prose during Thaw and Stagnation conditioned readers to see literature as an allegedly truthful commentary on everyday life and, by extension, the gendered problems inseparable from it. This implicit social commentary, limited in the works of Baranskaia and Grekova, became sharper in the prose of Petrushevskaia and Vasilenko and the small explosion of women's literary anthologies in the early 1990s. The fiction of Tolstaia and Ulitskaia, however, envisions *byt* more as an artistic resource in which ethics combine with esthetics.

Understanding literary treatments of everyday life helps in charting the transformation of women's writing as well as gauging critical responses and authorial approaches to the quotidian. During Thaw and Stagnation, critics employed *byt* as a code word for women's writing and its discussions of female experience. In the late- and post-Soviet periods, however, such mediated references vanished as both supporters and opponents of women's prose explicitly invoked gender as the major criterion for literary talent—or lack thereof.

Women's prose from Khrushchev to Putin moved from documenting the everyday to a systematic critique of *byt*'s inequalities and then to a more stylistically sophisticated and thematically diverse approach to daily life. This trend is inseparable from contemporary literary crises, such as the reduced post-Soviet role of the intelligentsia. Examining authors' changing conceptions of the quotidian exposes this main theme of Russian women's writing and reveals the basis of its reception in the last five decades.

1

Documenting Women's *Byt* during the Thaw and Stagnation

Natal'ia Baranskaia and I. Grekova

Art is a strange thing. We notice it when it is reflected in great
things, but from day to day we live surrounded by petty, forgotten, transitory little things. In a sense these, too, are art.

I. Grekova

The task of the artist is thus to find the immortal in the ephemeral.

Iurii Trifonov

In 1966 the deputy director of the Pushkin Memorial Museum in
Moscow abruptly retired after officials criticized her for inviting
dissident poet Joseph Brodsky to an exhibit featuring the photo-
graphs of the poet Anna Akhmatova and her family, all of
whom had suffered under Stalin.[1] Upon leaving her cherished
position, the former director turned to a new pursuit: writing.
Within three years her novella *Nedelia kak nedelia* (A Week Like
Any Other, 1969) had redefined Russian women's writing, and
the author—Natal'ia Baranskaia—had become internationally
famous.

From the early 1960s to the mid-1980s female authors employed images of supposedly innocuous everyday life to raise

women's issues in mainstream Soviet prose. Baranskaia (1907–2004) and I. Grekova, the literary pseudonym of mathematician Elena Venttsel' (1908–2002), used the post-Stalinist focus on documentation to depict a gendered quotidian existence illustrating the problems of female Soviet citizens. Their protagonists, drawn from the USSR's showcased scientists and engineers, were usually single mothers or widows (as were the writers themselves).[2] This similarity between creator and character parallels the strong relationship women's writing tried to create between the quotidian and its fictional counterpart during the Thaw and Stagnation.

Baranskaia and Grekova worked within their era's emphasis on sincerity, documentation, and the new focus on the everyday to illustrate the divergent ethics of male and female characters and relations between the sexes. What resulted was a picture of numerous inequalities in Soviet society that, because of the writers' modes of depiction, paradoxically legitimated some of the gender differences whose extremes the authors critiqued. Relying on what one critic snidely termed the "Procrustean bed of *byt*" seemingly limited options for representing women's lives.[3]

Critics responding to this prose assessed its success in categories that unwittingly reproduced the authors' tactics: a focus on *byt* as the main building block of narrative and the belief that fiction shows what is typical about Soviet reality. Such seemingly straightforward critical strategies revealed a host of cultural anxieties. These issues stemmed from the everyday as a women's realm and the legacy of Stalinist socialist realism, with its quixotic claim to simultaneously depict and transform reality.

Baranskaia and Grekova draw heavily on the daily lives of women, leading most critics (both Western and Russian) to restrict their discussion to assessing the sociological accuracy of their fictional images.[4] This approach, while valid to a certain degree, is limiting and naive in its assumption that women's writing is little more than the unproblematic representation of what happens outside the narrative (i.e., *byt*). Indeed, the reader's conflation of fiction with its actually existing referent is a key goal of women's writing, warranting critical examination rather than facile acceptance. However, since the appeal to "real" social conditions is such a striking part of Baranskaia's and Grekova's approach, no discussion of their works would be complete without a brief survey of the women's experiences that the authors have selected to illustrate the female quotidian.

During the Thaw and Stagnation the USSR professed gender equality while displaying a series of imbalances that, to varying degrees, surfaced in literature under the rubric *byt*. Despite the state's policy of hiding, distorting, or simply never gathering unfavorable statistics, some figures suggest marked discrepancies between men's and women's quality of life. Both Baranskaia and Grekova were widows when their relatively late literary careers began. (Baranskaia's second husband died in the Nazi invasion, while Grekova was widowed in 1955.) After 1945 there were twenty million more women than men in the Soviet Union. This gap, along with a woman's longer life span, made males a "deficit" item for the next generation, one to be carefully guarded if procured. The resulting obsession with the vanishing man had several results, none boding well for stable families or, for that matter, gender equality. Divorces increased from 3.2 per 100 marriages (1950) to 27 (1973), with the husband's alcoholism blamed for 20–40 percent of divorces. One third of Soviet women had extramarital affairs in 1969, a proportion that increased to half in 1989. Prenuptial attitudes help to explain this lack of connubial harmony: whereas 70 percent of future brides believed that spouses should know everything about each other's plans, only 21 percent of the grooms agreed.[5] This backdrop provided Baranskaia and Grekova with a steady stream of characters who are single mothers, widows, or unmarried. The happy couple is a rare find in this fiction.

A decrease in familial stability, along with overcrowded living conditions, helps explain the USSR's high number of terminated pregnancies: an average of nine during a Soviet woman's life, as abortion was the primary method of contraception for Soviet women. And 81 percent of women had one or no children, a situation exacerbated by the urbanization affecting Russians more than non-European ethnicities within the Soviet Union.[6] The declining Russian birthrate, which alarmed the state, emerges as a theme in Baranskaia's *Nedelia kak nedelia*: overworked mothers fill out questionnaires to determine why Muscovites are not having more children, with one woman observing that higher maternity pay and fewer surveys would be better.[7]

It is difficult to quantify another issue much more cautiously reflected in women's prose, namely, violence against women. The scanty statistical evidence suggests that rape may have been fairly common: there were 17,658 reported rapes and attempted rapes in 1988, a 60 percent increase since 1961. The number of cases not reported to the (usually unsympathetic) authorities was probably much higher. Alcoholism, another theme hesitantly depicted by Baranskaia and Grekova, periodically entered the public spotlight as a serious problem: 18.6 percent of male and 2 percent of female drinkers in the early 1970s were alcoholics, conveying a gendered difference in leisure time and the social acceptability of heavy drinking.[8]

Low wages meant that most (intact) families needed to have two incomes, a situation women's writing illustrates in terms of mothers struggling with the "double burden" of work and household. Ol'ga in *Nedelia kak nedelia* epitomized this problem for readers and critics. One underlying cause dates from the 1920s, when Bolshevik feminists such as Aleksandra Kollontai did not sufficiently assert that housework constituted sexual inequality. The state thus concluded that it did not owe its female citizens a replacement for the failed communal laundries and cafeterias it had initially proposed. Lack of male help at home, as well as technology geared to industry instead of the consumer sector, perpetuated the problem.

State policy nevertheless tried to promote higher ethnic Russian birthrates and stable families. To this end, Soviet culture endorsed strict gender roles, with such informal policies implemented through de facto wage discrimination, legal and administrative channels, and advice related to family and "proper" behavior. The state feared a destabilizing scenario of gender reversal and the prospect of effeminate men and mannish women. Literature was a crucial arena for airing these anxieties. Sergei Chuprinin exemplifies conservative concerns with his warning that early 1980s prose "reveals" women to be sexually aggressive, a presumably inappropriate trait that could be corrected if women emulated their counterparts from twenty or a hundred years ago. This retrograde viewpoint assumes women to be the sinning sex needing instruction, a charge also dominating advice literature in the perestroika and post-Soviet periods.[9]

Men also stray from the strictures of gender, but women's writing confines depictions of these errant males either to exaggerations of "acceptable" behavior (alcoholic war veterans) or absence (some children simply do not know the identity of their fathers). Homosexuality, a more serious threat to conservative gender roles, does not exist in published literature before perestroika.[10] This absence exemplifies the Soviet Victorianism dominating official public discourse from the 1930s to the mid-1980s. However, eliding gays and lesbians also shows that post-1953 private life was less a sphere than an edifice. Certain levels of this structure (mainly those open before and during Stalinism) were accessible in women's writing, while others (homosexuality, female alcoholism, incest) remained sealed for decades. Private life may have been the right of every Soviet citizen, but this variegated space also had its dark corners. Perestroika writers (most notably Liudmila Petrushevskaia) would later mercilessly illuminate these murky recesses for shocked yet fascinated readers.

Fear of gender reversal hints at anxiety over the results of postwar urbanization and, by extension, Russian modernity. The capital, the most common setting for Baranskaia's and Grekova's works, was a particularly extreme example. Moscow's growth from 1970 to 1990 was largely due to *limitchitsy* (female temporary workers from the country) and to the city's incorporation of outlying villages.[11] Conservative authors and critics warned that such displacement of the rural women, who embodied authentic "Russianness," imperiled cultural memory. Increased migration to the city was also profoundly unsettling for the urban intelligentsia populating the works of Baranskaia and Grekova. These intellectuals found their everyday world invaded by often less educated newcomers, who struck Muscovites as singularly uncouth.

Hidden worries over social transformation and the future of the Russian (not Soviet) people caused consternation over gender roles, with women authors depicting and often fueling these fears through their putatively objective descriptions of daily life. Portraying *byt* by means of the era's emphasis on documentation ironically limited representation. Such methods of depiction either ignore problems too risky for print (poverty, incest, rape) or

transform "typical" moments (marriage, childbirth) into meto-
nyms of women's existence, reiterating conservative gender expectations in the process.

Women authors both shaped and were influenced by the
overall context of post-Stalinist culture. Following Nikita Khrushchev's ouster (1964) and the Prague Spring (1968), official views
on writing and politics became more consistently conservative.
This change affected literature earlier than other forms of art. The
explicit anti-Stalinism of Aleksandr Solzhenitsyn's novella *Odin
den' Ivana Denisovicha* (One Day in the Life of Ivan Denisovich,
1962) and Evgenii Evtushenko's poem "Nasledniki Stalina" (The
Heirs of Stalin, 1962) fell out of favor: direct critiques of the recent past were no longer safe. Depictions of Soviet political experience now diffused their commentary through images of
personal life, as in Iurii Trifonov's novel *Dom na naberezhnoi* (The
House on the Embankment, 1976), with its retrospective view of
moral compromise under Stalinism. These portrayals, operating
through the reduced scope and quasi-direct narratorial discourse
dominating literature after 1953, valued individual experience
over direct social commentary. While these authors' works favored the apparently insignificant realm of the everyday, their exposition and content showed that the quotidian was key to understanding Soviet society. As critical responses to Baranskaia and
Grekova revealed, *byt* and its representation quickly emerged as
anything but harmless.

Documenting *Byt*: Impasse or Obstruction?

The move away from Stalinism's limitless optimism toward
the reduced scale of Thaw and Stagnation literature was crucial
to rediscovering *byt*, a mundane universe of small crises. These
minutiae tend toward "muddle" rather than organization and
coalesce around individual experience instead of the collective
significance of Stalinist culture.[12] The combination of *byt* and literary documentation in the 1960s and 1970s shaped women's
writing at the thematic level (with its emphasis on "real-life"
problems) and style (marked by an accumulation of detail and a
lack of overt commentary by the narrator).

As Boris Groys argues, post-Stalinist fiction moved out of the utopian dreamscape of socialist realism and into a more problematic reality.[13] However, this shift led to another idealistic scenario, namely, literature's drive to use documentation to join verbal art and the world it depicts. This paradoxical drive displays a willingness to recognize the gulf between representation and reality while at the same time trying to bridge this gap with more sincere and "objective" portrayals. While documentation signaled rejection of discredited Stalinist varnishing (*lakirovka*), its more "authentic" prose also proved successful at hiding various agendas. For instance, Grekova's story "Bez ulybok" (No Smiles, 1975) fictionalizes how colleagues shunned her after authorities discovered that she had been writing prose under a pseudonym. Sometimes documentary works either claimed to be nonfiction, as with Baranskaia's politicized family chronicle *Stranstvie bezdomnykh* (Wanderings of the Homeless, 1999), or fictionalized what was previously recognized as fact, as with Baranskaia's narrative about Natal'ia Goncharova, the widow of the romantic poet Aleksandr Pushkin.[14]

Exposition contributes to this union between fiction and the universe it illustrates. Grekova grounds this overlap in personal terms, asserting that her prose reflects what she knows based on personal experience: the life of scientists and *byt*, a pair she is careful to distinguish. Baranskaia and Grekova appropriated the style that Roland Barthes denotes as "zero degree of writing": a purportedly "neutral mode" of realistic representation that fit the mimetic goal of women's writing during the Thaw and Stagnation.[15] This seemingly commonsensical pairing (neutrality, documentation) masks several underlying assumptions that indicate how this prose viewed its place in the world. Representation reveals itself to be far more than art's mirroring of reality, as Tzvetan Todorov and Mikhail Bakhtin note when they caution against confusing verisimilitude with what actually exists.

Rita Felski offers the tantalizingly reasonable argument that objective depiction imparts women's experiences in an easily understandable manner, persuading readers to adopt the author's subtly conveyed opinions as the "objective" reality of everyday life.[16] For Felski this molding of progressive ideology and mimesis heightens one's awareness of women's problems.

The style that Felski lauds dominates works such as Baranskaia's little-known story "Provody" (The Farewell Party, 1968), which shows how society discards an older woman no longer useful in terms of labor.[17] Following this type of logic, one post-Soviet critic optimistically argues that this story was a subversive forerunner of glasnost feminism. Readers must first identify the problem (an exploitative state whose inequities Baranskaia's transparent style discloses) before arriving at a conclusion (the need to oppose combined gender and political oppression). While such a close connection between response to the narrative and social reform is far too optimistic, in one sense it does validate Felski's argument: quasi-journalistic style highlights small-scale gendered discrimination, while the unobtrusive third-person narration asserts the story's veracity.[18] Content, from this point of view, is the undisputed master of style.

By ignoring the politics of selecting content and the subsequent shaping of reader reactions, Felski unwittingly substitutes the deceptive allure of the real for the poststructuralist glitter she denigrates. In "Provody" Baranskaia focuses on the dramatic end of Anna Vasil'evna's career, a part of her life that characterizes her as a victim of the state. The reader does not learn anything substantive about the character's former work, which, as the narrator observes, takes the place of religion in providing meaning.[19] A similar omission shapes Grekova's "Bez ulybok." While the narrative details M. M.'s hurt at being ostracized by her coworkers, it sheds little light on the supposed errors that motivated her censure. These missing portrayals should remind critics of the inherently subjective nature of portraying daily life. With respect to a work such as "Provody" or "Bez ulybok," Felski's argument exemplifies the attitude of the naive reader, who, in Todorov's scenario, mistakes manufactured verisimilitude for reality.

In order to create the illusion of objective documentation, Baranskaia's and Grekova's prose firmly subordinates form to content. Nothing must interfere with conveying the hectic nature of the lives of such characters as Ol'ga in *Nedelia kak nedelia*. Moving from the hated Monday to Sunday's reprieve, the narrative even uses the protagonist's flashback to her idyllic honeymoon to underscore the quotidian's crushing force.[20] *Byt* structures the diegesis just as it constricts the lives of Ol'ga and her family.

Form also reiterates content in Baranskaia's novel *Den' pominove-niia* (Remembrance Day, 1989).[21] Here, however, it operates by means of moral imperatives connected with the essentialist trinity of peace, remembrance, and motherhood, embodied in widows commemorating husbands who died in the Great Patriotic War.[22]

Daily life inspires narrative form. It is no surprise that women authors chose to operate within the staid style of the *byt* prose (*literatura byta*) popularized by Trifonov.[23] This framework provided a ready-made arena for "objectively" depicting women's experiences in an everyday newly reclaimed from the margins. Baranskaia used the quotidian to heighten awareness of selected problems in women's lives—a key strategy of reporters. However, her disdain for journalistic style was only surpassed by her strident refusal to be labeled a feminist.[24] Grekova likewise shied away from literature as a didactic forum, suggesting she opposed both journalism's and feminism's appropriation of the everyday—despite her own prose using *byt* as a backdrop for women's problems. (One critic, however, who paints a fairly sympathetic picture of Grekova, opines that the deep psychological issues she explores through daily life redeem her often uninspiring prose.) For her part Helena Goscilo pairs 1960s and 1970s women's writing with realism. However, contrary to Felski, she links this perceived stylistic staleness with acceptance of underlying gender inequalities.[25] This view is more insightful, yet one should recall that during the Thaw and Stagnation women's themes and *byt* were still somewhat suspect. Baranskaia and Grekova could not combine these with shocking stylistics or a wholesale indictment of the Soviet state and still hope to appear in print. On a thematic level, neither author endorsed such iconoclasm—a situation that changed with perestroika writers.

Baranskaia's scorn for journalism hints that the bare prose of reporters' style (Barthes's "zero degree of writing") was to her mind insufficient. A parade of facts does not constitute literature and, as Iurii Tynianov argued, even opposes "true" art. Grekova and her contemporary, the prose writer Viktoriia Tokareva, recast the argument in slightly more abstract terms when naming the authors who influenced them: the humane realist Anton Chekhov (Tokareva) and mystical realist Fyodor Dostoyevsky

(Grekova).[26] Both predecessors made *byt* respectable, transforming writing about everyday life into far-reaching discussions of the human condition. Hailing from such august (male) company legitimates Tokareva and Grekova. Along these lines, an early review of Baranskaia compared her to Leo Tolstoy, albeit with the weighty (and erroneous) caveat that ethics and artistic representation are incompatible in literature.[27] The above assertions convey a key commonality that runs throughout criticism of women's writing: the raw material of *byt* must be transformed into the finished product of literature.

Typicality is another concern. This unresolved problem of typicality, a crucial issue encompassing content as well as exposition, was inherited by post-Stalinist authors through critical and socialist realism. Two conceptions of typicality—what I term a transformative and reflective approach—dominated literary criticism from the 1960s through the mid-1980s. The first of these echoes Georg Lukács's contention that the typical is what will be or should be in a given era (i.e., representing reality in fiction can transform said reality, an axiom of socialist realism). Within this schema the everyday beyond the narrative is a temporary obstacle, as critic Vladimir Rozanov avers, criticizing Grekova's novella *Na ispytaniiakh* (On Maneuvers, 1967) and its emphasis on supposedly uncharacteristic shortcomings (dead dogs and toilets) besmirching the image of the Red Army. Nina Dikushina amplifies this note, implying that the atypical is suspect in terms of representation and ideology: the USSR's overgeneralizing enemies base their attacks on the anomalous (a category she carefully does not specify). This paranoid logic explains why authorities pressured the novella's author to leave the Zhukovskii Military Academy after realizing that the school's mathematician Venttsel' was using the pseudonym I. Grekova to "defame" the Soviet military in *Na ispytaniiakh*.[28] The supposedly neutral realm of *byt* became a touchstone for critical debate over illustrating everyday life, authorial responsibility, and the reputation of the USSR's armed forces during the Cold War.

Women writers' rhetoric of documentation, however, implicitly rejects Rozanov's and Dikushina's stance. Instead, it posits typicality as reflective: describing what exists, which must be conveyed to the reader. The Thaw value of sincerity is important in this context. After 1953 the intellectual caste viewed sincerity—honesty, loyalty, and the union of appearance and reality—as an antidote to Stalinist varnishing.[29] Sincerity, like typicality, appealed to a generation wary of the yawning gap between everyday life and its distorted image on page and screen.

This viewpoint justifies depicting both the familiar and the exceptional: both constitute the human condition and thus represent reality. Women readers identified with the first term of this binary and saw works such as *Nedelia kak nedelia* describing their own everyday existence. (One reader even complimented Baranskaia on knowing so much about the reader's life.)[30] Baranskaia and Grekova imply that women's experiences are both statistically and morally typical in a reflective sense.

It is unsurprising that critics such as Rozanov are loath to support the reflective function of typicality. This endorsement would ultimately create a disastrous chain of causality. To admit that typicality is reflective—part of existing reality and not its transformation—implies that women (the majority of the population) constitute this reflected reality. This majority, mired in the quotidian and embracing the corporeal over the ideational (according to Soviet orthodoxy), had long been deemed the most backward segment of society. As Yuri Slezkine observes, stressing the ideologically marginal viewpoint of women indicates that the USSR is one huge communal apartment. Here, however, it is gender, not ethnicity, that threatens the Marxist-Leninist radiant future with its constant petty crises.[31]

Critics' responses to depiction of everyday life in the works of Baranskaia and Grekova fell into two categories. The first group, implying that literature as a whole should be transformative, recalled Roman Jakobson's description of *byt* as a swamplike realm, swallowing and suffocating any aspirations to higher meaning. One irate critic accuses Baranskaia of perpetuating *byt* through its description. While the characters in her story "Partnery" (Partners) are ballerinas, they are nonetheless described through "trivial" speculations about infidelities and a woman's worries of how a child will affect her career on the stage. A cafeteria and other accoutrements of banality clutter the work, with no ideational significance attached to them. Baranskaia, the critic carps, first protests the material "stereotypes" of everyday life and then perpetuates them.[32] This viewpoint combines and dismisses three traditionally separate categories—love, the world of objects, and the body—as dead weight encumbering the narrative. Literature should transform and not merely depict, such logic notes, and these mainstays of *byt* do not help this goal.

Another critic echoes this view in an extremely formulaic reading of Grekova that begins by citing the latest congress of the Communist Party. While conceding that life was difficult during the Great Patriotic War, he chides the author of the novella *Vdovii parokhod* (A Ship of Widows, 1979) for portraying the bleak reality of widows after 1945: "In art it is not only important how it was but also how it should be." He then qualifies this apodictic phrase by assuring readers that he refers not to a "violent normative process in literature" but to a search for creative potential.[33] Despite his coded critique of Stalinist varnishing, he affirms the socialist realist maxim of transformative typicality, for which *byt* is anathema.

Some critics see *byt* as tolerable if it does not dominate a work. One argues that Maiia Ganina's novella *Uslysh' svoi chas* (Know When It's Your Hour, 1975)—which describes an actress, her daughter, and the husband the actress betrays—should assert that daily life is a part but not the limit of experiences. The critic is likewise disturbed by the unmotivated and aimless narrator, whose meanderings do not display the clear intentions and logical plans apparently needed to inspire the builders of communism.[34] Worse yet, he argues, the everyday obfuscates the author's motivation and frustrates attempts to explain the present. Here is another lingering effect of socialist realism and, by extension, Russian literary tradition as a whole: a work's attitude to contemporaneity should be clear to the reader. According to this reasoning, *byt* is isolated from existence, leading neither to a reliable image of the present nor to the posited brighter future.

Denial of finalized meaning is also problematic, as V. Lysenko shows when noting that Tokareva's ethical relativism is the ·modus vivendi of the philistine. Tokareva's lack of values, the glut of everyday life in her fiction, and the writer's status as a practitioner of *byt* unite to produce amoral literature. In the intriguingly titled "Lzheromantika obshchikh mest" (False Romanticism of the Commonplace), another critic makes an overt accusation foreshadowing post-Soviet criticism of Tokareva: "This 'romanticism' turns into a crassly philistine condition, co-existing quite well with a false sense of being the elect, not resembling other people, etc."[35] The underlying issue, the critic implies, is an elitist lack of transparency, with muddied authorial intent sabotaging the supposedly straightforward relationship between narrative and reality.

A second group of critics diverges from the above opinions, arguing that *byt*'s presence is either useful per se or acts as a stepping-stone to loftier goals. From this viewpoint daily life can be described through reflective typicality: there is no need to mask everyday experiences through transformation. With his analysis of "Provody" Ia. El'sberg hesitantly admits the necessity of *byt* and sets the tone for later discussions of Baranskaia. Conceding that Soviet literature should describe the quotidian, he hastens to add that one must not overlook "the everyday's spiritual and ideational content [*dukhovnoi, ideinoi soderzhatel'nosti byta*]."[36] Two other critics make a similar comment when applauding Tokareva for making the everyday "ideational" (a watchword of socialist realism). The writer herself asserts that her works use the everyday to create *bytie*, the spiritually significant counterpart of *byt*.[37] Descriptions of the quotidian, this reasoning avers, must connect it with higher meaning, whether through ideology or by revealing the soul, as one critic claims for Grekova.[38]

This second group of critics recalls the narrator in Grekova's early story "Za prokhodnoi" (Beyond the Checkpoint, 1961), who sees *byt* as either intrinsically valuable or at least as a conduit to more significant topics: "Art is a strange thing. We notice it when it is reflected in great things, but from day to day we live surrounded by petty, forgotten, transitory little things. In a sense these, too, are art." Such an assertion parallels Maurice Blanchot's deliberately vague description of the quotidian as lacking truth but being a part of Truth: the everyday contains a significance that is not immediately visible.[39] Blanchot envisions the everyday as a hotbed of political and intellectual rebellion. "Za prokhodnoi," however, deals with the inspired *byt* of presumably loyal young scientists at a secret military research institute.

Trifonov was *byt's* best-known defender from the 1960s through the 1980s. Not surprisingly, he sees the everyday as inseparable from great art: "The interaction of [fact and artistry] is the interaction of life and art. In this sense no one has said it better than the ancient Greeks: one is ephemeral; the other is immortal. And the task of the artist is thus to find the immortal in the ephemeral." The true artist, Trifonov avers, fuses the *byt* and *bytie* long estranged from each other in Russian culture. *Byt* is not a conduit but itself a resource for the patient and talented writer capable of finding meaning in what others deem trivial.[40]

These disparate ideas about representing *byt* are all based on the assumption (whether explicit or covert) that the everyday is above all a female experience. Critic L. Zhukhovitskii approvingly notes how Tokareva uses a woman's sense of detail and male skill in imagining unusual situations that reveal the extraordinary.[41] Here Trifonov's ephemeral/quotidian is joined with female minutiae, which stern masculine resolve renders artistic.

This transformative relationship between raw facts and polished fiction underlies the rhetoric of documentation and its proprietary approach to *byt*. A stronger and more rational force must subdue the feminized expanse of the everyday in order to distill its meaning, whether that force is the guiding hand of the party or the elusive genius of "true" art. In depicting daily life, women writers also replicated all the anxieties Russian culture espied in the quotidian. Long-standing worries over *byt* and its threat to *bytie* combined with post-Stalinist culture's drive for documentation and sincerity. The result was a necessary yet antagonistic relationship between the formlessness of everyday life and literature's desire to control its fictional universe.

Women's Time and Space: Scale, Crisis, and Memory

During the Thaw and Stagnation specific issues relating to women's conception of time became a key feature of female authors, especially Baranskaia and Grekova. These problems stem from *byt*, which Russian culture has long seen as a vortex of small tasks, cramped spaces, and trivial concerns. The peculiarities of female temporality, with its self-erasing, ateleological time of domestic chores, are inseparable from the Soviet Union's gendered spaces (the abortion ward, mothers waiting for groceries in long lines, and so forth). It is difficult to pinpoint how time and space operate in the quotidian. The elusive yet pernicious nature of *byt* makes it formless and threatening, a problematic factor within the ordered schema that proponents of documentation tried to impose on literature and its representation of reality.

Conjoining time and space gives a special quality to both *byt* and the women's literary works devoted to its representation. For Bakhtin such combinations create the chronotope, which shows the "intrinsic connectedness of temporal and spatial relationships that are artistically expressed in literature. . . . Time, as it were, thickens, takes on flesh, becomes artistically visible; likewise, space becomes charged and responsive to the movements of time, plot and history."[42] This confluence of space and time organizes literature through character experiences, with the everyday being post-Stalinist literature's favored venue for gathering such knowledge.

As Iurii Lotman notes, *byt* is most identifiable during times of crises. Such moments shape women's writing and determine how it uses the quotidian to convey specifically female problems. In this context, the threshold chronotope, which Bakhtin links to a life-changing event for a character, is of special interest to the present discussion. Baranskaia's and Grekova's female characters inhabit the chronotope of crisis, which is a subset of the threshold, the moment when *byt* is most visible.[43] The chronotope of crisis became a model for women's battles with time and place, undergoing a series of changes as women's writing itself diversified in the late- and post-Soviet era.

For Baranskaia and Grekova women's temporality is fragmented, cyclical, and self-erasing—traits that arise from *byt*, with its magnification of mundane concerns. The smaller scale of crisis within this context distinguishes women authors from their male counterparts. Vasilii Grossman's mammoth novel *Zhizn' i sud'ba* (Life and Fate, published abroad in 1980) illustrates how Stalinism and the Nazi invasion threatened an entire society, while Grekova's novella *Malen'kii Garusov* (Little Garusov, 1970) describes the epic siege of Leningrad through the experiences of a single child. The "little things" scrutinized by women's prose imply an inductive approach to understanding life: these objects and actions are grounded in the banal details of *byt* and oppose the deductive and often sweeping scope of male contemporaries such as Grossman.[44]

Fragmented time heightens intensity as the narrative examines crisis on a microscopic level. In Grekova's novella *Damskii master* Mar'ia Vladimirovna, dean of a Moscow scientific institute, makes surprisingly little headway at work: "A scientific problem demands complete attention, and mine is torn, ripped to shreds."[45] This lament reflects the pressures of the modern workplace and continues the battle with time inherited from the shock workers of the socialist realist production novel. Mar'ia Vladimirovna, however, experiences temporality as a disjointed series of events instead of the continuous flow ascribed to the construction projects literally and symbolically remaking the USSR. Unlike the socialist realist protagonist, she experiences no moment signaling the end of the struggle: her immature grown sons and naive young secretary need constant care. Likewise, while such positive heroes as Nikolai Ostrovskii's Pavel Korchagin focus on a future that will presumably redeem humanity, Grekova's dean battles with the present and more modest goals (assuaging angered colleagues, cooking dinner). It is no coincidence that there is very little discussion of research in this narrative.

Implicitly invoking documentation and its conflation of author and characters, Grekova notes that she mentally worked on her fiction in fragmented fashion: between tasks, before going to sleep, and so forth. This common observation of women writers is a temporal equivalent of the room of one's own whose absence Virginia Woolf laments. Writing during isolated moments may be one reason for the less lengthy literary forms (short and long stories) dominating women's prose, a prominent factor even given the post-Stalinist move away from the stolid novel to less monumental genres.[46]

The fragmentation of women's time accompanies exhausting, cyclical activity. In Baranskaia's *Nedelia kak nedelia*, working mother Ol'ga, whom Goscilo describes as waging a (losing) war with time, travels from home on the outskirts of Moscow to work in the city. The week as temporal structure indicates that her commute, arguments with husband Dima, and children's sicknesses are inevitable and unending. Indeed, Ol'ga none too happily observes: "So another week is over, the next-to-last week of the year."[47] In Baranskaia's story "Krai sveta" (The Edge of the World) Elizaveta Nikolaevna has a similar sense of time: she is retired but still lacks time to care for her shiftless relatives. On a morning resembling Ol'ga's week, she worries about the son who did not return home to his wife the previous night: "The day was like any other. She fixed breakfast, woke the children, had them exercise, fed them and walked them to school. She ran to the store, put soup and compote on to boil. She did some cleaning. Then she began to darn the socks for Petia's felt boots."[48] The morning consists of a string of domestic duties rendered stark by short sentences, perfective verbal aspect, and few pronouns. As in *Nedelia kak nedelia*, a series of discrete actions creates an aura of hurry characteristic of the chronotope of crisis in women's writing. In an underlying sense there is no clear dividing line between crisis and noncrisis: the everyday is an unending travail of missed buses, hungry children, and omnipresent lines. For Elizaveta Nikolaevna there is only one escape from the race against time: the death that delivers her to the "edge of the world" she longs to visit. Women's *byt* is a series of recurring problems whose ordinariness does not help Baranskaia's and Grekova's characters solve them.

Repetition and the appeal to typicality recall the conclusion of Solzhenitsyn's *Odin den' Ivana Denisovicha* and its enumeration of the days in the prisoner's sentence. Baranskaia's Elizaveta Nikolaevna and Ol'ga will never escape from their maternal duties, just as the gulag prisoners often had another prison sentence added to the one they had just completed. Despite manifold differences, Solzhenitsyn and Baranskaia skillfully craft a typical routine that strengthens the documentary allure of their narratives, as the storm of publicity accompanying these two works attested. The inmate Shukhov and Baranskaia's women base their identities on inherently unequal battles with everyday life. The protagonists' persistent dilemmas also have a metaphysical dimension: *byt*'s cyclicality erodes individual resolve and ultimately the characters' sense of self.

Time as problem is one way women authors depict *byt*. The wait in line to purchase often scarce foodstuffs and goods, a familial and familiar necessity, links two deficit items: necessary things and the time needed to obtain them. The narrator in Tokareva's short story "Iaponskii zontik" (A Japanese Umbrella) witnesses a bewildering transformation after waiting in line to buy a Japanese umbrella. Looking at the line reveals something startling: "The people and things had changed places. The things had stretched out in a long line and were choosing people. The people were sitting in the kind of cardboard boxes that you pack televisions in, sticking their heads out and breathing in the fresh air."[49]

At first glance this story cleverly critiques the ubiquitous shortages in the USSR. This initial interpretation—the humorous metamorphosis of buyers and sellers—displays the light irony critics prized in Tokareva's early (and better) works. A closer examination brings to mind Marx's critique of capitalism's reification, a "conversion of things into persons and the conversion of persons into things."[50] However, this unsettling change occurs not in the exploitative West but during the period of Soviet "developed socialism," as Stagnation was then optimistically called. The line as locus suggests loss of individual identity in a nation where the constant searches for basic necessities (or the luxury of imported goods) dehumanized the consumer. For women, responsible for home and family as well as their own shopping, the situation was even worse.

The line resembles the semiprivate space of the ubiquitous Soviet communal apartment in that both involve unwanted social interaction stemming from shortages. One of Grekova's best-known works, *Vdovii parokhod*, chronicles the lives of five female residents of a *kommunalka* from the Great Patriotic War until the 1970s. The women come from varying socioeconomic backgrounds (another trait uniting the communal apartment with the line). These differences and the confined space of the apartment create a state of permanent conflict, as Grekova's intellectual narrator Ol'ga Ivanovna sadly recounts:

In general the atmosphere in the flat was tense and always on the verge of a crisis. There was always someone at war with someone— Kapa with Panka Zykova, Panka with Anfisa, Ada Efimovna with Kapa—and I was involved in various confrontations too, however

sincerely I craved peace. . . . In these domestic battles coalitions and
alliances were formed. The coalitions changed like patterns in a ka-
leidoscope, more often than not for unknown reasons. Sometimes
everyone would take up arms against one person. And then there
were dreadful periods when everyone was at war with everyone
else. There were also periods when everyone was at peace with each
other, but these were rare, and only in exceptional circumstances.[51]

Although the campaigns, alliances, and plots mirror the male-
dominated epic of war or politics, they exist on the small scale
of *byt*, exaggerating every gesture, remark, and action. Reduced
scope and magnified impact increase the chronotope of crisis's
unrelenting pressure. One result is constant uncertainty and sim-
mering anger, a morass of misinterpretations, petty vendettas,
and shifting allegiances. Such turmoil recalls the spontaneity
that is the problematic starting point in a socialist realist novel.[52]
Grekova portrays this unenviable environment as the inescapable reality of Ol'ga Ivanovna and, by extension, the intelligentsia: formerly a piano player, she now yells in the kitchen. The
narrative downplays her role in the apartment's hostilities, with
the unstated assumption that she tries to distance herself from
the crass actions of her uncultured neighbors. Ol'ga Ivanovna
strives for dialogue instead of strife; her consideration of others'
opinions is indicative of Grekova's later prose and how intellectuals see themselves within it.[53]

Men are an absent yet problematic force in the *kommunalka*. In
Vdovii parokhod the alcoholic veteran Fedor sows discord and
jealousy among the women by his very appearance, a situation
that ends in tragedy when he falls under a tram and Anfisa
blames herself. In his seminal study Il'ia Utekhin notes that, while
men were initially the informal leaders of *kommunalki,* one re-
spondent later pigeonholed this function as "broads' business."
The communal apartment, like the family, is an everyday zone
men abandon to women when they leave home to visit a lover,
get drunk, or both.[54]

The *kommunalka*'s crowded living conditions exposed the unsavory secrets of private life, rendering them a topic for others'
conversations. When Pan'ka's lover leaves her, the other "widows" debate his action without any clear demarcation between
what may and may not be discussed. Such distinctions are not

operative in the communal apartment.[55] The rare moments of peace caused by overwhelming individual or collective tragedy (e.g., a husband's death) illustrate that the women are not inherently vicious but are merely reacting to the close quarters, constant contact, and poor living conditions, all of which promote strife. War and postwar privation are experiences common to all Soviets of Grekova's and Baranskaia's generation. However, while the bloodshed of 1941–45 was often invoked to unite the Soviet Union's citizens, the vicissitudes of *byt* divided them. *Vdovii parokhod* suggests that the nation is indeed one big communal apartment, a feminized metaphor that parallels the more famous comparison of the USSR to a vast labor camp. While such an image would have been impermissible to convey explicitly in print, Grekova's work makes this unflattering link by accessing the same insignificant realm of *byt* that hindered Soviet attempts to remake society.

The hospital ward is another, even less pleasant feminized locus where time and space intersect through crises and forced interaction with strangers. After breaking her leg, doctor Kira Petrovna, in Grekova's novella *Perelom* (The Breaking Point, 1987), at first cannot withstand the pain and lack of movement. The insufferable becomes bearable and then routine as she begins to notice the ward's peculiarities. These are filtered through the special burden of hospital time, as Kira Petrovna observes.[56] She notes that "it's surprising how a stay in the hospital narrows your horizon. More precisely, there is no horizon, but instead something rectangular: the walls of the ward, a ceiling, door, window. Any little thing becomes an event. They've put someone on crutches, they've discharged someone. They've brought in a new patient. . . ."[57]

The outside world has no meaning for the patients. It has been replaced by a *byt* where "they" (doctors and nurses) control everything. As in the communal apartment, scale matters: the petty becomes paramount due to immobility, close quarters, and unavoidable contact. The woman's freedom is restricted, except for the ability to think and worry about the home she cannot supervise.

The protagonist's changed life after her fall constitutes the metaphorical and literal breaking point of the work's title, a key theme in Grekova's later works.[58] As with the repentance of Anfisa's prodigal Vadim in *Vdovii parokhod,* Kira Petrovna's callous son Valiun repents after his thoughtlessness has symbolically and physically inscribed itself on his mother's body. According to the didactic mimesis of documentation that dominated this stage of women's writing, character transformation must be made legible. This guides the reader to the correct conclusion, which, in the case of *Perelom,* means recognizing the conjoined problems of maternal love and infantilized male children.

While the characters' fates are sometimes crudely obvious, history is a more subtle force in women's writing. The predilection for things past is not peculiar to female authors, but its mode of exposition is gender-specific. At times women's prose filters memory through specifically female moments connected with the body, a tendency that becomes more pronounced during and after perestroika. Grekova's story "Letom v gorode" (Summer in the City, 1962) assesses Stalinism through a flashback to the consequences of the 1936 ban on abortion. Mother Valentina Stepanovna's suffering symbolizes the human costs of totalitarianism; the link is understated, making the story acceptable for publication. Her past shows that sometimes the personal is not itself political, as Nancy Armstrong famously notes, but parallels the political: Valentina Stepanovna lacks control over her reproductive health in a way that mirrors all citizens' diminished agency and autonomy under Stalin. For women, however, this control operated through the body (e.g., criminalization of abortion), a factor men did not experience. This corporeality of control defines and limits personal autonomy, a theme amplified by Ulitskaia's post-Soviet prose.[59]

"Letom v gorode" implies that an individual's sense of temporality structures the connections between memory and collective experience. The results are far from positive. This personal perception of time ties Valentina Stepanovna's inability to have an abortion to daughter Lial'ka's birth and the latter's plan to terminate her own pregnancy many years later. The doubled fate of mother and daughter suggests that women's problems did not end after Khrushchev legalized abortion. The narrative hints that male irresponsibility, state indifference, and the difficulties of *byt* continued to make women the victims of their own bodies.

Repetition is even more damning in Grekova's masterful novel *Svezho predanie* (In Recent Memory), written in 1962 but not published until almost thirty years later. Tsarist anti-Semitism, the Holocaust, and Stalinism exterminate the relatives of protagonist Konstantin Isaakovich Levin, whose name simultaneously evokes Tolstoy's truth-seeking hero and Russia's Jewish population. As the critic Iuliia Govorukhina notes, similarities reiterate common fates. Vera, Levin's mother, dies while giving birth to Tsilia, named for a sister murdered in the 1905 pogroms. Tsilia herself is killed in occupied Ukraine after someone informs the Nazis that she is Jewish. After the war, Levin's friend Iura is arrested because of his association with the "cosmopolitan" (viz. Jewish) science of cybernetics.[60] Explicit connections between Stalinism, anti-Semitism, and Nazi genocide made this work more daring than *Odin den' Ivana Denisovicha*, as Aleksandr Tvardovskii signaled when he declined to publish it in *Novyi mir* but accepted Solzhenitsyn's work. While "Letom v gorode" depicts an ordinary mother-daughter conflict in order to mask its claims on history, Grekova's novel openly shows anti-Semitism to be a constant in Russian culture. The various temporal layers negate the possibility of progress for both Soviet Jewry and humanity as a whole, thus denying a key tenet of socialist realism's legacy.

Like *Svezho predanie*, Baranskaia's *Den' pominoveniia* relates past to present through grief and suffering. The novel portrays widows literally and symbolically moving between memory and reality as they journey to the graves of husbands who died during the Great Patriotic War. Memory is the only theme where female writers at times approximate the large-scale aspirations of their male colleagues, as when Grossman's *Zhizn' i sud'ba* depicts the horror of war as a portal to the past. For Baranskaia mourning takes on gendered form as memory binds present and past through a series of flashbacks to ordinary life during evacuation and under occupation.

However, Baranskaia's work reveals that memory, too, is disjointed, with connections absent or willfully suppressed despite the documentary tendency associated with the war theme. In decrying Nazi aggression and US saber-rattling during the Cold War, *Den' pominoveniia* ignores the Soviet occupation of Eastern Europe and Afghanistan, where the very Russians who purportedly "lack the capacity to hate" nonetheless became the aggressors.[61] In this sense Baranskaia's novel unwittingly parroted the era's official platitudes of peace even as the author herself was becoming increasingly estranged from the state. Her narrative implies that recollection is not a solution to the fragmented and ateleological nature of women's time. Rather, memory reproduces unresolved tragedies within a scope that renders them less immediate but still painful. Everyday problems and their refraction in national tragedy indicate how temporality and setting destabilize rather than support female characters.

Women's time and space combine a series of set locales with a temporality of fragmentation, self-erasure, and repetition—all aspects of the quotidian Baranskaia and Grekova depict. While memory spans past and present, this bridge is formed by a grief and loss that challenge any lasting sense of progress, leaving a painful legacy of widows and single mothers. In this sense commemorating the Great Patriotic War is the apotheosis of collective female mourning. As *Den' pominoveniia* reveals, this gendered sorrow can fall prey to official visions of events that relegate women's voices to a supportive chorus intoning the monologic state view of history.

The Vicissitudes of *Byt*: Defining Women's Themes

Documentary ambitions, an emphasis on *byt*, and the post-Stalinist reemergence of the private created conditions for the discussion of "women's" issues in officially sanctioned literature. To this end Baranskaia and Grekova emphasize, to varying degrees, five interrelated topics: work, love, abortion, rape, and the cult of motherhood. While these all involved men, critics and authors characterized most as belonging to the female sphere of daily life. The prose of Baranskaia and Grekova posits that these themes (with one notable exception) are typical in a reflective sense and are thus worthy of documentation. What is deemed emblematic for the reality of one group (women) is intrinsically worth depicting. The authors whose works I analyze appropriate this logic to justify illustrating the problems of female characters in the prestigious "thick" journals that have long dominated

Russian high culture. Baranskaia's and Grekova's focus on these themes established a trend that later shaped perestroika and post-Soviet women's writing.

Work is the least controversial of these topics. In many ways images of women's professional lives—the careers of the intelligentsia—attest to what Beth Holmgren describes as the successful equal opportunity policies accompanying the retrograde gender roles of Stalinist and Thaw culture. The work community is a parallel family for many women, including the fatigued but enthusiastic Ol'ga in *Nedelia kak nedelia* and Grekova's scientist-mothers in the novella *Kafedra* (The Faculty, 1978). In this respect Birgit Fuchs, in her monograph on Baranskaia, greatly overstates the case when she labels the author anti-Soviet. Baranskaia's and Grekova's characters enjoy work: it represents genuine involvement in a professional world created by the women themselves.[62] In a telling example, Grekova's "Za prokhodnoi" shows male and female scientists joyfully advancing the cause of the Soviet military-industrial complex, demonstrating that individual creativity and intellectual camaraderie coexist with Cold War ideology.[63]

The image of the professional woman, however, harbors a host of controversies rooted in distinctions between *byt* and *bytie*. First, Russian culture views successful professional women as worth depicting because of their anomalous status. In Vladimir Men'shov's film *Moskva slezam ne verit* (Moscow Does Not Believe in Tears, 1979) single mother Katia becomes a factory director through hard work and state support, while her less fortunate female friends languish in the working class. Sometimes these exceptional women are unwelcome. In *Damskii master* Mar'ia Vladimirovna's assistant resents his female supervisor.[64] Professional men, such as careerist Glebov in Trifonov's *Dom na naberezhnoi*, are not discussed through gender; they are the norm and thus need neither explanation nor justification. Women, however, exist at the margins of the work hierarchy and invite comment, if not criticism.

Economic necessity as well as enthusiasm made the working woman a constant in Baranskaia's and Grekova's prose. Ol'ga in *Nedelia kak nedelia* never questions why neither husband nor government takes more interest in her problems; her struggles with groceries, children, and transportation imply that caring for the family justifies such everyday trials. This acceptance of the status quo accompanies what Tat'iana Rovenskaia perceptively labels a gendered guilt felt by women when beset by the domestic and professional obligations they cannot fulfill without more state support.[65]

Baranskaia has suggested that such career women are symptomatic of masculine behavior, which threatens the gendered binarism of Soviet society. This stance contradicts clear narrative endorsement of successful women in *Nedelia kak nedelia*, where Ol'ga derives meaning from using her university education and experience. Neither implied author nor characters can resolve the issue of women taking on a "male" role (breadwinner) while maintaining "female" duties (wife, mother). Grekova supplies a more ironic image of the working woman. Tat'iana Vasil'evna in the story "Pod fonarem" (Under the Streetlight, 1963) is a self-professed bad housekeeper who focuses on scientific work instead of being feminine: "She was not a woman by profession. Just as one might not speak French or English, she did not speak the language of women."[66]

Like work, the search for love is a major topic in post-1953 prose, albeit one inherently evoking private life and explicit gendered differences refracted through divergent male and female ethics. Nicholas Žekulin insightfully notes that a woman's "right" to love, while an age-old expectation, was repackaged by late-Soviet culture under the rubric of personal happiness. This happiness, as Grekova's and particularly Baranskaia's characters demonstrate, assumes marriage and children. Love, however, usually ends badly. Often the very conditions of relationships promote inequality and male irresponsibility—if not worse. In Grekova's *Kafedra*, for instance, Nina's lover is a married alcoholic actor who is both the father of one of her three sons and has another woman.[67]

For women such as Mar'ia Vladimirovna constant responsibility (a moral equivalent of the double burden) results from broken marriages and failed relationships. Her absent husband and platonic relationship with the young hairdresser Vitalii substantiate Svetlana Boym's conclusion that after Stalinism intimacy referred to friends rather than to couples: emotional contact supplants sexualized closeness (at least for female characters).[68] Interestingly enough, Baranskaia and Grekova provide no examples of wives having affairs, suggesting a monopoly on fidelity that tells the reader more about how the authors differentiate female and male values than about "real" behavior. Women's love is synonymous with a higher ethical standard and the moral duties it entails. Despite their commitment to documenting everyday life as typical in a reflective sense, Baranskaia and Grekova emulate a transformative approach when they imagine women not as they are but as they should be.

In this subtly schematic context, negative characters embody the individual symptoms and consequences of undesirable male behavior. Unlike in some perestroika works, there is no claim that men per se are the collective enemy. In the novella *Fazan* (Pheasant, 1984) Grekova's sole dubious protagonist, the spendthrift Fedor Filatovich, lies dying in bed. Tortured by a dripping faucet that symbolizes his wasted life (a rare cliché in Grekova's prose) he remembers past infidelities and mistakes with women. Such painful ethical stocktaking, one facet of Stagnation-era introspection, resembles the gloomy recollections of Tolstoy's Ivan Il'ich.[69] What is different is the emphasis on Fedor Filatovich specifically as an erring male who reviews his life by focusing on how he has deceived the opposite sex.

With its rogue's gallery of unpleasant men, *Nedelia kak nedelia* provides another harsh look at male ethics: Shura's husband drinks, Dark Liusa's husband wants her to stay home (an affront to Baranskaia's female intellectuals), and Light Liusa's husband has another wife.[70] Each embodies a problematic male behavior, creating a portrayal of "typical" men whose deficiencies contrast with the more positive female characters (almost all of whom are mothers).

Female characters are stronger as well as more ethical. Abandoned by her husband, Magda in Grekova's novel *Porogi* (The Rapids, 1981) is more stable and self-reliant than the ironically named Neshatov, who is occasionally cruel and often unstable (*shatkii*). Many of Grekova's women exhibit the Tolstoyan ethics Gary Saul Morson and Caryl Emerson connect with Bakhtinian prosaics: "[Characters] discover that they can make correct moral decisions without a general philosophy. Instead of a system, they come to rely on a moral wisdom derived from living rightly from moment to moment."[71] (Interestingly enough, two male characters—*Kafedra*'s caring Professor Fliagin and the stunted Garusov—exhibit the same self-sacrifice as they assume maternal roles.) While Grekova's women act according to the subtler ethics of Tolstoy's earlier period, Baranskaia's rigid characterizations follow the moral absolutism of his last decades. Motherhood, whether in its sacred (*Den' pominoveniia*) or mundane (*Nedelia kak nedelia*) manifestation, dictates maternal characters' actions and thoughts. Based on this logic, maternity is the sum total of women's positive ethical system.

The sincerity of Baranskaia's and Grekova's mothers is one of the core values of the post-Stalinist intelligentsia and, not coincidentally, a key tenet of Thaw and Stagnation fiction. Female genuineness predictably counters male duplicity. Fedor Filatovich in *Гажа* is the clearest example: a chronic imposter, he tricks German POWs and sleeps with both a neighbor and her teenage daughter during the New Economic Policy, an era condemned for its amorality. The predatory and insincere male infects his (often unintended) offspring, as illustrated by Maika in *Kafedra*. Maika is Grekova's only psychologically complex female villain. Seduced by her high school music teacher, Maika never knew her father, who presumably abandoned his family. As she shamelessly exploits kindly professor Enen, the reader is led to the inescapable conclusion that amorality breeds more of the same.[72] As with the erring sons, whose selfishness causes their mothers' hospitalization in *Vdovii parokhod* and *Perelom*, female characters' bodies and psyches legibly reflect the signs of male malfeasance. Even Grekova's less strident prose has an ethical agenda inseparable from representation: exposition must reaffirm content.

Characters are sometimes stylized, recalling socialist realism's transformative typicality and its subordination of psychologically nuanced representation to a dubious script for remaking reality. Baranskaia and Grekova pursue an analogous goal through the subtler means of post-Stalinist documentation by employing "objective" descriptions to persuade the reader that reality is not as it should be. However, neither author considered a systematic critique of Soviet culture based on the episodic gender inequalities they identified. Instead, Baranskaia and Grekova emphasized symptoms, such as the need for compassion toward women or the problems of (male) alcoholism.[73]

Baranskaia and Grekova demonstrate that few male or female characters are either unequivocally punished or essentially evil. While their actions may be despicable (e.g., hippie freeloader Valiun in Grekova's *Perelom*), the narratives document their irresponsibility as an inevitable feature of *byt* and gendered interactions. Truly atrocious actions are ascribed to an a priori identified enemy (e.g., German rapist soldiers in *Den' pominoveniia*). This tacit limit on the illustration of evil disappears during perestroika.

Divergent male and female ethics lead to constant conflict in everyday life. Baranskaia and Grekova do not allow their female characters recourse to alcohol, the traditional male alternative to *byt*. In post-Stalinist literature men's drinking both liberates them (for a short time) and unites the relationships and personal interests comprising private life as they gather (usually outside the home) and enact an imagined escape from tedious responsibility.[74]

Women's alcoholism remains invisible not merely because of the reflective approach to describing reality and the small percentage of female problem drinkers. More important, alcoholism reveals a dereliction of duty; it violates Baranskaia's maternal dicta and, less obviously, the case-by-case ethics of Grekova's positive characters. Neither overworked Ol'ga in *Nedelia kak nedelia* nor Mar'ia Vladimirovna in *Damskii master* can indulge in the transcendental oblivion of the intellectual protagonists in a work such as Venedikt Erofeev's *Moskva-Petushki* (From Moscow to the End of the Line, written in 1969). Male drinkers in women's prose burden their wives and mothers, as the alcoholic son in Baranskaia's "Krai sveta" amply demonstrates. Unable to escape through drink, female characters are trapped in the mind-numbing sameness of sobriety. Always responsible (and liable for those who are not), they cannot take advantage of the carnivalesque release that drinking sanctions: women are entrapped by their responsibility for others.[75]

The nonexistence of female alcoholism in Baranskaia's and Grekova's narratives has several implications for a literature that purports to document *byt*. First, the two authors imply that such women either do not exist or are unimportant: they have no place in writing that allegedly portrays reality. This stance, a mainstay of the transformative approach to literature, ironically resembles the attitudes certain critics held about the description of women's "anomalous" issues in fiction. Likewise, pre-1985 authors shy away from the physiological details (e.g., vomit, uncontrolled defecation) that are the unpalatable effluvia of Petrushevskaia's drinkers as she mocks the demand for "morality" and "spiritual life" (*dukhovnost'*) in Stagnation literature. Verisimilitude has its limits, suggesting that certain taboo actions could not exist in Soviet everyday life—and, even if they did, they would not be ascribed to Baranskaia's and Grekova's morally sound female characters.[76] While such reticent descriptions may also be a function of the age of these authors when they turned to fiction (Baranskaia was in her sixties and Grekova in her late fifties), their prose demonstrates that certain themes do not belong in literature.

Depicting a central alcoholic character, in particular, would violate the Soviet myth that *bytie* triumphs over the difficult material circumstances of *byt*, a scenario Katerina Clark describes as the victory of consciousness over spontaneity. The hopelessness of chronic drinking undermines the optimistic (Marxist-Leninist) future and the assumption that Soviet private life supports the public sphere.[77] These illusions and the gender-specific problem of female alcoholics limited permissible depictions of drinking.

Male duplicity, irresponsibility, and alcoholism mean that love—connoting a satisfying relationship that will lead to marriage and children—is a source of frustration in women's prose. The lingering lack of men some fifteen years after the war does not help this situation, as Mar'ia Vladimirovna sadly notes in Grekova's *Damskii master*. In *Vdovii parokhod* this deficit leads to various machinations and the pathetic coquetry of the neighbors over Fedor and even the child Vadim, while the narrator in Baranskaia's story "Vstrecha" (The Meeting, 1993) has sex with a stranger based only on his uncanny resemblance to the husband she lost in the war. This wish-fulfillment scenario, complete with one of the rare descriptions of coitus in the author's works, idealizes the male as strong and overpowering. This fantasy, however, only underscores the rarity of the eligible male and the endangered biological family in Baranskaia's and Grekova's prose.[78]

Women's writing in late-Soviet culture provides several examples of the reconstituted (non-nuclear) family that was a crucial force in Thaw film and literature. In Grekova's novella *Khoziaika gostinitsy* (The Hotel Manager, 1975), Masha and Vera raise Masha's baby, which one critic probably countenanced only because Vera's husband is away defending the motherland. In a similar vein, *Kafedra*'s Liuda cares for her illegitimate son with the help of friends.[79]

Male culpability, women authors opine, results from weakness. Baranskaia summarized her personal view, which colors male characters such as Shura's husband in *Nedelia kak nedelia*, as follows: "Our men are rather weak. Perhaps here the problem is that they have ceased to be the head of the family; they no longer feel the responsibility of feeding and clothing their family. Their wives receive as much, perhaps more money than they do. They feel aimless and take to drink." She implies that men are disappointing and immutable and that women must change to ensure family stability. This viewpoint echoes Stagnation-era fears of male children infantilized by maternal love and an educational system dominated by women. Baranskaia deploys the traditional critique of the powerful woman in arguing that men, stripped of their traditional "rightful" role of leader, have now lost their purpose. This attack on strong women reverses the pattern of the nineteenth-century superfluous man and his Turgenev maiden, where the latter's physical and moral beauty uplift the former from gloomy uselessness.[80] Now, Baranskaia implies, women's innate strength and willingness to suffer for others emasculate the men they try to aid.

Other thematic areas of Baranskaia's and Grekova's narratives diverge more strikingly from literary tradition. Abortion and rape are two aspects of women's lives that Soviet literature only hesitantly discussed before 1985. In women's writing both follow from willed transgression or women's status as victims of fate. After *Kafedra*'s Liuda escapes assault by the fashionable Gena, her otherwise sympathetic roommate reproaches her, claiming that Liuda's behavior and actions "invited" rape. Those adhering to traditional roles, however, deflect unwanted attention, as when Baranskaia's Ol'ga tells a young man on the subway she is a mother so that he will stop harassing her.[81]

As with rape, abortion highlights the lack of agency Iuliia Gradskova decries as hindering Soviet women in *byt*. Women are subject to male power and the potential for physical violence. This control comes from the state through blocking or limiting access to decent health care, practical information, and contraceptives. In an atypical moment for Baranskaia, her Dark Liusa hints that she may have had an illegal abortion, while Ol'ga fears getting pregnant again (her daughter Gul'ka was not planned).[82] As a crucial part of state policy on reproductive health and fertility, discussion of abortion could not be banned from public discourse despite its unsettling implications. Why would a woman not want to give birth in a country with no official poverty, legislated gender equality, and a caring state? The unstated answers suggest that these egalitarian ideals remained far from everyday reality.

Rape, however, is essentially absent from official discussion, and both film and literature ascribed it to easily identifiable enemies. Baranskaia's story "Fotografiia Zoiki na fone dvora" (Zoika's Photograph with the Courtyard in the Background, 1993), while published in the post-Soviet era, models morality little changed by perestroika. Zoika's "shocking" biography is the only feature distinguishing this publication from the author's earlier work. After she is nearly raped by a furniture collector, Zoika remembers the night her drunken stepfather sexually assaulted her. "Zoika remembered that night when her mother was at work and her stepfather crept into her room and attacked her while she was asleep. She promised to tell her mother everything, but her stepfather lied, telling his wife that Zoika had been after him for a long time and was behaving shamelessly. There was a scandal. Tamara believed not her daughter but her husband."[83]

While the narrator clearly sympathizes with Zoika, this feeling exists alongside the story's disturbing moral, revealed after the incident with the furniture collector: women who behave decently are rewarded with marriage and children, while those who do not may be assaulted. The rapist is not a blood relative but a stepfather who, in this case, is also an alcoholic. These factors permit the unrealistic assumption that under other circumstances sexual assault by male relatives does not occur. Connecting this action to marginal characters (Zoika's stepfather) or groups (Nazi soldiers) removes it from *byt,* suggesting that rape is atypical and thus merits representation neither in a reflective nor a transformative sense. Literature distinguishes itself from the reality it supposedly documents: for Baranskaia morality is ultimately more important than verisimilitude.

Images of maternity best exemplify the ties between representation, ethics, and conservative gender roles. The mother in post-1953 women's writing is the epicenter of the chronotope of crisis, a prism for national memory, and above all an icon of responsibility and self-sacrifice. Baranskaia provides some of the few urban counterparts to the infamously idealized maternal figures in village prose: those characters in *Den' pominoveniia* living in the cities and the less stoic but still self-effacing Ol'ga in *Nedelia kak nedelia.*

Grekova's *Vdovii parokhod* presents an insightful look at the problematic consequences of sanctifying motherhood. Anfisa gives birth to her illegitimate son, and her future subservience is unambiguously foretold: "Anfisa fed her son. She overflowed into him, her master. No one had ever mastered her like this, neither Fyodor nor Grigorii. No one but Vadim." "Master" implies a sense of independence and dominance that Russian culture tropes as male. Vadim's freedom will have dire consequences for his mother, leading to her stroke and early death. Ol'ga Ivanovna, the author's mouthpiece, believes that Anfisa suffers from maternal love, an illness the male doctors will never recognize. In this sense Grekova establishes a critical middle ground between the apotheosis of motherhood (Baranskaia) and its merciless dismantling during perestroika (Petrushevskaia). *Vdovii parokhod* offers no final answer concerning whether maternity emotionally helps or harms mothers, but it certainly questions pairing motherhood with redemption in works such as Baranskaia's "Fotografiia Zoiki na fone dvora."[84]

Baranskaia and Grekova present women whose husbands have died as a special subset of mothers within a culture that, as Goscilo argues, sees itself as a nation of widows. This image became demographic fact after decades of Soviet rule had drastically reduced the male population. *Den' pominoveniia* and *Vdovii*

parokhod show maternity and widowhood as the twinned fate of
an entire generation, where loneliness and deprivation are feminized. Although less directly than in Grekova's *Svezho predanie,*
Baranskaia's novel discusses Stalinism and collectivization, in
which millions of women lost husbands, brothers, and children.
The plot, however, subsumes these horrific losses within its overarching theme—the Great Patriotic War—which was the only
sanctioned outlet for national mourning during the Soviet era.[85]
    Within this charged cultural context, Baranskaia's depiction of
Pushkin's widow, Natal'ia Goncharova, was quite controversial.
Contemporaries and successors pilloried Goncharova for violat-
ing the unwritten widows' code, namely, not spending her remaining years as a demure living monument to her husband. As
one reader appreciatively noted after reading the novella *Tsvet
temnogo medu* (The Color of Dark Honey, 1982), Baranskaia "re-
habilitates" Pushkin's widow. This redemption occurs thanks to
Baranskaia none too subtly connecting Natal'ia with the Mother
of God.[86] The author thus employs one feminine stereotype
(Goncharova as holy mother) to counteract another (Goncharova
as merry widow), evoking the ritualized Thaw label (rehabilita-
tion) for those the state exonerates. The individual woman is almost erased as author and society assign her competing roles
that subordinate selfhood to function (wife, widow, mother, victim of persecution).[87]
    Depictions of love, abortion, rape, and motherhood stem from
traditional conceptions of women (e.g., as sexual object or unit of
reproduction), which Grekova cautiously critiques and Baranskaia largely upholds. These authors' use of documentary style
and "typical" female roles solidifies traditional expectations for
women even as the writers attack the excesses resulting from
these demands. Such instantiations of enduring gender roles in
Russian culture qualify the Soviet modernity project and its symbol, the career woman. Baranskaia's and Grekova's heroines
demonstrate that a woman's sense of self derives from the problematic private sphere and not public life, with its showcased female scientists and engineers.
    The posited egalitarianism of Soviet rhetoric carefully limited
divisive discussions of differences between men and women.
Byt, however, served as a code word for "natural" distinctions

between male and female experience. Literary critics after 1953 linked the quotidian to banality, reduced scope, ateleological time, private life, and anomaly. Such comparisons deformed assessments of women's lives and literature.

However, Baranskaia's and Grekova's fiction employed an appeal to realism and sincerity and claims of typicality in order to establish the quotidian as a legitimate, if controversial, literary topic. Female authors benefited from their appropriation of *byt*, making it a cultural space that rendered women's problems visible in mainstream prose. Perestroika-era women writers built on this precedent, using the everyday to move beyond a selective examination of gendered issues, resulting in an artistically diverse group of writings that critiqued Soviet society with brutal honesty.

2

Perestroika and the Emergence of Women's Prose

Liudmila Petrushevskaia, Tat'iana Tolstaia, and Women's Anthologies

Non-mother. Non-housewife. Non-wife. . . . This is a world where everything is its opposite.

Marina Abasheva

One can pull an entire world out of a single word.

Tat'iana Tolstaia

On a rainy Moscow afternoon in May 1988 author Svetlana Vasilenko happened to meet Larisa Vaneeva, another prose writer. As the two women talked, they compared their lives—a series of menial jobs, no opportunities for publishing—and realized they knew many women writers who, having previously garnered praise for their work, could now find no interested publishers. Vasilenko's and Vaneeva's chance encounter led them to create one of a series of women's literary anthologies that tried to correct this problem, in the process giving women's writing an unprecedented prominence and notoriety.[1]

From the early 1960s until roughly 1984 female authors had appropriated *byt* as a cultural space for selectively documenting gendered problems within mainstream literature. Perestroika

58

(1985–91) was a cataclysmic period for Soviet culture as Mikhail Gorbachev unleashed a series of economic and political changes that curtailed the role of the state, effectively ending censorship while also dramatically lowering the standard of living for the intelligentsia and Soviet citizens as a whole. Having long dealt with the idea of everyday crisis, women authors now existed within a context of national upheavals refracted through the prism of the quotidian. Both newspapers and "thick" journals published increasingly scathing exposés of past and current problems. Unlike during the Thaw, public criticism of the state began with attacks on Stalinism but went on to challenge Lenin and the allegedly democratic October Revolution. The Chernobyl disaster, ethnic tensions, and ongoing anti-Soviet protests in Eastern Europe added to an atmosphere of imminent catastrophe.

Appropriately enough, the first of these events to greatly influence women's prose was one firmly rooted in *byt*: Gorbachev's infamous sobriety campaign, which began in 1985 and was abandoned as a failure three years later. The policy both suspended the state's tacit support for the heavy drinking of the Stagnation years and implied that this private yet visible activity was now (once again) grounds for public intervention. This effort was more serious than its predecessors and women writers became less circumspect in their descriptions of drinking.

Women's prose came to be associated with the vitriol and conflict of perestroika. The phenomenal success of the authors Liudmila Petrushevskaia (1938–) and Tat'iana Tolstaia (1951–), coupled with the publication of six women's literary anthologies between 1989 and 1991, made female writers a visible and controversial feature of late-Soviet literature. Women authors responded to post-1985 cultural shifts while following the thematic precedents of the older Thaw and Stagnation authors who preceded them, using *byt* as common cultural context and focusing on female protagonists. Perestroika women's prose, however, abandoned the staid verisimilitude of Baranskaia and Grekova, who adapted poorly to the new conditions and were all but forgotten by 1991; these authors' conservative styles and virtuous heroines no longer captivated readers overwhelmed by political and cultural upheaval.

After 1985 women's prose, like Soviet society as a whole,

introduced previously private, taboo, or politically suspect
topics into the public arena for discussion, often digging into the
past to do so.[2] These themes, while shocking those readers accus-
tomed to the more circumspect approach of previous decades,
continued the post-Stalinist rhetoric of documentation by foregrounding an appeal to truth, contemporaneity, and the importance of the everyday. However, many of the era's female authors
now openly and systematically critiqued gender differences,
claiming that the state neglected or even actively victimized
women. Some writers (Petrushevskaia, Tolstaia, Nina Gorlanova)
addressed this problem by emphasizing collective crisis over personal tragedy. Others (Vasilenko, Marina Karpova) directly attacked a state their narratives showed to be misogynistic.

The appearance of women's anthologies in both Moscow and
the provinces created a prominent cultural space within which
authors and critics could discuss women's prose. These reactions
to female writers raised now familiar issues of typicality and
neutrality, anxieties inherited from socialist realism and appropriated by post-Stalinist women's writing. Unlike in previous
decades, however, critics used gender per se as an artistic and
ideological criterion, with *byt* no longer serving as a coded reference to women's experiences and creative abilities. Instead, critical supporters and opponents saw this writing as a distinct literary trend arising from the authors' identities as women.

Exposing Everyday Life: The Intelligentsia and the Theatrics of *Byt*

Perestroika women authors, like their male counterparts, exploited the era's new openness. Scrutinizing areas of private life
previously off limits, they identified a new target during the late
1980s, namely, the intelligentsia, which predecessors had supported despite occasional misgivings. The irreverent manner
with which women's writing addressed intellectuals paralleled
its approach to two other constants inherited from Stagnation:
gender roles and the state.

After 1985 national crises and increased freedom caused
the private cynicism of Stagnation to spill out into the open.

Reevaluating past and present, perestroika fundamentally changed the content and style of public discourse. The legacy of the socialist realist esthetic asserted a worldview focusing on life's hopeful essence instead of problematic phenomena. Discussions of *byt* from the 1960s through the 1980s had thus subordinated the everyday to typicality and its promise of a radiant future. The Gorbachev era destroyed this scenario. As crisis after crisis shook the Soviet empire, public discussion of the quotidian became a harbinger of destruction. Perestroika propounded an esthetic of negation, which envisioned reality as rapidly worsening. Mikhail Zolotonosov summarized the zeitgeist graphically yet accurately when he labeled this negative trend in glasnost literature and culture a "cacotopia."[3] The positive Soviet worldview no longer proved viable and was supplanted by its antithesis, which female writers helped to create.

Petrushevskaia, together with Tolstaia, is the author most often identified with women's prose during perestroika. Born just after the height of the Stalinist purges, she first attracted attention as a dramatist. Despite many difficulties arising as a result of her "inappropriate" material, in 1977 she was admitted to the Writers Union as a playwright. Her elevated profile was largely due to her shocking themes and exposition, whose bleak vision of private existence accompanied the death of optimism in public life. For one critic the author's novella *Svoi krug* (Our Crowd, written in 1979 and published in 1988) was a chamber of horrors masked by realism, an image evoking an exhibitionistic array of terrors. Petrushevskaia's themes make the rogue's gallery of irresponsible men in *Nedelia kak nedelia* seem tame. As Helena Goscilo observes, the physically and morally repulsive becomes banal in the author's work: "Suicide, alcoholism, prostitution, one-night stands, fictitious marriages, unwanted pregnancies and abortions, neglected children, crushing poverty, theft, physical and psychological violence constitute the 'norm.'"[4]

Petrushevskaia's prose exemplifies perestroika's negation of idealism and obsession with exposure. These trends and the author's focus on the body privilege material *byt* over ideational *bytie*, with the preponderance of female characters underscoring the dubious trinity female-physical-quotidian. The body is far from a unified whole in these works. Petrushevskaia mixes actions associated with the upper and lower bodily strata. Despite various critics' assertions to the contrary, this scenario diverges from Bakhtin's conception of carnival owing to two key missing elements: "an authentically celebratory dimension" and a feeling of community (however temporary). Indeed, in complete opposition to Bakhtin, Petrushevskaia's prose links corporeality and human enslavement to its animal instincts. Her narratives' famously brutal frankness led critics to pair her with the *chernukha* (sexually explicit or violent material) prevalent in the late 1980s and 1990s.[5]

Petrushevskaia's works manifest the desperate fate of her characters as starkly as possible. Transgression has highly visible consequences: readers, the narrative implies, must clearly connect misstep and tragedy. Accidental pregnancy, a noticeable result of (usually illicit) sexual activity, is a trope that perpetuates the cycle of single mothers and unwanted children populating the author's works.[6] Such behavioral causality develops a trend begun in women's writing of the 1960s and 1970s (e.g., Valentina Stepanovna's child from philandering Volodia in Grekova's "Letom v gorode" or the seduction of teenage Alka in Maiia Ganina's novella *Sozvezdie bliznetsov* [The Gemini Constellation, 1974]).[7] As with the uneasy blending of documentation and morality in this earlier prose, immorality leaves legible traces on women's bodies and lives. Petrushevskaia's works, however, do not claim there is a gap between male and female ethics. Instead, they place the reader at the edge of the chasm separating actual human actions from an unspoken ideal only visible through its horrifying antithesis.

Petrushevskaia's worldview fundamentally differs from that of Tolstaia, the other female author shaping perestroika literature. Tolstaia, firmly rooted in the Saint Petersburg intelligentsia, is one of the daughters of a family with authors Aleksei N. Tolstoi and Leo Tolstoy among its relatives. An early reviewer praised Tolstaia's prose as revealing life to be a gift that all too many squander as they look for meaning beyond the everyday.[8] The variegated wonders of existence—whether fascinating or terrifying—shape her rich and textured language, a prose devoted to elucidating *byt*'s opportunities instead of the repeated dead ends marking Petrushevskaia's narratives.

For Tolstaia the reader is a creature of textual response rather than visceral reaction, as her story "Poet i muza" (The Poet and the Muse) implies. In her prose it is more often female characters who are predators, peddling platitudes to justify their schemes:

Nina was a marvelous woman, an ordinary woman, a doctor, and it goes without saying that she had her right to personal happiness like everyone else. . . . She needed a—you know—an animal passion, dark windy nights with streetlamps aglow. She needed to perform a heroine's classical feat as if it were a mere trifle: to wear out seven pairs of iron boots, break seven iron staffs in two, devour seven loaves of iron bread, and receive in supreme reward not some golden rose or snow-white pedestal but a burned-out match or a crumpled ball of a bus ticket—a crumb from the banquet table where the radiant king, her heart's desire, had feasted.[9]

Nina emerges through the careworn clichés of late-Soviet *byt*: a woman's right to personal happiness; the implication that men are disappointing; and a catalogue of romantic adventures plagiarizing Russian folklore. As with Petrushevskaia's characters, Tolstaia's would-be original heroines quickly blend into a sea of similarities: doctor Nina resembles nurse Zoia, who in the story "Okhota na mamonta" (Hunting the Wooly Mammoth) wants to woo a surgeon but fails to trap even that most boring of beasts, the male engineer. What these protagonists mistake for authentic experience is an ironic reworking of Vladimir Maiakovskii's suicide note, in which the vessel of love is shattered on the rocks of *byt*. These women's relationships end due to a lack of compassion and a refusal to recognize their beloved as an autonomous human being. It is this callous egocentrism, not life itself, that dooms their love.

Indeed, Nina's grief following the death of her beloved Grisha is quickly forgotten when a widowed friend remodels her former husband's room in "traditional" peasant style. The narrative's juxtaposition of such mismatched categories (death and interior design) confused at least one critic, who assumed this final evidence of Nina's vapid callousness to be an attack on intellectuals' appropriation of peasant culture.[10] This attempt to determine the political meaning of *byt*'s knickknacks recalls Gary Saul Morson's "semiotic totalitarians," including the Soviet subspecies that policed the politicized semiotics of the quotidian. For Tolstaia the meaning of everyday activity is inherently diffuse and defies a single, moralizing interpretation.

Byt in Petrushevskaia's prose is more visual and causal. Her catalogue of crime and punishment, with its penchant for publicly portraying the consequences of transgression, connects the author to a long tradition in Russian literature. In this sense she recalls Fyodor Dostoyevsky and his description of "the human animal, the simultaneous victim/victor, and the murdering mother," along with another, overlooked commonality: the Dostoevskian proclivity for public suicide. Like the spurned Svidrigailov, Petrushevskaia's characters end their lives in as visible a manner as possible. The two favored methods are hanging and defenestration: former convict Andrei threatens to throw himself out of the window (again), while the teenage outcast in "Batsilla" and the husband in "Gripp" (The Flu) act on this impulse.[11]

Defenestration is public and irreversible, while hanging oneself presents an opportunity to be saved and comforted while engaging in the emotional manipulation on which Petrushevskaia's characters feed.[12] Natal'ia Ivanova remarks that Petrushevskaia treats Baranskaia's content in an existential manner: Zoika could have hanged herself had she not been transformed into a demure and chaste wife. Petrushevskaia, however, would have seen such a resolution as the artificial and unlikely rebirth that it was. While her characters and narrators constantly indulge in theatrical displays, they are of an entirely realistic sort— at least in her perestroika-era prose.[13]

An often incongruous mystical element entered Petrushevskaia's later narratives, as in the bizarre novel *Nomer odin, ili V sadakh drugikh vozmozhnostei* (Number One, or In the Gardens of Other Possibilities, 2004). The narrative highlights a cannibal raping and eating an actress, with this scene caught on a videotape that the protagonist hopes to sell to an American university. Such sadistic voyeurism is a classic Petrushevskaian trope, as is the chronotope of the road encompassing the work's characters while they move from Moscow to the north, battling over a relic that has the power to transpose human souls.[14]

This novel illuminates a key Petrushevskaian conceit: characters are pawns in their own self-defeating games of desire and destruction, which give them little more autonomy than the items (animate or otherwise) they fight over. By contrast, Tolstaia's dichotomy between human and object is more descriptive than prescriptive: things tell us about their owners, revealing the hidden universe of each individual's *byt*. In the story of the same name Sonia's enamel dove brooch symbolizes her naive passion for the fictitious epistolary amour the vicious Ada Adol'fovna creates for her. Ada Adol'fovna herself becomes attached to the pin after Sonia sends it to her imaginary lover. With its Christian overtones the dove suggests both the purity and devotion of its owner and the longevity of good intentions. While Ada probably burned Sonia's letters, the dove escaped destruction since, according to the narrator, doves don't burn.

This provocative claim recalls Mikhail Bulgakov's more famous statement ("Manuscripts don't burn"), which sees literature as a repository of human values. Tolstaia's story, by contrast, ends with the meaning of these values themselves. It does not matter that this significance is embodied in a keepsake sent by a feeble-brained woman to a man who never existed.[15] Here, as often in Tolstaia's works, readers must reevaluate their assessment of what makes a life worth living. Sonia's brooch suggests that, while its naive owner probably perished during the siege of Leningrad, her life was fuller than that of her intellectual "friends" who survived.

Objects reflect their owners—with often unsettling results. In Tolstaia's story "Krug" (The Circle) elderly Vasilii Mikhailovich stands in a crowd outside a stall whose owner sells cosmetics and laments the female penchant for artifice:

Woman, woman, do you exist? . . . What are you? . . . High up a Siberian tree your hat blinks its eyes in fear; a cow gives birth in suffering so you can have shoes; a lamb is sheared screaming so you can warm yourself with its fleece; a sperm whale is in its death throes; a crocodile weeps; a doomed leopard pants, fleeing. Your pink cheeks come from boxes of flying dust, your smiles from golden containers with strawberry filling, your smooth skin from tubes of grease, your gaze from round, transparent jars. . . .[16]

This description, deceptively direct for Tolstaia, at first glance resembles the esthetics of Petrushevskaia in the sense that the narrative reveals the bestial underbelly of human beauty. Such is the fate of Ada Adol'fovna: the desperate pursuit of elegance in an attempt to halt time. The impatient buyers, like Vasilii Mikhailovich and his wife in the beauty salon, have forgotten that life itself is a gift that renders makeovers redundant.

The narrative's message, however, is multivalent. Vasilii Mikhailovich criticizes the cruelty involved in women maintaining their outward appearance while perpetuating an analogous gap between facade and reality in his adulterous affairs. "Krug" depicts this duplicitous universe through an array of objects—things that, like the *byt* they constitute, hide the importance of the ordinary.[17] In a rare instance of one generation of women writers commenting on another, I. Grekova notes that details—whether physical, oral, or aural—are the building blocks of Tolstaia's prose. Grekova and Baranskaia, who legitimated *byt* and its objects as part of mainstream literature, implicitly endorsed a focus on the material. Unlike these earlier authors, Tolstaia pays more attention to the entangled relationships between characters and their possessions, giving things in these narratives both temporality and morality. In her prose the material world is more than the storehouse of documentation.[18]

Tolstaia's objects draw the reader inward, while Petrushevskaia's horrors externalize, reminding readers that they are unwitting voyeurs peering in from outside the narrative. Her post-Soviet story "Kredo" (Credo) carries this uncomfortable situation to an extreme as members of a medical seminar watch slides of undressed patients. The most intriguing of these shows an older woman clearly uncomfortable with her nudity. As the narrator breathlessly adds, resistance is always more interesting than consent.[19]

Petrushevskaia's themes, which created a scandal when they first appeared during perestroika, are hardly unique in world literature. Instead, as Karla Hielscher and others have demonstrated, the author's novelty lies in a narrative style fueled by rumor, gossip, and polemic as cornerstones of oral communication. Petrushevskaia's best-known work, the novella *Vremia noch'* (The Time Night, 1992), represents the apotheosis of her overly active storytellers. Through communication with her (unwilling) interlocutors, middle-aged Anna Andrianovna assumes the mantle of public morality in addition to her role as maternal savior.

The narrator is a conduit for the communal voice and its prejudices, rendering *Vremia noch'* and other works even more startling owing to the often matter-of-fact comments on their horrific content.[20]

Petrushevskaia's garrulous narrators reveal others' faults as dramatically as possible. These monological storytellers combine the verbal habits of the nosy *kommunalka* neighbors in earlier prose with perestroika's muckraking journalism. Blurring the boundary between public and private, they imply that even the most intimate details are fair game for public discussion. Although this worldview continued the documentation beloved by critics during Thaw and Stagnation, it now suggested a compulsive search for social ills instead of a healthy culture admiring itself in the mirror of literature. In both instances the artifice of narrative masks itself through the representation of reality.

Tolstaia's narrators, however, signal the fact of storytelling with an irony that is more complex than the totalizing delusions of Petrushevskaia's gossips. Petrushevskaia's storytellers critique others' actions and thus indirectly reveal their own weaknesses. Tolstaia's works rarely yield a unified picture of her raconteurs: they exist only at the level of milieu, allusion and, above all, in their response to language.

This response exposes her characters' hypocrisy even as they cry out for truth and justice. In "Krug," quasi-direct discourse echoes the protagonist's outrage at the blood and suffering behind women's quest for beauty. However, Vasilii Mikhailovich's adultery and refusal to approach his former lover Izol'da (now a homeless alcoholic) show that he, too, is immoral.[21] His anger reveals that pitying animals is an ethical commonplace sometimes commensurate with mistreating one's fellow human beings.

Tolstaia's use of folkloric motifs leads to similar results as her narratives expose the genre's potential to devolve into triteness. Much like Vasilii Mikhailovich's internal monologue on the cost of beauty, fairy-tale ideas about happiness and romance, while inherently valid, lose their vitality in the hands of patently inauthentic characters. Zoia, who sees her name and appearance embodying a lively happiness, is as morally dead as Nina, Grisha's warden-wife. Folklore is not the object of attack. As her post-Soviet novel *Kys'* (The Slynx, 2000) makes clear, Tolstaia views traditional Russian culture as a wellspring of creative potential. Rather, her works savage those who reduce it to cliché or "anti-tale." This critique questions one of the most sacrosanct features of Soviet *byt*, namely, the voice of the collective, whether embodied in gossip or the pithy sayings conveying culturedness.[22]

Petrushevskaia's narratives deploy quotidian speech for other reasons. In *Deviatyi tom* (The Ninth Volume, 2003), her overlooked collection of essays and memoirs, she advances several explanations for adopting garrulous narrators steeped in Soviet language: "[Before perestroika] there was much that I hid, camouflaged under passionless, stale, untalented storytelling. Sometimes I even spoke in the voice of the collective—the voice of the crowd and gossip. (I did not know then what has become clear to me now: all those stories were theatre.)"[23] Such disingenuous narrative strategies did not increase her small number of pre-1985 prose publications. Voluble storytellers could not disguise Petrushevskaia's vision of *byt* as an existential hell annihilating any higher purpose in life.

The appropriation of a collective voice was more successful in evoking theatricality. By putting others' lives on display, the Petrushevskaian storyteller inflates her own importance as she eagerly relates tragedy. Suffering becomes a stage; theatricality is crucial to all her works, regardless of their putative genre. Within this context traditional distinctions between tragedy (preserving dignity) and comedy (loss of dignity) are unimportant since few of her characters have any lasting self-respect. Petrushevskaia argues that infusing humor into tragic moments presumes that both are compatible in the human condition, a concept connecting her to a long Russian tradition of depicting suffering through laughter.[24] For the author *byt* is a stage from which there is no escape—even death is public and revealing.

Several stories highlight this dramaturgical tendency. The narrator of "Ioko Ono" (Yoko Ono) remarks that several generations of alcoholic Khazar women could be a "Greek tragedy," while "Teshcha Edipa" (Oedipus's Mother-in-Law) by its very name evokes doom, indecent comedy, and the inescapable conflicts between generations. Writing before the latter story appeared in 1995, Mark Lipovetskii astutely observes that the Oedipal myth implicitly informs all of Petrushevskaia's works.[25] As with the plays of Sophocles, they link individual fates to familial and collective tragedy, leading the reader to infer that humanity's spiritual and intellectual strivings are as pointless as the horrible *byt* of her characters. Following the logic of *chernukha*, Petrushevskaia uses a grim external reality to suggest an even more frightening internal wasteland.

Shakespeare's unsettling image of the family provides another model for Petrushevskaia. Her story "Novye Gamlety" (The New Hamlets) articulates what for the author is an uncharacteristically straightforward narratorial hypothesis: "The problem with Hamlet was probably the severing of temporal connections. And what are temporal connections if not the connection of father-mother-child?" Petrushevskaia explicitly connects the individual's sense of time and space to family relations, with the recurring threat of homelessness shaping the narrative. Her characters live on the threshold in their search for metaphorical and literal homes, a liminal state Goscilo relates to Dostoyevsky's fiction.[26] This borderline existence, combined with familial crises, renders it almost impossible for them to improve their lives.

Privileging dramatic genres indicates that Petrushevskaia envisions life as a stage that presents undesirable alternatives. This image fits perestroika's esthetic of negation: bettering society through identifying and attacking the impermissible. At the same time Petrushevskaia accesses Russian literature's proclivity for using plays as social commentary when she terms the novellas *Vremia noch'* and *Svoi krug* comedies.[27] Her "comic" prose, however, sooner resembles a new type of Shakespearean tragedy in which characters survive physically yet are spiritually dead.

The audience, Petrushevskaia maintains, is the hero in her works. More precisely, as she notes, it is the "positive hero," which suggests imparting a higher consciousness to the reader. Viewers unwittingly follow a scripted response: (1) Recognition of others' misery; (2) Ensuing empathy for the characters; and (3) Recognition of oneself in the characters.[28] Petrushevskaia's narratives operate under the assumption that readers transform themselves by responding to a negative model, an ironically optimistic assessment within perestroika's worldview.

Outrage will hopefully lead to change. One critic partially follows this script when linking the author to the pessimism of

Tolstoy, Chekhov, and Dostoyevsky, whose *byt* and gloom guided the reader to action. She also compares Petrushevskaia's attitude toward her characters to the humanity formalist critic Viktor Shklovskii espied in Nikolai Gogol's Akakii Akakievich.[29] This interpretation reflects sympathy for both the "little man" and his Petrushevskaian equivalent, using the everyday as a backdrop. As with critics' assessments of Baranskaia and Grekova, the quotidian purportedly leads to the worthier goal of *bytie*: readers examine the everyday and, according to Petrushevskaia's scenario, attempt to correct the problems they find.

In her study of women's alternative prose, Carol Adlam argues that Petrushevskaia's writing highlights the problematics of the communication central to her oeuvre. Petrushevskaia, she observes, is both within and outside of *byt* prose: her works simultaneously attempt and sabotage characterization from the viewpoint of her famously unreliable narrators. In *Vremia noch'* Anna Andrianovna and her ilk reveal too much (Anna Andrianovna's comments on her daughter's diary) while obscuring what is important (the diary shows Alena repeating her mother's mistakes with men).[30]

Petrushevskaia questions the degree to which realist narrators can explain the nuanced characters they describe. In raising this issue, her works attack the main principle of documentation, which assumes a meaningful and consistent relationship between what we are told (whether by character, narrator, or author) and what we experience in reality.[31] The narrator's constant manipulation of characters and reader reaction draws attention to the artifice Tzvetan Todorov sees as central to mimesis. Petrushevskaia's histrionic narrators deliberately undermine their tales by reminding us of the stage on which their crises unfold.

While Petrushevskaia's identity is that of an ultimately self-conscious director, Tolstaia sees herself as a viewer. In a 1991 interview she stated: "I am by nature an observer. One watches and thinks: 'My Lord, what an amazing theatre of the absurd, theatre of stupidity, theatre of fools . . . Why do we, grownups, play these games?'"[32] The opposition Petrushevskaia/director and Tolstaia/spectator helps explain the second author's more mediated approach to *byt*: life's disappointments are diffused within language instead of being concentrated and conveyed by the narrator.

Petrushevskaia as consummate director relies on the audience. Language is the hero in Tolstaia's work, leading Grekova to ascribe an almost physical pleasure to reading her stories. What dominates these narratives, she remarks, is a phrase forgotten by perestroika—the literary device (*priem*), a concept recalling the formalists and the lush modernist writing of their contemporaries.[33] Despite various attempts to enlist her prose in the nebulous ranks of Russian postmodernism, her privileging the word and personal ethics in literature connect Tolstaia more to the generation of Andrei Belyi.[34]

Tolstaia's multilayered language makes even her "viscous *byt*" inviting, as Zolotonosov admits. Besides evoking the dichotomy between the wasteland of *byt* and the artist's imagination, this formulation implies that the everyday itself is of interest, an argument developed in the post-Soviet prose of Liudmila Ulitskaia. For Tolstaia the greatest tragedy is waiting for something beyond life: existence itself is a gift. This permanent longing, a feature of her negative characters, appears through an enduring dissatisfaction with *byt*.[35]

Realizing that time is dwindling, the cold, intellectual Rimma in the story "Ogon' i pyl'" (Fire and Dust) exemplifies this frustration as she schemes to get a separate apartment.[36] Her erratically erotic nemesis subordinates temporality to imagination. Pipka's narratives harness geography and a bizarre kind of logic to the desire-based discourse motivating her wild tales. These fantastical stories constitute a female picaresque, a genre almost unknown in Russian literature. Mastering discourse gives Pipka an alternate control over temporality, a power that Rimma lacks. Time, like language, is a way for Tolstaia to transform the mundane quotidian into a realm of infinite possibilities.[37]

This type of imagined narrative also appears in Petrushevskaia's post-Soviet mystical story "Nagaina," only here it signals hopelessness and loss instead of escape and possibility. While talking to a girl, the nameless protagonist describes an impossible trip to India, only to realize that the girl is his Indian girlfriend, who has recently died half a world away.[38] Pipka's lies clearly bring her joy, while "Nagaina" uses speech for its classic function in Petrushevskaia's works: conveying the inner emptiness characters long to ignore.

No one escapes this void. Usually living in Moscow, her characters come from all sections of a metropolis that personifies migration and social flux. Petrushevskaia was especially notorious for her irreverent treatment of intellectuals. In *Svoi krug* would-be rapist Zhora is writing his dissertation, while the short story "Ali-Baba" describes the bed-wetting alcoholic scientist Viktor. These characters are far more reprehensible than their intellectual counterparts in the works of Grekova, Baranskaia, or Iurii Trifonov. As one critic succinctly noted, neither Petrushevskaia nor Tolstaia feared describing the intelligentsia as "freaks."[39]

This characterization often led to surprising reversals. "Ogon' i pyl'" contrasts Pipka's earthy sensuality with the repressed jealousy of intellectual Rimma. The former is a prevaricating nymphomaniac, but the latter is deceitful on a more fundamental level of interaction, namely, friendship. Illustrating the incongruity between image and act demythologized the intelligentsia, suggesting it was closer to *byt*'s petty passions and problems than it cared to acknowledge.

Characters such as Rimma and Nina are not only morally inadequate but embody the twin anathemas of the intelligentsia: *poshlost'* and inauthenticity. In "Poet i muza" Nina's use of folkloric motifs smacks of triteness as she pursues Grisha's former lover, Lizaveta. Nina envisions herself wearing out seven pairs of iron boots, breaking seven iron staves over Lizaveta's back, and gnawing on seven kilos of iron wafers as she attempts to destroy her rival.[40] At the end of the story, her friend's "peasant" room is another emblem of *poshlost'* that, like Nina's persona, radiates the falseness of convention becoming cliché.[41] The art of dissembling, of assuming another's values, was unavoidable for the intelligentsia in late-Soviet culture. Precisely because of this inevitability, it was a sin for those raised on the putative Thaw values of honesty and courage.

There are two reasons for women authors' critique of the intelligentsia. The first relates to intellectuals' collective self-image and their dominance in literature published before the early

1990s. Almost all of Baranskaia's and Grekova's heroines come from the intelligentsia; the enthusiastic but bland scientist-engineer was a mainstay of post-Stalinist literature. Linked by common background to both character and implied reader, female authors before perestroika highlighted the predicament of the well-educated woman managing home and work. Writers such as Petrushevskaia and Tolstaia had no need to establish women intellectuals as legitimate characters: they could rely on ready-made patterns and reader expectations. Indeed, their prose rebelled against the Baranskaia/Grekova ethical intellectual mother as a cliché, ironically duplicating the disgust at unrealistic depictions of working women that had prompted Baranskaia to write *Nedelia kak nedelia*.[42]

While Baranskaia and Grekova had selectively depicted the moral shortcomings of the intelligentsia, their characters are far less repugnant (and memorable) than the physically and spiritually crippled heroine in Elena Tarasova's story "Ne pomniashchaia zla" (She Who Remembers No Evil), who comes from an intellectual family that does not understand her.[43] Critics decried the evident lack of morality in the "lumpen" intelligentsia depicted by perestroika women writers. However, the prose of an author such as Petrushevskaia did not expose the intelligentsia's immorality so much as it used physiological metaphors (drinking, sex, deformity) to reveal its inner decay. As Goscilo observes, "Since the violation of the psyche, which is [the author's] ruling obsession, carries the taboo of ultimate sin, it cannot be represented directly, and therefore gets displaced onto the body."[44] When Petrushevskaia and Tarasova made the private public by depicting corporeality, they echoed the axiom that the body expresses the sufferings of the soul. However, envisioning the intelligentsia as incarnating this relationship separated perestroika-era women writers both from their male counterparts and from the more staid accounts of Baranskaia and Grekova. This difference signified the revenge of the material world, hinting that the intellectual was both fallible and redundant. What is the role of ideas in a world of poverty, drunkenness, and violence?

Indeed, the intelligentsia felt itself increasingly besieged by the falling standard of living and chaos of the Gorbachev years. Natal'ia Doroshko's story "Dvadtsat' piatoe fevralia" (February

Twenty-fifth), published in the women's collection *Abstinentki* (The Abstainers, 1991), describes Jews awaiting a perestroika-era pogrom that never comes. The pogrom is an archetypal nightmare for both the Jewish and gentile intelligentsia. As the discussion of anti-Semitism in Grekova's *Svezho predanie* makes clear, for Jews the pogrom is an omnipresent (if remote) possibility confirming their marginal place in Russian culture.[45] For gentiles it signals the same elemental forces—the common people—that could destroy the intelligentsia as a whole.

Evoking similar unease, Nina Gorlanova gives a wryly humorous account of living in the industrial city of Perm. Her story "Pokaiannye dni, ili V ozhidanii kontsa sveta" (Confessional Days, or Waiting for the End of the World) opens the *Novye amazonki* collection. Its autobiographical intellectual narrator attempts to support her family during perestroika, when Perm is awash with rumors of natural catastrophe (an impending flood) and civil unrest (news items documenting the rise of anti-Semitism). As in Doroshko's story, time first thickens around an expected event, then returns to normal when the tragedy does not occur. Both works pair anti-Semitism with an assault on Soviet-era stability, when pogroms were condemned as tsarist racism. Narrator Nina Viktorovna notes that her family must be fed despite the possible disasters; the intelligentsia is at the mercy of *byt* and its banal materiality. While earlier images of crisis in women's prose centered on domesticity, during the Gorbachev period these combined with uncertainty, tragedy, and shortages at the national level.

Within this unflattering focus on things, Tolstaia's secret life of objects emerges as a rare, optimistic image of the material. As the author notes, one word can bring forth an entire world, a creative potential that Grekova applauded when discussing details as the building blocks of Tolstaia's first stories.[46] However, given Russian culture's constant striving for *bytie*, a worldview where things have the potential to decenter people is heretical. Foregrounding the object over the character is as threatening as the disturbing corporeality of Tarasova's and Petrushevskaia's physically and emotionally deformed characters. In both instances the spiritual is no longer the arbiter of human significance.

Tolstaia's prose does, however, provide two synecdochal images that link this preponderance of the physical to larger themes in perestroika-era culture: the meat grinder and the newspaper. Her story "Samaia liubimaia" (Dearly Beloved) discusses school-teacher Zhenechka and her fruitless efforts to edify local children, attempts lost in the oblivion that eventually claims Zhenechka herself. Indeed, as the narrator wistfully notes, only small things survive the meat grinder of time's passage, which destroys larger objects such as "wardrobes, pianos, and people." However, the dynamics of past and present are not merely destructive. History's material embodiment is also stratified, as the autobiographical protagonist in "Belye steny" (White Walls) discovers. While renovating the family dacha, she uncovers layer upon layer of newspapers beneath the wallpaper, representing a visual record of Soviet history.[47]

These two images—meat grinder and newspaper—encapsulate the representation of Soviet history during perestroika. The USSR as viewed through the era's esthetic of negation resembled a series of calamities, sacrifices, and atrocities, a merciless iron contraption that had decimated the Russian people. At the same time, however, assessment of the past exhibited the archeological impulse Goscilo ascribed to unearthing previously repressed cultural figures, emerging from invisibility like the layers of newspaper in the family dacha. In addressing history—Russian literature's favorite disaster—Tolstaia's works belong to the intellectual tradition of literature commenting on society, even if the intelligentsia itself may often seem repulsive in her narratives.

Not surprisingly, critics were shocked by women authors' treatment of the intelligentsia. Scandalized readers "recognized" themselves in fictional form and hastened to complain that they were not as the works portrayed them. While these responses in a sense followed Petrushevskaia's claimed expectations for the reader, identification with the characters caused defensive outrage instead of compassion for the less fortunate. Some critics even conflated authors with their unsavory characters, recalling Bakhtin's caveat about distinguishing writers from their fictional personae.[48]

Ironically, such mistakes buttressed the documentation shaping earlier women's writing, a tendency that Petrushevskaia both appropriated and critiqued. Documentation touted a transparent relationship between reality and its depiction within the narrative, as well as between authors' "real" opinions and those of their fictional counterparts. Confusing Petrushevskaia with her abusive maternal characters was both a testament to the author's carefully crafted verisimilitude and an indication that the biographical approach is dangerous in such cases.

An opposite but congruent tendency marked the first critical responses to Tolstaia's stories, where critics went to great lengths to indicate that life—not the author—was the source of brutality in her work.[49] Both cases evince a struggle to determine the author's relationship to narrative immanence, an ultimately fruitless stance that ignores the complex linguistic and structural autonomy the authors' works possess. Ultimately this formal variety is the greatest innovation of perestroika-era women's prose in describing *byt*. Together with a broadened and intensified critique of gender roles and the state, this originality distinguished Tolstaia, Petrushevskaia, and their contemporaries from earlier writers. These authors' exposure of the quotidian revealed an often disturbing but vibrant realm. Everyday life was emerging as art in its own right, not simply raw material for the talented author.

New Iconoclasms: Critiquing Gender Roles and the State

During the late 1980s and early 1990s women's writing addressed traditional gender roles in a manner resembling its treatment of the intelligentsia: a systematic critique through exposure of previously unmentionable weaknesses. Discussion was more sustained and critical than that by earlier generations, which had accepted strictly prescribed (and proscribed) behavior while selectively depicting the shortcomings resulting from such strictures.

It is far from surprising that perestroika-era women authors described their male contemporaries in extremely unflattering terms. Negative models predominate, uniting various generations and roles. The literally and psychologically greedy son Andrei in *Vremia noch'* is a recidivist revision of Grekova's Vadim in *Vdovii parokhod*. Characters' fates overlap: the hard-drinking son in Petrushevskaia's story "Pchelka" (Little Bee) regularly passes out in his mother's kitchen, while the sculptor in Viktoriia Tokareva's novella *Piat' figur na postamente* (Five Figures on a Pedestal, 2000) does the same in his studio. In her novel *Nomer Odin* Petrushevskaia presents characters who validate the sad realization of the protagonist, namely, that a son is more like a husband than the husband himself.[50]

As could be surmised from the previous paragraph, depictions of drinking were less circumscribed than in previous women's writing. Men's alcoholism reflected entitlement as well as the failure of Gorbachev's sobriety campaign, which merely restricted access without meaningfully addressing causes. In *Vremia noch'* Andrei's drinking is culturally sanctioned as reprehensible but normal male behavior, while his sister's and mother's drinking would be unacceptable because of their "natural" obligation to care for home and children. Indeed, one reader of the newspaper *Komsomol'skaia pravda* argued that nagging wives often drove husbands to drink, with these rebukes no doubt increasing along with the amount consumed.[51]

Sober men were also more disappointing than in earlier works (e.g., the relatively hardworking Dima in *Nedelia kak nedelia*). Absent or dubious fathers predominate. In *Vremia noch'* the father of Alena's unborn child is probably the married assistant director, who will never see her again. The taxi driver in Petrushevskaia's story "Medeia" (Medea) may have slept with his fourteen-year-old daughter, causing her mother to kill her with an axe. This scenario of incest is starker than anything previously published. Baranskaia's Zoika was raped by her stepfather—not a biological relation—and was ultimately redeemed by a happy marriage and children of her own. On a more metaphorical level, Uncle Boria violates the rules of the childhood world in Tolstaia's story "Svidanie s ptitsei" (Date with a Bird) when he has sex with the "princess" Tamila, who has befriended Boria's nephew.[52]

In many cases perestroika women's writing enunciated the tantalizingly simple thesis implied in works such as Venedikt Erofeev's *Moskva-Petushki*, namely, that the Soviet system emasculated men. The Karelian author Mar'a-Leena Raunio summarizes this idée fixe in an article that also details her failed writing career: "In a society where all members are beaten down and crushed, men cannot be generous to the 'weak sex.' . . . A humbled, crushed person can derive at least some satisfaction from knowing that there are some who are weaker and more exhausted."[53] Raunio simultaneously defends and critiques the "unnaturally" weak Soviet man. Robbed of his innate masculine dignity, he exploits women as the only group more downtrodden than himself. The result is the author's own domestic situation, in which husband, children, and ailing mother function as a trio of dependents for whom Raunio alone is responsible. In blaming the Soviet state for oppressing and supposedly emasculating men, she, like Baranskaia, ultimately exonerates males from accepting responsibility for their actions.

Lina Tarkhova posits another cause undermining the Soviet male: the phenomenon of the "strong" woman. Imploring women to reverse men's tendency to surrender responsibility, Tarkhova argues that families headed by women are the culprits. This situation can only be rectified if wives give up leadership and focus their energy on nurturing their husbands with love. Tarkhova's advice, allegedly gleaned from sociological and psychological research, repeated a demand made of female characters in 1950s literature: women must retreat from public life and compensate for men's shortcomings. Gorbachev seemed to endorse a similar scenario, arguing that female Soviet citizens should "return to their purely womanly mission."[54]

Tarkhova and, to a lesser extent, Raunio imply that a change in social roles could restore man's (presumably) invigorating essence. Nina Sadur's "Chervivyi synok" (Worm-Eaten Sonny), however, dashes all such hope. This short, *skaz*-influenced sketch attacks man, who has been bitten by a demon, causing him to consume women and then leave them. The narrator laments that women were not assigned this destructive role: "It would have been better to bite women. So that she could corrupt man, deprive him of *his* innocence and future, drink him down, leave him to grow old alone. So that men would become women, and women men."[55] Sadur appropriates postlapsarian rhetoric to revise the Adam/Eve dichotomy. The narrator is interested in reversing gender inequality, not erasing it; the unequal power dynamic remains, but the balance of power now favors women.

Tarasova's short story "Ty khorosho nauchilsia est', Adam" (You've Learned How to Eat Well, Adam) also equates males with rapacious behavior: men destroy their health, relationships with women, and even the exotic pets they bring home for their children.[56] Unlike the males whom "Chervivyi synok" describes, however, man also consumes himself through the institution of the army. For Tarasova he is both destroyer and victim. In contrast to Grekova and Baranskaia, Tarasova and Sadur permit no redemption for their male characters: man's own appetites devour him, a bodily metaphor that looms large in Petrushevskaia's works as well.

No women's writing published before 1985 offered such a harsh and systematic assessment of masculinity. Aside from the political implications of Tarasova's critique of the Soviet army—much more damning than Grekova's *Na ispytaniiakh*—both she and Sadur offer gendered polemics threatening permanence and meaning. If man, the architect of the October Revolution, is merely a lecherous glutton, then physiology will always frustrate his dreams of social change. Female authors' assertion of the quotidian's corporeality impedes the ideational struggle to build communism.

Perestroika-era women's prose also criticizes traditional conceptions of femininity, as Tolstaia's negative female characters show in their self-defeating quest for emotional security. As might be expected, however, it was Petrushevskaia's heroines who aroused more critical ire. Oleg Dark described *Svoi krug* as inhabited by "not-quite men" (*nedomuzhchiny*) and "not-quite women" (*nedozhenshchiny*), while Marina Abasheva was starker: "Non-mother. Non-housewife. Non-wife. In general, an anti-world is described. . . . This is a world where everything is its opposite."[57] While Dark suggested the possibility of improving his grown-up Mitrofanushkas, Abasheva sees no escape from the anti-world.

Women authors in the late 1980s and early 1990s sharply questioned the validity and viability of gender roles in a way that their predecessors during Thaw and Stagnation did not. While Baranskaia and Grekova displayed an assortment of irresponsible fathers, truly "bad" mothers did not exist for them: this type of character would have been ontologically impossible. In Gre-kova's *Damskii master* Mar'ia Vladimirovna's children jokingly characterize her as a broodsow who may eat her piglets. Such alarming images, however, remain at the level of humor, without the disturbing overtones of later portrayals, as when Anna An-drianovna describes Grandmother Sima as a devouring half-shark/half-Nazi in *Vremia noch'*.[58]

Petrushevskaia's works brutally laid bare the rhetoric of ma-ternity, a discourse that supported Grekova's (and particularly Baranskaia's) prose. These two authors documented the central-ity of mothers: plot and the accretion of details encouraged the reader to make connections between the specifics of one woman's life and generalized experience. Petrushevskaia, however, sub-stituted speculation for such amassing of evidence. In *Svoi krug* the conniving first-person narrator gives the reader no choice but to accept her view of what occurs. Very little transpires in the story—aside from the final scene involving Alesha, his mother, and her friends—with scheming and embittered reminiscence re-placing action. It is difficult to determine the main event in a Pe-trushevskaia work: temporality and the events it orders are less real than the narrator's verbal onslaught. This tendency unites an oeuvre that at first seems fragmented—colloquialism, slang, and jargon locate a character's space in time.[59]

Anna Andrianovna, the most masterful of Petrushevskaia's egomaniacal narrators, reveals the close relationship between maternity, discourse, and self-representation. From the very beginning of *Vremia noch'* she establishes her narrative as a con-fession of faith, where maternal love is the overarching rationale. A semiprofessional poet, Anna Andrianovna is no stranger to twisting words. In her ceaseless battles with the family she pur-ports to cherish, she reads and rewrites Alena's diary from her daughter's viewpoint, complete with a scene detailing "Alena's" opinions of a conflict between mother and daughter.[60] *Vremia noch'* is ultimately an elaborate series of self-justifications, where the reader is pretext and audience. These mental peregrinations conclude with a nonevent exposing the emptiness of the nar-rator's existence: the decision not to bring Grandmother Sima home is followed by the realization that the rest of the family has abandoned Anna Andrianovna.[61]

Perestroika women's prose destroyed the "terrible perfection" of Baranskaia's martyr-mothers as the hope of family and country. Two related variants dominated this negation of the traditional feminine image: the holy fool (*durochka*) and the freak (*urodina*). The *durochka* is a key image in Tolstaia's story "Ogon' i pyl'," in which Pipka attracts men despite her rotten teeth and lack of material possessions.[62] Svetlana Vasilenko's post-Soviet "novel-hagiography" *Durochka* (Little Fool, 1998) would later provide the best developed example of the female holy fool in modern Russian literature.

The *urodina*—a *durochka* without God's guidance—is a more prominent figure in perestroika prose. The nameless protagonist in "Ne pomniashchaia zla" is hideously misshapen due to a mysterious illness that began when she was a child. Her identity derives from the suffering ironically expressed in the title and final line of the story: not only does the main character remember evil, but she also uses these thoughts to structure reality. Nothing exists outside her physical and spiritual torment. Within this context the narrator amends the traditional concept of the soul being mirrored in the body: "She used to think that the soul is a reflection of the body and its shape, that it is equally palpable. When the body loses a finger, the soul loses one as well. But the body can use prostheses, while the soul remains toothless, legless, fingerless."[63]

This formulation suggests a heretical correlation between physical loss and spiritual mutilation. On a theological level Tarasova undermines the idea of the immortal soul, a concept supporting the opposition between the eternal *bytie* and the ephemeral *byt*. While Stephen Hutchings posits that *byt* derives from the gap between Orthodox icon and image, Tarasova implies that both can be harmed by the physical world. The fact that these thoughts occur to a thirty-three year-old woman seemingly hints at a parallel between her and Christ. The protagonist, however, is interested neither in saving her own life nor in redeeming anyone else's. The suffering she embraces is pain, not kenosis.[64]

Women's prose also revised the literary depiction of the wife. As Abasheva observed, satisfied wives and mothers are rare in this writing. This paucity continues a trend evident in the fiction of Baranskaia, Grekova, and the early works of Tokareva.

What distinguishes childhood is its endless potentiality, where the quotidian is a forest of enchantment and danger. Children, Tolstaia notes, must find their own language—and consequently their own identity—presumably to avoid the fate of grownups such as Rimma and Zoia, victims of a perpetually disappointing *byt*.[71] Life is a gift whose enjoyment shows that the everyday is less a series of obstacles than a range of opportunities.

Childhood's temporality is ateleological and diffuse, often associated with summers spent at the dacha. Tolstaia's story "'Na zolotom kryl'tse sideli' . . ." (On the Golden Porch) begins with an evocative image: "In the beginning was the garden. Childhood was a garden. Without end or limit, without borders and fences, in noises and rustling, golden in the sun, pale green in the shade, a thousand layers thick—from heather to the crowns of the pines: to the south, the well with toads, to the north, white roses and mushrooms, to the west, the mosquitoed raspberry patch, to the east, the huckleberry patch, [bumblebees], the cliff, the lake, the bridges."[72]

This space is the prelapsarian realm of childhood, an organic unity missing in the modern world. While Petrushevskaia (and Grekova before her) masterfully depicted the inward-looking cosmos of the apartment, the dacha is a world that opens outward.[73] The chronotope of the dacha and its broader context, the decentered temporality of childhood, resemble the fantastic stories of Pipka, who regards imagination as *byt*'s greatest treasure. These characters' sense of time is more viable and rewarding than others' goal-oriented and ultimately self-defeating temporality (e.g., Zoia's marriage schemes in "Okhota na mamonta" or Rimma's fear that Pipka will ruin her plans to gain control of the apartment). This aura of potentiality, alien to Petrushevskaia's perestroika-era works, is the most significant difference between the two authors.

Discussion of children and family is inseparable from how the state supported this fundamental social institution. Before 1985 negative representations of the government in women's prose were restricted either to corrupt local figures or (during the Thaw) the cult of personality as a phenomenon presumably removed from the present regime. Perestroika, however, opened the floodgates as female authors envisioned the state unflatteringly as neglecting women or countenancing violence against them.

Neglect of women in post-1985 works frequently involved the much-maligned medical system. Indifference toward women within the hospital topos underscored humiliation and loss of agency in everyday life. Both of these issues existed in pre-perestroika works but (to borrow a description of gulag writing) were survivable and limited in their horrors.[74] Goscilo observes that incarceration and hospitalization share a reliance on clock time and small-scale tasks. The camp and medical systems likewise rob the individual of the autonomy traditionally paired with masculine roles; in this sense they highlight the limited freedom marking Soviet society as a whole. In Petrushevskaia's novella of the same name vindictive Malen'kaia Groznaia (Little Terrible, 1998) experiences the psychiatric hospital as the nadir of degradation. Much like Solzhenitsyn's scientists in *V kruge pervom* (The First Circle, published abroad in 1968), the elderly woman moves from the mild "first circle" (an ordinary hospital) to a more torturous realm of hell.[75]

Petrushevskaia is not unique in comparing the penal and medical systems. In Tolstaia's story "Spi spokoino, synok" (Sweet Dreams, Son) veterinarian Pavel Antonych vigilantly exterminated diseased animals in the 1920s and 1930s. During the Thaw he fell out of favor, signaling that during Stalinism he liquidated the metaphorically infected as well.[76] This same premise—the paradoxical position of doctors under a regime dedicated to wholesale eradication—recurs in a different vein in Ulitskaia's post-Soviet novel *Kazus Kukotskogo* (The Case of Kukotskii, 2001).

At times authors critique the medical system through the sardonic lens of irony. In Gorlanova's story "Istoriia ozera Veselogo" (How Lake Jolly Came About) Masha gives birth alone inside a decrepit hospital that, along with the town itself, has on paper been converted into a lake.[77] Neither the medical facility nor its surroundings matter to the Moscow bureaucrats, who abruptly resettle the local population, destroy the area, and create the planned lake (complete with fish). This arbitrary act stresses lack of individual agency more than any benevolent concern on the part of the state.

Other works sacrifice humor for heavy-handed description, recalling the charges of journalistic style leveled at Baranskaia and Grekova. The telling title of Marina Palei's novella *Otdelenie propashchikh* (The Bloody Women's Ward, 1991) precedes an account of how overworked and unpaid personnel maim, insult, and simply ignore patients in the abortion ward. Tat'iana Rovenskaia identifies one result of this neglect: a specifically female sense of shame associated with the body in public institutions.[78]

In a complete break with their predecessors, some women writers active during perestroika also indicted the state for systematic violence. At times this critique occurs through images that characterize the environment as the victim. Vasilenko's short story "Suslik" (Gopher) portrays sixth-grade students flushing out and killing gophers in a competition to collect their skins. Her "video-novella" *Shamara* shows one possible result of inculcating such violence in adolescents: the albino officer Maks and rapist Ustin. Their town is poisoned by the factories on its outskirts, which are staffed with prison labor. The use of convicts in industry recalls the gulag, a toxic legacy leaching into Soviet public life. In the opening scene Shamara dances on the sandy bank of the Akhtuba River: "Suddenly, on the other bank, the armored troop carriers appeared. Languid but quick, like crocodiles, they entered the water, their snouts staring vacantly at her as she danced. They moved right toward her, overcome by lust. They moved fast, in a herd." Violence infects the community. The consequences of Shamara's rape reverberate in a locale based on the labor of the rapists and other convicts. While the protagonist remains in the city, the assault is reenacted several times: first through the metaphor of the predacious personnel carriers and then by Ustin himself, who this time shouts commands in German.[79]

As in "Suslik," state activity disrupts the natural world. The Soviet government, metonymically reduced to armored personnel carriers, resembles a herd of single-minded predators converging on Shamara.[80] For Vasilenko these images constitute a gendered division, where men can destroy the world while women have the ability to save it. This realization came to her during the Cuban Missile Crisis. Vasilenko and other children were evacuated from their military town, while her father sat in one of the command posts responsible for launching the USSR's nuclear arsenal.[81] The state, troped as male, has the power to end the life its female citizens create.

Marina Karpova's story "Lovlia maiskikh zhukov" (Catching May Bugs), virtually ignored by critics, is another narrative structured around state-sanctioned violence against women. Beginning with the narrator's music teacher putting his hand down her pants, the work immediately establishes itself as publishable only after 1985. Guards from a nearby labor camp accost the narrator's older sister on the road, initiating a flashback to the narrator's earlier, Stalinist childhood, when guards from the same camp threatened her mother while she took the narrator to kindergarten. The flashback ends with the scene of the guards' crude proposal to the narrator's sister. Using prison slang, they convey a word (*matsat'*) unfamiliar to the girls but clear in meaning to the narrator: "It was the same thing as when I was just beginning to jealously look over her body with furtive glances through lowered lashes when my sister undressed to sleep. . . . And that was also impossible to talk about, one could not give it a name." The narrator cannot put this new knowledge into speech, just as her childhood has been "hollowed out," silenced and deformed by sexual abuse and the threat of rape within the general dissipated terror of Stalinism.[82] Karpova's narrative is shaped by sexual violence and a fear similar to the shame Rovenskaia relates to women's bodies in public.

Elena Glinka's documentary story "'Kolymskii tramvai' srednei tiazhesti" (Kolyma Streetcar, Medium Size) connects the state to violence even more explicitly.[83] Glinka, imprisoned in 1950 for being in Nazi-occupied Novorossiisk, describes a likely autobiographical encounter between political and criminal prisoners. Local "free" men and prisoners, having heard that women have arrived, come to greet them. In the main event of the story an unspecified number of women prisoners are dragged into a nearby building and raped for two days.[84]

Glinka prefaces this account with a denunciation of both the Stalinist gulag and those supporting the dictator. "'Kolymskii tramvai'" appeared only a year after Leningrad teacher Nina Andreeva penned her pro-Stalin letter, one of the key conservative reactions against perestroika. Throughout the story the first-person narrator contributes generalizing comments underscoring the brutality of the Stalinist camps via the narrative's status as a documentary story. These moments reinforce the work's anti-Stalinist message while giving it an overbearing didacticism, with both aspects exemplifying the perestroika tendency to critique systematically.

In 1989 *Dodnes' tiagoteet* (Till My Tale Is Told), a collection of women's memoirs of the gulag, appeared in the USSR. In "O proshlom" (About the Past) Khava Volovich, one of the few non-intellectuals to write about the labor camps, describes the period following her arrest and imprisonment in 1937. Although the camp as a space is a priori removed from everyday reality, her formulation applies to a certain extent to Soviet women's lives in general. There is "a wish to wipe from memory the years of torment and privation, but also a feeling of shame. This is the same feeling experienced by a girl whose honor has been stolen by the man she loves."[85] Volovich implicitly politicizes both the shame Rovenskaia identifies and the powerlessness Iuliia Gradskova and Raunio ascribe to the Soviet woman. This feeling of group victimization by the state sharply divides perestroika women authors from those who came before them. Ol'ga in *Nedelia kak nedelia* took pride in advancing Soviet science, as did Grekova's female researchers. However, the rhetoric of documentation draws these dissimilar authors closer together, with all employing the allure of the real as a persuasive device.

Women's writing after 1985 attacked assumptions that the state attempted to support women. Authors such as Petrushevskaia and Tarasova likewise destabilized the cult of motherhood, the ascendancy of beauty, and other elements of femininity. Critique of traditional roles, however, had its limits. In Petrushevskaia's story "Peregrev" (Overheating), middle-aged Vera is refreshed after a stay on the beach that has bronzed her skin and made her attractive once more. However, while watching her niece shower she realizes that her body cannot recapture the past. Upon returning to Moscow, she is diagnosed with skin cancer and learns that her husband has impregnated her niece.[86] As in Solzhenitsyn's *Rakovyi korpus* (Cancer Ward, published abroad in 1968), cancer is a moral metastasis that reiterates the message of earlier female authors: middle-aged women must ensure others' happiness, not their own. Indeed, for Baranskaia's and Grekova's generation—with its widows, single mothers, and privation—there was little or no alternative to self-sacrifice as the woman's worldview.

Petrushevskaia was less interested in critiquing gender roles than in examining how their extremes signify inner decay, as her negative depictions of same-sex love hinted. In *Vremia noch'* Andrei was probably raped in Butyrka Prison, while Serezha's long homosexual affair in the story "Shato" (The Chateau) costs his family time and money. These works see homosexuality as abnormal and often coerced, grouping gays and lesbians with the homeless and alcoholics as victims of Soviet society.[87]

As with depictions of male homosexuality, lesbianism in Petrushevskaia's writing is far from positive. Drunken coworkers rape Gulia, the unattractive lesbian in Petrushevskaia's story "Muzyka ada" (The Music of Hell), after she unsuccessfully attempts to seduce the female protagonist. In the story "Muzhestvennost' i zhenstvennost'" (Masculinity and Femininity) the androgynous Nadia suffers because doctors believe that she falls between the definitions of male and female.[88] Deviation entails either medical incarceration or sexual violence. The kind hermaphrodite Lera in *Shamara* is a rare exception to this brutal enforcement of gender norms, hinting that Vasilenko is a less strident defender of clear divisions between male and female (despite lauding women as preservers of the world).

Homophobia presupposes linking male and female identity to procreation. Such a sharp demarcation of traditional gender roles is not a case of separate but equal. Eve Sedgwick observes how "categories presented in a culture as symmetrical binary oppositions—heterosexual/homosexual, in this case—actually subsist in a more unsettled and dynamic tacit relation according to which . . . term B is not symmetrical with but subordinate to term A."[89] Normative heterosexuality marginalizes homosexuality and ossifies conceptions about gender. Sedgwick's formulation is a bit too optimistic for perestroika literature, where homosexuality is less a recognized opposition than a shadow, frightening in its dark and amorphous nature.

Women's prose during perestroika systematically critiqued traditional gender roles within the era's esthetic of negation and exposure of the taboo. This acerbic assessment occurred alongside an indictment of the Soviet state for neglecting and victimizing women. Images of homosexuality, however, suggested that writers such as Petrushevskaia discarded some stereotypes (loving mother, ideal homemaker) while upholding others (prison

"bitch," ugly lesbian). As with the prose of Baranskaia and Grekova, critique had its limits. Once again these boundaries were
carefully hidden under the guise of objectively portraying reality. While this reality was clearly more threatening than its Thaw
or Stagnation counterpart, tacit limits on its depiction remained a
constant.

Inventing Women's Prose: Problems
of Definition and Association

Before the late 1980s, authorial perception and critical reception
resembled views of Russian women writers in the nineteenth
century: while individual works by women authors existed, they
did not constitute a distinct category. In 1991 Irina Sliusareva
equivocated by contending that, while women can and do write,
to insist on a separate women's literature invites hostile generalizations from critics.[90] This argument implied the existence of
women's writing based on the undeniable fact that critics debated its status and merits. Such recognition plus reservation
dominated critical assessments of the newly visible female authors and the six women's collections published between 1989
and 1991.

In the introduction to one of these collections, *Ne pomniashchaia zla,* a banal but crucial assertion appears that would have
been impossible before perestroika: women's prose "exists as a
necessity, dictated by time and space." Both dimensions stem
from everyday life: "We must remember that for women the
closed circle of *byt,* the circle of hell, is also the circle of life, offering the never-ending journey that is its constant." *Byt,* infinite
within its confines, both provides opportunities and delimits
women's experiences.[91]

These anthologies depicted previously suspect or taboo
themes, such as infidelity, abortion, violence, poverty, rape, prostitution, ecological disaster, and (both male and female) alcoholism. As with women's issues in the prose of Baranskaia and
Grekova, foregrounding these topics asserted their typicality.
Common content and increased critical attention constituted a
reinvention of women's prose after decades of writers such as

Vera Panova, who had subordinated it to a vision of women as female Soviets.

Why did women's writing only expand, diversify, and gain prominence during perestroika? First, in the 1960s through the 1980s Baranskaia and Grekova had created a precedent by focusing on women's concerns in mainstream writing—despite the fact that neither author viewed herself as a woman writer. Russian women's writing has always suffered from alienation and the absence of a stable identity: glasnost women authors never mentioned female predecessors, nor did they assume that such writers might be awaiting rediscovery. While Petrushevskaia and Tolstaia continued the thematic concerns of earlier women authors, they never identified them as a source of inspiration. Elaine Showalter has noted in a different cultural context that such lack of tradition makes women's writing derivative in the eyes of critics and authors alike. A perpetual newcomer, it must constantly reinvent its identity.[92]

Critic and editor Natal'ia Perova cited time as a simple reason why more women had not written for publication or "the drawer" and thus could not be discovered during the late 1980s. Raunio gives the reader a starker and more specific picture in "Kak ia ne stala pisatel'nitsei" (How I Did Not Become a Writer):

> Work, family, keeping house, a poet husband who needs to have the 'right environment' created for him in the crowded space of our small single room heated by the stove. (They say that some people manage to write in the bathroom. I am not going to talk about the kitchen since we didn't have such a thing.) Then children, my husband's university studies, divorce and my mother's illness, which lasted for years, as she died slowly and painfully before my eyes. Who is not familiar with these scenes?[93]

This grim description deploys the accrual of facts and documentary rhetoric familiar from Baranskaia and Grekova to convey an image of crushing poverty. Raunio's article made two claims indicative of the new approach female authors took under Gorbachev. On an obvious level she depicted how daily life for women differs from that of men, with this divergence a function of male irresponsibility and an apparently indifferent state. What was more shocking is that making writing (or the lack thereof) dependent on *byt* undermined a crucial myth of the intelligentsia, namely, that genius triumphs over difficult material circumstances.

The reinvention of women's prose occurred during a period of polarized cultural change. Two opposing tendencies marked the overall gender climate of 1985–91: critique of traditional roles by some intellectuals and the reinforcement of these same identities by state and economic forces. Several factors in Russian academe led to a questioning of perceptions of masculinity and femininity: surveys dealing with marriage and sexuality; an increase in the number of articles relating to women's issues; the 1990 creation of the Moscow Center for Gender Studies; the publication of past and recent women's literature; media coverage of feminists such as Ol'ga Lipovskaia; and the appearance of a small number of women's and feminist organizations. In 1989 Larisa Vasil'eva created the short-lived Federatsiia pisatel'nits (Federation of Women Writers) as part of the state Writers Union. She opened her organization's first event by asking why women, who accounted for more than half the world's population, were absent from art.[94] These developments had less of an impact outside Moscow and Leningrad/Saint Petersburg.

There was, however, an opposite tendency, partially rooted in Gorbachev's observation that society should give women the chance to stay at home. Whether intended as edict or suggestion, this paradoxical formulation emboldened those who subscribed to an essentialist interpretation of female roles. Perestroika's dramatic cultural changes precipitated a search for a stabilizing constant, which many Russians harnessed to a conservative interpretation of "proper" gender roles.[95]

Perestroika's new freedom of the press also led to a dramatic increase in sexual exploitation of women's bodies in advertising and pornography. Publicizing prostitution, the USSR's first beauty pageants, and fashion models rendered Baranskaia's and Grekova's earnest scientists invisible as readers reoriented their image of women. Previously seen as full (if flawed) participants in society, women in the late 1980s became linked to a small number of unfulfilling roles.

In this polarized context three principal literary trends shaped the reinvention of women's prose. First, one must qualify the

influence of *byt* prose. While female authors' main concerns derived from the topics of Trifonov, Baranskaia, and Grekova, the
provincial women's almanac *Mariia* (1990) emphasized a strong
affinity with the more traditional village writers. The 1980s trend
of alternative prose (*drugaia proza*) was a second influence on
female authors and critics' perceptions.[96] Petrushevskaia and
Tolstaia were among the most visible writers of *drugaia proza*, a
catchall term applied to innovative fiction that distinguished itself from the legacies of socialist realism as well as *byt* and country prose. *Drugaia proza*'s lack of pathos and skeptical approach
to verisimilitude marked 1980s literature in several ways. The
fiction of this era refused to honor stereotypes created by previous authors, challenged the hypocritical standards of Soviet
morality, and pursued stylistic innovation. Critics later applied
these attributes to women's prose through the age-old principle
of guilt by association, considering it a subset of alternative
prose.[97] However, denying the ties between women's prose and
realism dehistoricizes its development, particularly the earlier
documentary style of Baranskaia and Grekova, which helped legitimate women's issues.

The third factor concerns the six collections of women's
prose, poetry, drama, and nonfiction published between 1989
and 1991: *Zhenskaia logika* (Women's Logic, 1989), *Mariia* (vol. 1,
1990), *Ne pomniashchaia zla* (She Who Remembers No Evil, 1990),
Chisten'kaia zhizn' (A Clean Little Life, 1990), *Novye amazonki* (The
New Amazons, 1991), and *Abstinentki* (The Abstainers, 1991).[98]
The idea to publish such untraditional prose in the form of anthologies may have derived from the 1970s underground tradition, which had produced the samizdat anthology *Zhenshchina i
Rossiia* (Women and Russia, 1980).[99]

These collections directly or indirectly critiqued one another.
Vasilenko, a main organizer of the more feminist *Ne pomniashchaia zla* and *Novye amazonki*, implies that *Zhenskaia logika* and
Chisten'kaia zhizn' were published without any rationale, that
is, they did not employ women's prose as an organizing principle. *Mariia*'s compilers claimed that *it* was the first almanac of
women's prose, without mentioning *Zhenshchina i Rossiia*, *Zhenskaia logika*, or the two other collections published in 1990.[100] This
solipsism reflected the breakdown in communication between

Moscow/Leningrad and the provinces, a situation that worsened during and after perestroika due to economic decline. However, it also showed the atomistic beginnings of women's prose, which, as a literary trend, was isolated both from the past and contemporaneous trends.

The anthologies had several genesis stories. A 1989 women's literary meeting in Karelia eventually produced *Mariia* (1990, 1995), the collections *Zhena, kotoraia umela letat'* (The Wife Who Could Fly, 1993), and *Russkaia dusha* (Russian Soul, 1995), as well as the local television show *Komnata dlia sestry Shekspira* (A Room for Shakespeare's Sister, 1992). Vasilenko ascribed the creation of *Ne pomniashchaia zla* and *Novye amazonki* to a 1988 meeting with the writer Larisa Vaneeva, at which both authors realized that women were increasingly being excluded from the literary world.[101]

Women's anthologies added a key sense of alterity to the documentary style marking most of their content. The editors of *Novye amazonki* made this otherness explicit: "For reasons connected to the irregular life in the field of combat, the Amazon did not emerge from under Gogol's *Overcoat*. Everyone else did, but she did not." Revising Dostoyevsky's formulation about the Gogolian roots of modern Russian literature, they rejected an "alien" past while suggesting the importance of this same discarded legacy. Literary tradition legitimated its opponents, who gained in stature by association through opposition.[102]

These authors identified themselves through gender, suggesting that women's anthologies were what Rovenskaia terms a collective identity, "a 'summative' [*summarnaia*] personality on the path toward forming its own cultural tradition." The collections stimulated intense debate over the existence and attributes of women's writing, which was judged as a presumably unified whole. Critic Irina Savkina woefully summarized the general response: "All critical articles begin in different ways . . . except those devoted to women's literature. The latter, as a rule, open by considering whether it is worthwhile to divide literature by sex, whether this notorious women's prose actually exists."[103]

Labeling this writing was surprisingly problematic. Following Sliusareva, both Rovenskaia and Elena Trofimova made the basic but convincing argument that the extensive controversy over the existence and characteristics of women's prose proved that there was such a body of fiction. According to this logic, the term "women's prose" (*zhenskaia proza*) must be used since it remains the most common designation, being frequently employed by the contributors themselves. Publishing the first theoretical article on this subject in a major journal, Nina Gabrielian cast her net even wider in stating that women's prose includes any work written by a woman. This seemingly self-evident statement posits a set of common styles, themes, and attitudes; critics did not assume such connections before 1987. Amplifying and expanding this definition, Adlam sees women's writing as united by internal characteristics (e.g., questioning realism, identity formation, a "submerged modernist heritage," textual transgression) and a key external factor, namely, difficulty being published.[104] I view women's prose as writing by women, who often (but not always) focus on female lives, which differ from men's lives largely because of gender inequality.

The vociferous Pavel Basinskii was one of the few opponents of women's prose to devote substantial thought to its alleged characteristics, attacking *zhenskaia proza* as both esoteric and ateleological. He identified women's writing as a distinct trend that, like *drugaia proza,* tried to distance itself from Russian literary tradition. For Basinskii this alterity was a self-deluding publicity stunt, whereas Vasilenko saw it as the creation of a new literary identity.[105] Indeed, ascribing difference to women's writing was a key distinction between perestroika authors, who recognized and often asserted their otherness, and Baranskaia and Grekova, who sensed their alien status but attempted to minimize it.

While Vasilenko paired women's prose with literary and gendered alterity, *zhenskaia proza* continued Baranskaia's and Grekova's documentation, albeit filtered through perestroika's proclivity for systematic critique. The introduction to the almanac *Mariia* connects literature, policymaking, and women's survival, implying that women's writing must, first and foremost, reflect life and its problems. These sentiments formed a basic tenet of women's prose during the Gorbachev era, namely, that literature can and must express female collective experience.[106] This axiom in turn owed a great deal to authors before 1985, who modified previous ideas about verisimilitude to establish prose as a venue for representing women's daily lives.

Perestroika critics shared this conception of literature as essentially mimetic, which partially explains their hostility to the more extreme depictions in women's prose; such authors overemphasized the purportedly anomalous grimness of women's lives. As was the case during Thaw and Stagnation, opponents and supporters of women's prose stressed its relation to typicality, defining this concept in contradictory ways. When critics attacked *Shamara*'s abortion scene or accused Petrushevskaia of privileging the physiological, they invoked the transformative typicality lingering after socialist realism.[107]

Others, however, argued for reflective typicality, that is, describing what actually exists. Verisimilitude may justifiably illustrate shocking problems if this is the present state of reality. From this viewpoint, Tolstaia's fancifully bleak vision of outlying Moscow neighborhoods as a wintry wasteland (complete with wolves) was acceptable to one critic since it allegedly reflected representative conditions.[108]

In women's prose the typical comprised either what was often present (the shortages Gorlanova and Vasilenko describe) or an extreme situation metonymically conveying a truth of everyday life (e.g., Sima's fate indicates neglect of the elderly). *Chernukha* combined these two tendencies. As Lipovetskii suggests, this concept derived from a journalistic approach to literature, which depicts an extreme image of *byt* that contains recognizable types (e.g., abused prostitute, impoverished mother).[109] These representations combined Baranskaia's and Grekova's legitimation of women in Soviet prose with shocking depictions of the violence and hopelessness comprising the reality of this "typical" group.

As in previous eras, critics under Gorbachev attacked the neutrality of women's prose, recalling the Orthodox division of the world into the moral and immoral (with any middle ground vulnerable to the latter). From this standpoint Petrushevskaia and her contemporaries wielded what one critic bemoaned as "merciless neutrality." Such perceived coldness was symptomatic of *drugaia proza* as a whole, which, having allegedly lost its roots with the Russian people, will end in tragedy. This approach saw literature as either imparting or inhibiting morality: conservative critics assumed that writing must reflect what should be (or provide an alternative to what should *not* be).[110] Nontraditional male writers such as Viktor Erofeev garnered their share of hostility. What distinguishes reception of women's prose was the critics' emphasis on gender qua gender—an unsurprising response given the collision of specifically women's collections and the more conservative gender roles resurfacing during perestroika. Before 1985 almost all critics had discussed women authors through *byt,* which was coded as a female and trivial realm. Critic Vladimir Bondarenko demonstrated the longevity of this thinking when he made the bizarre accusation that Petrushevskaia's plays relied on the "cozy" world of women's everyday life.[111] This phrase, while clearly inaccurate, signaled the continuing Thaw and Stagnation penchant for linking women to the quotidian's crass materiality. Basinskii, however, epitomized the new critique of gender when he suggested that the existence of a woman's soul was merely a trick invented by male writers. In an even stranger attack, a conservative critic lambasted Tolstaia, consigning her to the ranks of those women authors who draw mustaches on themselves.[112]

Supporters of women's prose also used the explicit rhetoric of gender, albeit with predictably different results. Rovenskaia proposed gender as its defining characteristic, asserting that documenting the female's everyday existence in literature furthers awareness of inequalities and the need to address them. Her assessment reiterated the introductions to *Mariia, Ne pomniashchaia zla,* and *Novye amazonki*: female *byt* shaped women's prose as a distinct reality, which in turn hoped to improve the quotidian it depicts.[113]

Baranskaia's and Grekova's documentation of individual women's daily lives was replaced by a literature encompassing a collective vision of female *byt.* As Adlam argues, Petrushevskaia provides the most extreme examples of this milieu, with the shattered lives and endless misery of her prose recalling a work such as *Odin den' Ivana Denisovicha* more than the "petty" concerns of earlier women writers. However, there is another similarity between Petrushevskaia and Solzhenitsyn: documentation as the "instrumental intent" that Adlam claims is lacking in the female author's writing.[114] The paradox of Petrushevskaia lies in the narrative questioning the possibility of meaningful communication even as her dramaturgical tendencies exploit it to the utmost. The problem of representing everyday life only intensified during perestroika.

From 1985 to 1991 women's prose emerged in the context of tentative academic feminism and a broader conservative backlash limiting women's functions and image in society. The combined influences of *byt* prose, *drugaia proza*, and the appearance of six literary anthologies gave women authors distinct styles and themes. As was the case during the Thaw and Stagnation, critics debated the role of typicality and neutrality in these works, with the added problem of *chernukha* exacerbating perestroika's gloomy worldview.

The political and economic turmoil of perestroika made *byt* a synonym for crisis and permitted frank discussion of the Soviet quotidian. Female authors appropriated the era's emphasis on exposure, negation, and systematic critique to challenge gender roles in a manner unthinkable for earlier generations. These attacks helped produce the women's collections, which, in turn, reinvented women's prose as an identifiable trend in literature. While previous authors and critics had used everyday life as a proxy for open discussions of women's issues, both supporters and opponents of this literature now addressed such problems directly.

3

The Artistry of Everyday Life
Liudmila Ulitskaia, Svetlana Vasilenko, and Post-Soviet Women's Anthologies

A woman's gaze is always fixed, unexpected, and paradoxical.
Svetlana Vasilenko

I accept everything that is given.
Liudmila Ulitskaia

During the Brezhnev years one of the young workers in a Moscow genetics laboratory was discovered reading and retyping underground literature. Fearful that the entire lab would be closed, her superiors fired her, citing the need for a reduction in staff. The woman, who had graduated with a degree in biology, abandoned her long-standing interest and began to devote more time to writing, her other passion.[1] In the 1990s this author— Liudmila Ulitskaia—began to gain international fame for her original prose, which fused everyday life with humane values, eventually winning the author Russia's most prestigious literary prize. The ultimately fortuitous career change of Ulitskaia (1943–) recalls the literary path of Natal'ia Baranskaia, another author who brought *byt* to the attention of readers. These two writers, each of whom defined images of the quotidian, shared a common beginning: the government that distrusted them unwittingly spurred their development as authors.

During perestroika women's prose had become a visible and voluble presence in Russian literature, accompanying hesitant academic discussion of feminism against a backdrop of conservative gender roles. Female authors used the era's tendency toward negation and exposure to broach taboo topics of private life, demythologizing the intelligentsia and critiquing the state with brutal frankness. Whereas before 1985 authors and critics employed *byt* as a coded reference to women's issues, during the last years of the Soviet Union supporters and opponents explicitly invoked gender as a criterion for artistic merit. After 1992 women's prose and literature as a whole changed dramatically as the economic and cultural shifts of perestroika gave way to the rapid disintegration of the USSR, the chaos of Boris Yeltsin's presidency, and a shift toward conservatism under Vladimir Putin. High culture and the intelligentsia, its keeper, found themselves struggling to remain relevant and soluble, especially during the impoverished early 1990s.[2] Women's writing, however, was an intriguing exception. It—and particularly the prose of Ulitskaia—was phenomenally successful in the post-Soviet era. Tolstaia and Petrushevskaia likewise remained a staple of intellectual readers despite the nation's lowered standard of living and reduced spending power.[3]

Novels such as Ulitskaia's *Medeia i ee deti* (Medea and Her Children, 1996) and *Durochka* (Little Fool, 1996) by Svetlana Vasilenko (1956–) were well received in great part due to their use of transhistorical time, a temporality distinct from the chronotope of crisis dominating the works of earlier women writers. This change paralleled a more fluid depiction of male and female interaction (including homosexuality), roles authors grounded in individual emotion and experience rather than in gendered expectations. Critics debated the relationship between women's prose and feminism as well as its place in the widening gap between elite and popular culture, a division in some ways bridged by female authors' images of the quotidian. Such treatment posited reader awareness of the type of gendered issues first cautiously documented by Baranskaia and Grekova and then brutally scrutinized by women's prose during perestroika.

Transhistorical Time: Humanizing Temporality

Ulitskaia and Vasilenko are post-Soviet Russia's two most original authors in terms of their depictions of *byt*. Such innovation in great part derives from imagining women's temporality as both an everyday phenomenon and something transhistorical, wherein families bound by emotional or spiritual ties unite different eras. Using kinship to shape temporality implies an indirect approach to history, with the narrative examining key events through the female quotidian. This viewpoint envisions *byt* as an ordinary yet unbounded realm whose very insignificance contains the secrets of human character.

Medeia i ee deti sharply diverges from the familial claustrophobia of a work such as Petrushevskaia's *Vremia noch'*, where relatives suffer through an endless cycle of unlearned mistakes. In Ulitskaia's novel the ironically named Medeia (Medea) shows that love is a different kind of continuity: her selflessness and kindness propel the narrative, which moves from the horrors of Stalinism to the turmoil of the 1990s. Medeia's relationships with her numerous relatives unify the plot. Focusing on such a character, the narrative presents love as more familial than carnal. Medeia never has sex after her husband dies, making her appear to adhere to the Russian widow's moral codex. However, the narrator implies that this chastity results from lack of opportunity rather than conscious choice to honor the deceased. Ulitskaia offers a marred but manageable model of a well-lived life. The protagonist is a character in whom human weaknesses combine with saintly virtues.[4]

Medeia, unlike Petrushevskaia's maniacal mothers, is a bulwark of family solidarity against common foes. While *Vremia noch'* ends with an empty apartment signifying existential abandonment, *Medeia i ee deti* concludes by evoking mutual support and endurance: "It is a wonderful feeling, belonging to Medea's family, a family so large that you can't know all its members by sight, and they merge into a vista of things that happened, things that didn't, and things that are yet to come."[5]

The open-ended final paragraph portrays a group united by feeling rather than blood. While relatives may not recognize

one another, they share a common sense of belonging that emanates from Medeia as a centripetal force (as opposed to Anna
Andrianovna, whose influence is centrifugal despite her "best"
intentions). Medeia's relatives represent the evolution of the reconstituted family prominent in Thaw culture—although her kin
associate out of desire instead of necessity.[6] Indeed, Medeia's
family has another, deeper level of connection: common ethical
responses to the small and large disasters that constituted Russian life in the twentieth century. Ethics in this novel signifies a
broad humanism restricted neither by social system nor faith.
(Ulitskaia herself is a Christian of Jewish descent.)[7]

The last paragraph of *Medeia i ee deti* reveals kinship's role in
the novel: family structures time, mediating between what Fernand Braudel famously termed the "short time span" and the
"longue durée." The short time span (for Braudel an alternative to
the narrow history of events) derives from Medeia's everyday
life, with its gardening and neighbors. In Ulitskaia's work the
longue durée, which Braudel measures in centuries, refers to how
family joins past and present. Medeia's legacy of goodness will
continue long after her Crimean home disappears. In this sense it
is appropriate that the narrative unfolds in this ancient region,
with its echoes of classical and Russian history. Temporal and
geographical unity establish a chronotopic parallel to the stabilizing longevity of Medeia's clan, combining to create a home
that moves in time.[8]

Medeia's strong connection to the peninsula gives the novel
a core analogous to the role of postwar Moscow in Ulitskaia's
more autobiographical works, such as "Vtoroe marta togo zhe
goda" (March 1953) and the cycle *Detstvo-49* (Childhood-49).
These stories share a space and time more compressed than that
of *Medeia i ee deti.* In *Detstvo-49* the universe is reduced to a grimy
courtyard that represents the entire world to the local children,
recalling the author's own early years. Focusing on children's
lives reveals Ulitskaia's connection to the documentary impulse
running throughout women's prose, fictionalized through the
Jewish characters persecuted during late Stalinism and the forced
cohabitation of intellectual and proletarian neighbors.

Human relationships subsume political events as the undercurrent of history. For Ulitskaia the family—particularly the strong connections of its Eastern or Jewish variant—is a powerful form of memory.[9] While links between family and memory also shape time in *Vremia noch'* and Grekova's *Vdovii parokhod,* these earlier works offer negative models of memory. Anna Andrianovna invents a delusional version of the past that, based on maternal megalomania, is more self-serving than helpful. Grekova's novel is also limited, trapped within the widows' reconstituted family, where the pair past/pain pollutes present and future; even Vadim's transformation recalls the price Anfisa has paid to enact it.

In *Medeia i ee deti* neither motherhood nor the past constrains memory, which evolves and expands with each member of the family. The incompleteness that results from such growth resembles the rejuvenation of the Bakhtinian novel and, more important, hints at hope for post-Soviet society. Leaving her home to the Muslim Ravil', Medeia explicitly atones for the Stalinist deportation of the Crimean Tartars and furthers one of Ulitskaia's goals for contemporary Russia, namely, increased understanding between different ethnicities.[10]

Kindness transcends time and space. Vasilenko's Nad'ka-Ganna, the orphaned protagonist of *Durochka,* shows that transhistorical temporality also coalesces around a family explicitly modeled on spiritual relations. Nad'ka-Ganna has a clear connection to Russian collective identity, beginning with the trope of the *narod*: she is breast-fed by peasants instead of by the mother lost during the artificial famines of the early 1930s. The protagonist unites the work's two plot lines (Stalinism and the Cuban Missile Crisis), which depict her as a maternal figure and comforter to both literal and metaphorical children. The conclusion of *Durochka* envisions Nad'ka-Ganna as the Orthodox Mother of God. After dreaming of this holy figure, she gives birth to the sun and stops the US nuclear strike—an act of intercession resembling the *Bogoroditsa*'s mercy. Nad'ka-Ganna is the *longue durée* of Russian history, bridging the pre-Christian, Kievan, appanage, and Soviet periods.[11] What binds these eras together is the image of Nad'ka-Ganna as spiritual mother and the Russian people as God's children: they often err but are ultimately redeemed.

It is no accident that in Vasilenko's fictional world salvation derives from a maternal character rather than the paternal figure of Christ. This revision is a much more effective appropriation of biblical legend than the shrill rant of Nina Sadur's "Chervivyi synok." Nad'ka-Ganna creates instead of wishing to destroy, providing a matrilineal mythology that opposes the male-oriented history of great events exemplified by the brinksmanship of Kennedy and Khrushchev.

Durochka conveys multilayered temporality through Nad'ka-Ganna's culturally overdetermined claims on historical traditions. Layered time helps the narrative continue Russian literature's age-old search for national identity while distinguishing the plot structure from that of previous women authors. Family as transhistorical temporality separates Vasilenko's and Ulitskaia's works from the small-scale time of Grekova's and Baranskaia's harried heroines.

Illustrating transhistorical time through the family involves "history by indirection," where, as Jerome Beaty notes, a narrative conveys historical information through "the everyday affairs of the fictional characters." *Durochka* and *Medeia i ee deti* combine quotidian hints at the past (e.g., the orphans' Black Maria game; Medeia's thoughts on the deported Crimean Tartars) with political events embedded in important plot moments.[12]

In Ulitskaia's novel *Kazus Kukotskogo* (The Case of Kukotskii, 2001) indirect expression of history occurs through specifically female experience. Gynecologist Pavel Alekseevich and his support for abortion during Stalinism link lack of reproductive freedom to loss of human rights, for "isn't this the essential boundary between human and animal, the ability and right to go beyond the bounds of biological law and create progeny because of one's own wish and not the will of natural rhythms?"[13] This polemic, amplifying Grekova's more cautious discussion in "Letom v gorode," asserts that Pavel Alekseevich aids those already born by helping women choose when to have children. Such a function distinguishes female gender roles (Pavel Alekseevich as comforter and healer) from female biology, a crucial departure from earlier women's prose, which often conflated the two.

It is no surprise that *Kazus Kukotskogo* addressed the connections between Stalinism and abortion more explicitly than did Grekova's 1962 story. Indeed, critiquing the Thaw's vaunted

liberalism, Ulitskaia's narrator notes the bitter irony of Khrushchev's decriminalization decision, which allowed women to
take the lives of their unborn children just as the Soviet state had
slaughtered the living.[14] The novel's use of history by indirection
ties changes in abortion policies to a state concerned more with
demographics than with personal freedom.

Traktorina Petrovna, the head of the orphanage in *Durochka*, is
a more obvious symbol of history filtered through corporeal experience. The director, whose laughable first name suggests she
was born during the misguided enthusiasm of the 1920s, has a
patronymic evoking the common people. Nad'ka-Ganna's own
doubled name ("Hope" plus the biblical Hannah), with its striking Christian overtones, opposes that of Traktorina Petrovna.
Their physical appearance underscores this dissimilarity: while
Nad'ka-Ganna is small and malnourished as a result of starva-
tion and her wanderings as a holy fool, Traktorina Petrovna typifies the Stalinist body, which is large, unyielding, and crushes
challengers. In Vasilenko's worldview, Nad'ka-Ganna's body,
doubled name, and subsequent fate confirm her symbolic status
as woman, while Traktorina Petrovna typifies the belligerent
masculinized force that may destroy the world.[15] As with Ulitskaia's Pavel Alekseevich, the orphanage director shows that gender and biology are demonstrably separable.

By the 1990s the Stalinist authority figure was a recognizable villain, allowing Vasilenko to rely on reader reactions not
available to Grekova. "Letom v gorode" has no stand-in for
the state, and even the scathing *Svezho predanie* lacks a central
negative character. Traktorina Petrovna parallels Nad'ka-Ganna
as a transhistorical and mythically evil figure. She survives de-
Stalinization and continues to deform the younger generation.
This longevity implies that the totalitarian impulse continued
after 1953. On a folkloric level, it recalls unnaturally old villains
such as Baba Iaga. While the Mother of God symbolizes a tradition that may save the Russian people, the director personifies a
monolithic force pushing humanity toward disaster.

Despite this, historical pessimism in *Durochka* is less overwhelming than Tolstaia's dystopian novel *Kys'* (The Slynx, 2000),
another work concerned with the past. Depicting a settlement of
Russians several hundred years after a catastrophic explosion,

the narrative presents a society with the superstitions and political apparatus of the Muscovite period (complete with a Great Murza). Through the eyes of the protagonist, Benedikt, an avid reader, we see a culture caught in the dark cyclicality of Russian history, where intellectuals debate whether the West will save Russia and Benedikt approves of how the state creates shortages so that its citizens ("golubchiki") will have simple dreams. True to the pattern of dystopia, Benedikt internalizes his culture's suspicions and prejudices to the point where he resembles the fearsome mythical Kys' giving the work its title. Despite Tolstaia's alleged attempt to keep the novel apolitical, the narrative is a damning satire of both Soviet culture and Russian national identity.[16]

Durochka provides an equally broad but more optimistic reading of history. The opposition Nad'ka-Ganna/Traktorina Petrovna evokes the Orthodox idea of redemption through suffering, a concept the novel's conclusion upholds when Nad'ka-Ganna gives birth to the sun, thereby tempering the horrors of Russian history. Transhistorical time shaped by women and families broadens the scope of *Durochka, Medeia i ee deti,* and *Kazus Kukotskogo.*

Unlike the cloistered paranoia of Tolstaia's novel, Ulitskaia's and Vasilenko's narratives expand outward, much like the multitudinous members of Medeia's family. Emphasis on transhistorical time signals the importance of the family as an emotional and spiritual as well as a biological nexus. In contrast to Petrushevskaia's oeuvre, here kinship is a supportive rather than a limiting commonality. Interweaving various eras, temporality joins Braudel's short time span and *longue durée* through familial relations based on belief as well as blood. History and folklore permit the narrative to filter history through *byt,* itself a shifting prism in the hands of post-Soviet authors. What distinguishes Ulitskaia and Vasilenko, however, is how specifically female experience grounds the treatment of the past in everyday life.

Gender: Diffuse Descriptions and Diversified Roles

Transhistorical temporality and history by indirection promoted a subtle engagement with personal and political events shaping female lives. Post-Soviet female authors also provided more nuanced and diverse roles for women, with Ulitskaia in particular employing diffuse and original portrayals to avoid the sometimes clichéd images of her perestroika predecessors. In a significant departure, women's sexual experiences now resembled exploration as well as exploitation (especially for young women). Destabilizing the equation between sexuality and transgression had other results. Ulitskaia normalized homosexuality instead of linking it to a tragic outcome. However, Vasilenko and Ulitskaia also provided two recurring character types—the female saint and the disabled woman—who resemble more traditional personages in women's writing.

Physical and emotional passions were inseparable for Ulitskaia. Discussing Sandra's sexuality in *Medeia i ee deti*, the narrator filters observations through diction and syntax stressing the stylistics of representation more than the content itself. The novel contrasts Sandra's and Medeia's lives and, in particular, Medeia's more modest successes with men, for which Sandra is partially to blame: "Her kid sister [*sestrenka*] was not missing out [*prenebregat'*] on anything, diving for pearls in any sea, and sipping honey from any flower." The narrator gives Sandra a role usually reserved for the (older) male in Russian literature, namely, the connoisseur of varied pleasures. The verb *prenebregat'* (to scorn, disregard), which is too formal for the diminutive *sestrenka* (kid sister), creates the disparity between content and expression that continues in the various metaphors for Sandra's escapades.[17] The erotic, a network of choices furthering individual development, is revealed by a humorous and refined description diverging from previous women writers' dire or disappointing descriptions of sexuality. Baranskaia and Grekova avoided the topic, while Petrushevskaia's narrators embedded the erotic in malicious gossip and physiological voyeurism.[18]

Ulitskaia's story "Vetrianaia ospa" (Chicken Pox) presented another quietly radical depiction of female sexuality as teenage Plishkina shows her friend Chelysheva how to masturbate. Such an unconventional scene is defused by framing it as part of the girls' wedding game (i.e., the traditional heterosexual initiation of women). The narrator notes that both girls were aware of this source of pleasure: "[Chelysheva] knew about that trick herself.

What she did not know is that others knew about it, too." The passage exemplifies what Goscilo terms Ulitskaia's "low-key acceptance of the body." As with the description of Sandra, linguistic innovation (teenage slang and colloquialism) palliates content.[19]

In depicting this marginal aspect of sexuality, Ulitskaia broke with a series of traditions in women's prose. Plishkina and Chelysheva show that masturbation is pleasurable, implying that female sexuality may be distinct from procreation, a thought beyond the ken of Baranskaia's mothers. Constructing female sexuality as personal growth also distinguishes Ulitskaia from authors such as Marina Karpova, whose "Lovlia maiskikh zhukov" binds a girl's developing body to sexual abuse and fears of rape shared by her sister and mother. For Karpova, a perestroika author, sexual exploitation and violence are inseparable from the overall oppression of Stalinism. While *Kazus Kukotskogo* also makes this connection, the era's impact on women's sexuality per se is not as stark. This shift was partially facilitated thanks to previous fictional depictions of how the Soviet state had victimized women. Ulitskaia's innovative representation built on these precedents, creating a space where sexuality could evolve independent of exploitation.

Through her characters Ulitskaia offered an alternative to the legacy of woman as victim, a heritage hinted at by Baranskaia and Grekova and elaborated upon during perestroika. Using exceptional situations and lively diction, Ulitskaia forged a ludic alternative to previous depictions. The result was a discussion of controversial themes far more complex than Ol'ga Tatarinova's attack on saccharine depictions of love in the post-Soviet story "Seksopatologiia" (Sexual Pathology): "Everything is a sham. . . . Love is the biggest sham of all, getting people to torture themselves and bear new guinea pigs" for God's experiments.[20] This denunciation bears the stamp of perestroika's proclivity for negation, whose authors dismantled existing stereotypes rather than provide alternatives. Tatarinova's story is more a literary manifesto than a work of literature as such. Although it diagnoses the problem (love as a trap), it provides neither a means of prevention nor a cure. As a result, it lacks the enduring interest of the multifaceted female sexuality in "Vetrianaia ospa" or *Medeia i ee deti*.

Imagining sexuality as discovery implied that it helped a woman's growth, even if her partner was significantly older. Years after the incident, seventh-grader Bron'ka in Ulitskaia's eponymous story claims she truly loved the elderly neighbor she "seduced."[21] The narrator presents this denouement—the explanation for Bron'ka's repeated pregnancies—as a mystery rather than as statutory rape, according to Soviet law. Her friend Irina Mikhailovna even feels a momentary pang of envy, as if her life were incomplete because it lacks such a hidden love. Unlike Baranskaia's Zoika, this misalliance is not ascribed to prior sexual abuse: Bron'ka's choice gave her life meaning.

Ol'ga Lobova's story "Lëniny sny" (Lenia's Dreams) provides a more elaborate (and contrived) example of precocious female sexual activity with an older man. Vassa became pregnant at sixteen after sleeping with the artist for whom she posed as a nude model. She explains to her husband, Lenia, that she wanted to experience as much as possible. Marrying Lenia under the condition that he not interfere with her art, she then has an affair with the presumably younger model Pavel. In a fairly obvious plot device, her sexual and artistic apprenticeship precedes autonomy.[22] The narrative asserts that Vassa's independence derives from her voluntary and early erotic experience. Although Lobova reverses the traditional dichotomy male/artist and female/muse, the gendered imbalance of power remains. While such role reversals were unthinkable during the Thaw and Stagnation and innovative during perestroika, in the post-Soviet context they seemed almost as trite as the misogyny they countered.

Ulitskaia's novella *Sonechka* (1992) juxtaposes the results of early voluntary and forced sexual activity. Tania, the protagonist's daughter, has a variety of lovers and sees herself as an equal partner while having sex. Her friend Iasia, however, was coerced into intercourse when she was twelve, making sexuality a vehicle to achieve the otherwise impossible: she is able to live first with Tania's father and then move to Paris.[23] These contrasting images of sexual initiation, atypically didactic for Ulitskaia, clearly link initial sexual experience and psychological development. Tania and Iasia are symbolic opposites, recalling documentary prose's types more than individual personalities valued for their own merits.

In one of the post-Soviet women's anthologies, Galina Skvortsova takes a much dimmer view of older men and younger
women. Her "Russkaia dusha" (Russian Soul) recounts how an
American named Michael has an affair with a married woman
named Ol'ga Kazanova, who, in turn, discovers the Westerner
with a buxom younger woman. This detail is especially galling to
Ol'ga, who, as the narrator disapprovingly relates, fed her child
from a bottle to preserve the shape of her breasts. The affair between Ol'ga's younger rival and Michael illustrates several patterns in post-Soviet culture, women's prose, and Russian literature as a whole: older men and younger women; the unfaithful
wife as doomed; and predacious foreigners exploiting Russian
women. None too subtly emphasizing the third issue, the narrator alludes to a dream where Michael sells Ol'ga.[24]

Ol'ga's symbolic first name ("holy"), last name (related to the
city of Kazan', with its famous icon of the Virgin Mary), and nick-
name ("Russian Soul") emphasize her "Russianness." However,
this identity is thoroughly corrupt since both she and her husband have affairs and the bottle-feeding decision implies that
Ol'ga has broken one of Russian culture's central maternal ta-
boos by placing physical appearance above her child's health.[25]
This context contaminates the idea of the "Russian soul," a problem presumably lost on those who chose this title for an anthology lauding provincial female identity. The carnal Kazanova exemplifies Tat'iana Rovenskaia's assertion that ideology operates
on women through their bodies—a truism extending to the
sometimes essentialist dicta of women's prose.

In Ulitskaia's narratives same-sex relations are less exploitative than Kazanova's heterosexual experiences. Her gay characters are complete individuals, unlike the marginal miscreants
populating the prose of Petrushevskaia and Viktoriia Tokareva.
These two authors' post-Soviet stories imply that same-sex relations are "unnatural" at best, as exemplified by the embittered
and conniving lesbian Barbara in Tokareva's story "Lilovyi kostium" (A Violet Suit).[26]

Ulitskaia's "Golubchik" (Angel), however, sees same-sex love
as a part of human experience and implies that homosexuals are
neither "temporarily" gay (e.g., while in prison) nor are defined

only in terms of their sexual orientation. From this viewpoint the narrator of "Golubchik" stresses the irrelevance of whether the protagonist, Slava, was born a homosexual or "made" one by Nikolai Romanovich. What is important is the series of consequences. First, Slava is clearly satisfied with many of his affairs, including his first sexual encounter with a man he meets on the street. The narrator describes it as follows: "They made love, strong masculine love, of which Slava had had only an inkling before. The place smelled of vaseline and blood. It was what Slava had been wanting and what Nikolai Romanovich had been unable to give him. It was a night of nuptials, of initiation, and of ecstasy beyond the reach of music. A new life began for Slava."[27]

The beginning of another phase of Slava's life provided the first description of consensual gay intercourse in mainstream Russian literature. However, Ulitskaia's earlier prose contained certain stylistic precedents. There are striking parallels between this description of first "real" love and Sandra's variegated sexual experiences. Both depictions stress how sexuality connects the physiological and mental worlds. For Slava sleeping with the stranger brings relief from his obsessive thoughts about music. Sex is not limited to the accretion of bodily functions and moral deficiencies that Petrushevskaia reveals. The sense of discovery is more pronounced than that which results from the wedding game in "Vetrianaia ospa." While Slava's affair does not lead to marriage in the conventional sense, it resembles the image of the heterosexual "first night" where one partner initiates another into the pleasurable mysteries of sexuality.

The body is a function of individual experience, not collective values. Indeed, "Golubchik" suggests that the culpable party in homosexuality is not the gay lovers but the state, which imprisons the protagonist several times under Soviet anti-sodomy laws and is indifferent to his murder.[28] Ulitskaia's gay men resemble the heterosexual female characters of Vasilenko and Karpova. Both face actual or symbolic violence from the state on the basis of gender and sexuality.

Humanizing homosexuality continued the trend shaping depictions of Medeia's family, where kinship connotes emotional ties more than biological connection. Gender, too, is a construct instead of a "natural" truth, a distinction Ulitskaia asserts in an interview when she connects literary images of homosexuality to blurred boundaries between masculine and feminine.[29] According to this logic, gender identity is a function of experience and emotion rather than anatomical causality.

The relaxation of gender roles had its limits, a delimitation that resembled perestroika women's prose with the following twist: in post-Soviet writing by female authors the characters reasserting traditional gender roles were positive and central, not negative and peripheral. Medeia and Nad'ka-Ganna are both beatified in various ways. The protagonist of *Medeia i ee deti* uses kindness to create a home that is more metaphorical than physical. This transcendence, which Rovenskaia associates with *bytie*, encompasses the Christian virtues of love and sacrifice. As with the novel's depictions of the erotic, Medeia's saintly characteristics are muted and diffused. As a result she emerges as a well-rounded character, contrasting favorably with Skvortsova's contrived and corrupt Kazanova.[30]

Vasilenko's Nad'ka-Ganna is a more complex figure. The protagonist of what the author terms a "novel-hagiography," Nad'ka-Ganna embodies several topoi from the saint's life. While still a child she helps the other orphans, and even Traktorina Petrovna, whose Stalinist cruelty resembles that of a petty Antichrist. As in the saint's life, Nad'ka-Ganna is beset by demons in the form of Leshka Orliak's men, who nearly rape her, and the three Soviet soldiers, who succeed.[31] However, instead of the typical posthumous miracles, she gives birth to the sun and thus forestalls death for herself and others.

As the novel's title implies, Nad'ka-Ganna also derives from the tradition of the holy fool, existing outside the norms of acceptable behavior and communicating with God in a way that others cannot. This implicit challenge to church hierarchy resonates with her two main Christian identities: martyr saint and Mother of God. Nad'ka-Ganna does not speak—Traktorina Petrovna has usurped such verbal discourse—but rather sings and shrieks.[32] Nonverbal communication has long been the provenance of women in folk tradition, such as those afflicted with *klikushestvo* (shrieking sickness) due to possession by evil spirits.

In *Durochka* the girl's screams imply the opposite: the unclean forces, embodied in collectivization and the arms race, are external to Nad'ka-Ganna.

Lack of speech connects Nad'ka-Ganna to a series of disabled female characters in Ulitskaia's prose. Elena in *Kazus Kukotskogo* experiences a bout of amnesia. After regaining her memory, she remains senile, a psychosomatic manifestation of the marriage that worsened following a bitter argument over abortion. In Ulitskaia's narratives being in a disabled state is a sign of protest: Elena foregoes the obligations of mother and wife. Anfisa in Grekova's *Vdovii parokhod* undergoes a similar transformation following a stroke, indirectly forcing Vadim to take care of her just as she formerly took responsibility for him. However, in *Kazus Kukotskogo* there is no redemptive transformation: husband Pavel Alekseevich is daily reminded of the irreversible damage he helped to cause.[33]

While Elena is a living reproach to her erring husband, Lialia's condition in Ulitskaia's story "Lialin dom" (Lialia's Home) results from her own transgression—a mistake resembling those of Petrushevskaia's psychologically stunted characters. During an affair with her son's friend, Lialia discovers her daughter in bed with the same teenage boy and in the same position. After recovering from this shock, she is constantly happy and pities all things living and inanimate. Formerly callous, she is now overly compassionate.[34] Unlike the author's other disabled characters, Lialia and her fate embody an incongruously pat element of justice, illustrating how immorality leads to self-destruction.

Female authors after 1991 employed a variety of devices to depict less rigid gender roles. For Ulitskaia this relaxation revealed itself through a style describing sexuality in an organic, non-threatening manner. Sexual activity (whether heterosexual or homosexual) can be an empowering process of exploration, while *Sonechka*'s Iasia indicates that early coercive experience is damaging. Female characters are no longer victims or predators but individuals for whom sexuality is only one aspect of a relationship. However, the potent symbolism embodied in the saint and the disabled woman emphasizes traditional feminine virtues, showing that the diversification of gender roles clearly had its limits.

Locating Women's Prose: Feminism and the New Cultural Divide

The post-Soviet era solidified the status of female authors. In 2001 Tolstaia and Ulitskaia were awarded the prestigious Triumf and Booker prizes, respectively. Although a series launched by the Vagrius publishing house established women's prose as a permanent fixture, its depictions of everyday life placed it in a nebulous zone between high and low culture as these antipodes became more pronounced.

For some critics ideological issues were paramount. A short story contest in 1992 had the ambitious but self-defeating goal of linking feminism and women's prose. Sponsored by the feminist journal *Preobrazhenie* (Transfiguration), the established "thick" journal *Oktiabr'* (October), Columbia University, and other groups, the competition received some five hundred submissions. The committee's makeup indicated that not only feminist critics but such "traditional" authors as Fazil' Iskander and Vladimir Makanin recognized the legitimacy of this literature.[35]

Diana Medman, sponsor of the now-defunct *Preobrazhenie*, was disappointed with the submissions: "As a rule the heroine constantly perpetuates the situation causing her degradation and suffering," which passes for women's "natural role" in society. What was lacking, she maintained, was the "positive cultural potential that is the feminist mentality." As a consequence of this shortcoming, the jury failed to award a first prize.[36]

Medman's vague yet dogmatic formulation had several implications. She tacitly acknowledged a basic characteristic of women's prose inherited from the 1960s through the 1980s, namely, the presence of a female protagonist whose life is unsatisfying due to (often unacknowledged) gender inequality. However, like Western feminists such as Rita Felski, Medman assumed that description of oppression led to recognition of this injustice and consequently to change. For her the key element of feminist literature was an explicitly theorized discussion of gendered oppression, which is absent in a story such as Tatarinova's "Seksopatologiia" despite generalizations concerning women's subordinate status. Medman believed a work to be unproductive from a feminist viewpoint if it contained no description of how to overcome gendered disparities. This doctrinaire standpoint ignored the creative blurring of gender roles in works by Ulitskaia and Vasilenko or, for that matter, Baranskaia's and Grekova's pioneering efforts to establish women's *byt* as a legitimate literary topic. Ulitskaia's story "Koridornaia sistema" (The Corridor System) illustrates the limits of Medman's approach: the daughter of an abandoned mother thinks feminist thoughts that never develop since, as the narrator sardonically notes, de Beauvoir had not yet been translated into Russian.[37]

Medman mischaracterized women's prose and the "feminist mentality" as a pair, where the first term produced the second, an ideologized relationship ironically recalling socialist realism's dialectic of spontaneity and consciousness. This approach explains why many of the best-known female authors—Petrushevskaia, Sadur, Tolstaia—ignored the contest, probably out of opposition to a project overtly connected to such an explicit agenda. The absence of their work from post-Soviet women's anthologies also indicates that the solidarity that Vasilenko saw in collections such as *Novye amazonki* was often only a quick way of getting published.[38] Medman's desire to meld feminist theory and women's prose did not reflect the reality of post-Soviet women's writing.

Although critic Tat'iana Meleshko refrained from defining feminist writing or overtly connecting it to female authors, she did identify eight common traits of contemporary women's prose: (1) authorial consciousness (either systematic or rhizomatic, with the second term connoting escape from patriarchal structure); (2) the opposition male/female and ways to overcome it; (3) connections between space and narrative; (4) nontraditional archetypes; (5) intertextuality as a support for gender-oriented narratives; (6) the body as a theme reflecting women's problems in society; (7) the presence of the holy fool; and (8) an ending emphasizing flight or departure.[39] These loosely defined characteristics did not dictate the purpose of women's prose. The vaguely phrased "authorial consciousness" in her first point recalled what Elaine Showalter saw as the third and most developed stage of feminist literary criticism, namely, recognizing a distinct body of women's writing while continuing to examine and rework how the image of women appears in male prose.[40]

For both post-Soviet and Anglo-American female authors, women's writing implied awareness of canonical (viz. male) images of women. All of Meleshko's typological descriptors stemmed from male-dominated Russian literature, which female authors almost without exception identified as the foundation for women's prose.

Meleshko, unlike Medman, did not advocate explicitly formulating a "feminist mentality" as the only alternative to naturalizing women's oppression. Instead, the critic's descriptors mapped a literature moving toward a different conception of women. This new image may also fulfill Medman's wish, albeit in a less obtrusive manner, as suggested by how Ulitskaia's and Lobova's young women equate the corporeality of sexuality with autonomy as well as exploitation.

Meleshko built on the tropes of perestroika criticism when identifying women's prose as a similar accretion of details, characters, and patterns. These features suggested independent women who were aware of gendered oppression yet did not espouse the feminist rhetoric that is anathema to most authors. While Medman prescribed a connection between women's prose and feminism, Meleshko provided a less intrusive link between the two.

Like Meleshko, Nina Gabrielian and Rovenskaia provided broader assessments of women's prose, envisioning a tripartite structure relating literature and feminist theory. Gabrielian distinguished three tendencies: mimicry, rebellion, and a blurring of self and other.[41] The rubric of mimicry includes Baranskaia and Grekova, who cast themselves as Soviet authors documenting specific problems of the female quotidian existence. The second tendency—rebellion—evokes the antiworld of such perestroika-era works as "Chervivyi synok." Post-Soviet authors' diversified image of gays and the emotional/spiritual family constitute the third trajectory, with its blurring of self and other (female/male, heterosexual/homosexual).

By default Gabrielian saw this blurring as the most productive path for women's prose: mimicry and rebellion replicated patriarchal culture, whether through support or opposition. Women's prose, she insinuated, must move beyond "gathering stones" or reclaiming lost traditions, that is, what Showalter labeled the first and second stages of feminist literary criticism.[42]

The work of Petrushevskaia and, in a less dramatic manner, Tatarinova validated the fear that women's prose would recycle traditional paradigms. Describing the bestial side of human existence, these two authors confirmed the physical/ideal binary informing Orthodoxy and its ersatz replacement, socialist realism. Because Russian culture binds the physical to the feminine, Petrushevskaia and Tatarinova paradoxically supported such restrictive categories by using the very same binarisms to challenge them.[43]

Rovenskaia also created a tripartite categorization of women's prose, albeit one based on chronology rather than representation. The first stage, beginning in 1979 and involving the Mariia group in Leningrad, stressed women's themes in literature and criticism. The period of women's anthologies followed in the late 1980s through the 1990s. The third stage, which began in 1994–95, encompassed increased contact with foreigners and saw the end of women's collections.[44] These stages resembled the three tendencies that Gabrielian saw existing simultaneously in women's prose: the mimicry of Baranskaia and Grekova dominated Rovenskaia's first stage, while the rise of women's collections accompanied rebellion as part of the perestroika esthetic of negation. The post-Soviet era contained authors who questioned the boundaries between self and other. Rovenskaia, like Meleshko and Gabrielian, provided flexible descriptors of women's prose and its relationship to feminism, as befits a literature that was developing.

During perestroika, when anthologies were making women's prose visible and controversial, Abasheva established a problematic pattern in assessing this literature. Claiming that Tolstaia, Sadur, Petrushevskaia, and Valeriia Narbikova were more talented than the collections' remaining authors, she characterized these other writers' works as "ladies' prose" belonging to mass culture. This critical strategy often appeared as critics divided favorite authors from their literary milieu, thus disregarding the stylistic, thematic, and historical characteristics women's prose shared.[45] There was a paradoxical cumulative effect of critics distinguishing "their" writers from those who were less talented: all maintained that talented women authors existed, yet including all the varying exceptions left very few.

Despite such assessments, beginning in the late 1990s women's prose established itself as a recognized component of high literature. The prestigious Vagrius and popular Eksmo publishing houses issued works by Ulitskaia, Vasilenko, Petrushevskaia, and Galina Shcherbakova, a milestone proving this literature's cultural value—and profitability. Vagrius's series *Zhenskii pocherk: Nastoiashchaia zhenskaia proza* (Women's Handwriting: Real Women's Prose, 1999–2001) featured Vasilenko, Ulitskaia, Shcherbakova, and Ol'ga Slavnikova alongside translations of works by Joyce Carol Oates and Iris Murdoch. Slavnikova, perhaps unsurprisingly, argued that the series charts the boundary between women's prose and other, less worthy writing. However, the inclusion of romance author Nataliia Medvedeva complicates this statement. The republication in the series of Medvedeva's works suggests that Vagrius saw women's prose as bringing together both high literature and "select" mass-market authors. This view located women's prose between high and low culture, a situation that would have been impossible in the more polarized environment that accompanied the collapse of high literature sales in the early 1990s.[46]

This variegated series revealed two commonplaces of post-Soviet literary culture. First, certain types of literature were deemed inherently "better." Echoing Iurii Tynianov's distinction between literary *byt* and "true" art, this conception asserted that high literature employed artistic depiction of life instead of allowing the content to determine representation.[47] However, the second part of this supposition had implications for the first: literature must either sell itself or eventually vanish. A book of women's prose not only discussed daily life but was itself a physical presence in *byt*, a unit sold on the streets.

For Tolstaia the positioning of reader and author between high and low culture played a crucial role. In *Kys'* Benedikt is the archetypal bad reader, whose literally and figuratively avaricious bibliomania leads him to imprison those he suspects of hoarding the forbidden books he longs to consume. Fedor Kuz'mych, the community's physically and morally stunted ruler, is no better: he sells literature dating from the nineteenth and twentieth centuries back to the people, claiming it as his own. The novel's language—a skillful *skaz* of archaisms and neologisms—recalls the language of children or, more precisely, the childlike language intellectuals ascribe to the *narod*.[48]

The weighty sin of plagiarism—which is abhorrent to the intelligentsia—goes hand in hand with graphomania as Fedor Kuz'mych peppers the populace with purloined prose. The ruler's semiliterate scribbling and Benedikt's lack of higher-order reading skills cry out for intervention by the intellectuals, whose leader is snatched from danger moments before being burned at the stake.[49] This deus ex machina leaves Benedikt and the other childlike *golubchiki* alone and bewildered, robbed of the guidance that, like post-Soviet readers, they had no idea they needed.

Kys' winning the Triumf Prize in 2001 marked the first major success of women authors in the dystopia genre long favored by the intelligentsia. Slavnikova asserted that the fact that the majority of readers were female explained the success of women writers. This reason, plus the engaging prose of authors such as Ulitskaia, helped clarify why women writers gained wider popularity in an era when the nation as a whole lacked time for overly serious reading.[50]

Literary images of *byt* were another reason. Diverse stylistic innovation provided consumers with sophisticated yet highly readable visions of everyday life.[51] While women authors still experienced difficulties getting published in the 1990s, these barriers were more likely due to overall economic crises than to prejudices against female writers. On the whole, however, after 1991 women's prose distinguished itself in terms of quality and print runs: in 2000–2002 Eksmo and Vagrius issued Ulitskaia's works in multiple editions of ten and even twenty thousand copies, while Petrushevskaia's 2003 collection of autobiographical essays reached eleven thousand.[52] This commercial success occurred alongside discussions by critics on the connections between women's prose and feminist issues. A broader debate attempted to locate this writing in the new divide between elite and mass literature.

Redeeming *Byt*: Everyday Life as Artistic Resource

From the early 1960s to the mid-1980s many critics saw women authors' depiction of *byt* as at best a springboard to more important topics. During perestroika depictions of the quotidian were attacked as reflecting the worst aspects of an increasingly chaotic external reality. After 1991, however, Nina Gorlanova, Vasilenko, and particularly Ulitskaia envisioned *byt* as a valuable resource in itself. Immersing themselves in the everyday, these three writers attempted to transcend what critics assailed as the quotidian's transience, banality, and physicality. This new approach used styles divergent from the occasionally journalistic depictions of Baranskaia or Petrushevskaia's gritty dramas. The new genre of the women's *detektiv* had its own designs on the everyday, incorporating the latter in a series of enormously successful detective novels.

Documentation nevertheless continued to inform how authors and critics saw the place of women's writing in Russian culture. In her introduction to the anthology *Bryzgi shampanskogo* (Splashes of Champagne, 2003) Vasilenko noted that women's prose arises from a specifically female view of the world, namely, literature documents reality, and the demonstrated differences in male and female *byt* produce correspondingly divergent prose. One critic echoed this assertion, approvingly characterizing the anthology as an encyclopedia of Russian women's lives.[53] The comparison continues the documentary tendency heralded in the introduction to *Nepomniashchaia zla*, which asserted the need to reflect women's *byt* in literary form.

Authors saw this necessity not only as compatible with good writing but as a precondition for it. Gorlanova's "Kak napisat' rasskaz" (How to Write a Story) maintains that neither documentation nor *byt* is incompatible with good fiction. In fact, the author dryly observes, the exhausting struggle to care for family and self provides "algorithms" for literary creation. This argument recalls the narrative strategies of works such as Baranskaia's *Nedelia kak nedelia* (A Week Like Any Other), where the demands of everyday life shape plot and style. Such a stance challenged Tynianov's distinction between "true art" and "*byt*-driven" literature. Gorlanova denies any division between literature and life since the latter provides its own comedies and tragedies.[54]

As Rovenskaia dramatically explained, women's prose after 1991 dove into *byt* in order to overcome the limitations of the everyday as a shallow backdrop. Like Gorlanova, she argued that the quotidian per se was valuable to the author. For Rovenskaia, however, *byt* led to still worthier things, as when *Kys'* uses the everyday to signal the general hopelessness of the *narod* and, particularly, *homo sovieticus*. (At various moments Benedikt philosophically ponders Soviet commonplaces: neighbors exist to torment us and widespread stealing eventually will make everyone equal).[55] Rovenskaia's assessment likewise recalls the vision of *byt* as a conduit to higher meaning, a tendency dating back to critics' early discussions of Baranskaia and Grekova.

One critic made a similar but broader argument in noting the doubled generic designation of *Durochka* (viz. novel-hagiography). Connecting these two dissimilar types of literature, she contended, shows that anyone's daily life can become exceptional. A Bakhtinian reading of this claim illuminates how Vasilenko moves between the world of the novel (banal, contemporary, still developing) and the realm of the sacred work (ossified in an epic, untouchable past).[56] *Durochka* depicts the novelization of the saint's life: the hagiographic topoi of a holy life are immersed in *byt*, thereby becoming part of a living quotidian existence instead of venerable relics.

The everyday was a constant problem in writers' lives. After 1991 *byt* became more important to women authors because of their falling incomes and precipitous drop in standard of living. This appropriately prosaic predicament validated Iurii Lotman's observation that the quotidian only becomes visible during crisis. The shock of the ordinary colors Tolstaia's autobiographical post-Soviet stories dealing with the 1998 currency collapse, hunger during the winter of 1991, and similar moments revealing *byt*'s unpredictability.[57] While for Tynianov the everyday opposed "true" art, for Gorlanova and Tolstaia it revealed the artistic potentiality of every moment.

Ulitskaia described her relationship to the everyday as coming from two seemingly different disciplines, namely, biology and applied anthropology. Both fields rely on accumulating details to construct more general theories, with Ulitskaia mining "private life" for empirical data in an inductive approach that resembled the documentary rhetoric of Baranskaia and Grekova.[58] Her oeuvre benefited from the efforts of these two predecessors since she did not need to gather evidence to prove that women's quotidian existence was "typical" and a legitimate topic. Instead, novels such as *Medeia i ee deti* and *Kazus Kukotskogo* were grounded on the conclusions of female authors from the Thaw to perestroika: society must make *byt* livable for both men and women, a transformation that Ulitskaia attempts through imaginative representation of the quotidian. What could have been a gloomy recounting of Medeia's loneliness becomes a vision of how daily life is largely what one makes of it. One critic posited that Ulitskaia's prose rendered *byt* survivable by describing it in abstract terms, an assertion that ignored the humble hegemony of little things in these narratives.[59] In the story "Pikovaia dama" (The Queen of Spades) Anna Fedorovna's precious early-morning hours provide another set of examples: "The whole house was asleep, and that was a blessing she had been granted—or perhaps stolen. Nobody was making demands of her. Completely out of the blue, two hours entirely her own had materialized, and she wondered what to spend them on: whether to read a book that a patient, a famous philosopher or philologist, had given her long ago or write a letter to her bosom friend in Israel."[60]

A bevy of details convey Anna Fedorovna's opportunities in the hours before her tyrannical mother, Mur, awakens. The scene's cozy domesticity expands beyond the boundaries of the apartment as the reader learns of former friends and patients, each suggesting another excursus beyond the four walls. The modest luxury of a few undisturbed hours is an occasion for recollection, hinting that even the most ordinary of moments can be rewarding. While the narrative ends with Anna Fedorovna's death, for now her life is peaceful.[61]

Ulitskaia's artistic approach to depicting *byt* recalls one of the first reactions to Vasilenko's prose. "This is a story about that which is secret . . . which encircles us with every step" and awaits an artist's eye. Such a formulation, key to understanding how the ordinary appears in Vasilenko's works, evokes Trifonov's defense of *byt* as the immortal in the ephemeral. The everyday comprises a myriad of opportunities within which the sublime and mundane coexist, a theme echoed in Slavnikova's story "Taina neprochitanoi zapiski" (The Secret of the Unread Note) when the narrator suggests that the work's setting is less important than the author's imagination.[62]

While Ulitskaia and Slavnikova depicted everyday life as an artistic resource, the hugely popular women's mystery novels (*zhenskie detektivy*) framed *byt* within a commercial context peculiar to post-Soviet culture.[63] In the early 1990s sales of mass-market literature (romances, *detektivy*, and so forth) eclipsed those of works by high-culture authors such as Solzhenitsyn and Nabokov—which proved a disheartening shock for the intelligentsia.[64] The presentation of daily life in a compelling and readable manner was a major reason for the success of author Aleksandra Marinina (pseudonym of Marina Alekseeva) and, later, Tat'iana Ustinova and the lightly "ironic" writer Dar'ia Dontsova (pseudonym of Agrippina Dontsova). All three writers, whose works were published in large quantities by Eksmo, the leading popular press, also had television serials based on their work.

Readers' passion for *detektivy* largely derived from the very banality of the works, which promote identification with imperfect heroines and the world they inhabit. This attraction is new neither to women's prose nor, for that matter, to literature as a whole. What is different is that these works present *byt* as an adventure or a puzzle to be solved: the *detektiv* creates a specific air of verisimilitude that becomes both theme and goal as the female detectives solve the murder according to the laws of the narrative's imagined reality.[65]

At first glance the life of Marinina's heroine, Anastasiia Kamenskaia, is anything but compelling. The middle-aged criminal investigator lives in a modest Moscow apartment, with weekend plans that are unexciting at best. When asked by her husband what she will do, she replies: "Be lazy." Here is her domestic routine: "Having stayed in bed until twelve, Nastia then moved into the kitchen to continue being lazy. She settled into a comfortable nook, made herself croutons with cheese, wrapped herself in a warm terrycloth robe and began the second phase: drinking two cups of coffee and a glass of orange juice."[66]

While such languor has its appeal for Russia's harried women, Kamenskaia's domestic routine is not novel. What gives her life (and Marinina's prose) meaning is how she analyzes her quotidian existence and that of her murder suspects. When Kamenskaia's colleague, Vladislav Stasov, congratulates her on having caught a particularly crafty criminal, she corrects him: "Don't exaggerate. . . . I have never caught a single criminal in my life. I can't do that. I figured him out [*vychislila*]."[67]

This "figuring out" is deduction and is dependent on the examination of everyday life and its hidden meanings. Solving a case thanks to minutiae is a commonplace of women authors and *detektivy* as a genre. A policeman assisting one of Dontsova's heroines observes that criminals are caught because of petty details. To find the wrongdoer one must correctly interpret the semiotics of everyday life.[68]

Such scrupulous attention to the trivial unites two antithetical approaches to *byt*. Kamenskaia is clearly attuned to the significance of ordinary things. She combines what Barbara Heldt in a broader context sees as feminine attention to detail with the "masculine" tendency to assemble these facts into a coherent whole. This combination challenges those earlier critics of women's prose who dismissed the quotidian as a women's realm estranged from higher meaning. For Kamenskaia daily life is a series of discrete clues befuddling the inattentive but rewarding the careful and patient. The quotidian contains the "local knowledge" crucial to closing a case.[69]

In contrast to Marinina's works, which are grounded in the documentary appeal of post-Stalinist realism, Dontsova's novels flaunt their humorously surreal moments. One of the author's "dilettante" detectives stumbles upon a murder while working as a New Year's folk character. In another narrative protagonist Dasha Vasil'eva sees a group of bewildered penguins waddling along the roadside.[70] These episodes pique reader interest, propelling the author's elaborate plots while commenting on the absurdities abounding in *byt*.

It is no coincidence that women's *detektivy* became a prominent genre in the 1990s. In Russia (as in the West) crime novels have long been popular during dramatic social change (e.g., the late imperial period, NEP, and the first post-Soviet decades).[71]

However, the fact that female authors contributed to the rebirth of this genre is remarkable. With a few notable exceptions, such as the widely translated Agatha Christie, women writers and characters have been peripheral in Russian crime novels. One reason is an adroit appropriation of *byt* as a source of humor during the difficult Yeltsin and Putin years. In the United States mysteries were hugely popular during the Depression, helping readers distract themselves from the national feeling of hopelessness.[72] Female authors' felicitous treatment of everyday life, rooted in late-Soviet culture's obsession with *byt*, is itself a peculiarity of the novel, that most flexible and contemporary of Bakhtinian genres.[73] These works unabashedly lay claim to post-Sovie realia. With their heightened anti-Americanism and half-joking fears of Chechen terrorists, Dontsova's novels appealed to the reader of the early 2000s. Topical xenophobia undermined one critic's hopeful claim that women's *detektivy* move beyond the division between the "familiar" and "alien."[74]

Women's *detektivy* exhibited another tendency that at first seemed opposed to contemporaneity yet also bolstered popularity: ritualistic elements from premodern culture. Katerina Clark has convincingly shown that folkloric and medieval narratives greatly influenced socialist realism. They also played a noticeable role in *detektivy*. Dontsova's complex plots begin with a *priskazka*—an opening action sequence or humorous episode. Her heroines then confront a series of improbable coincidences, reflecting the fortuitous encounters of folk heroines Elena the Beautiful or Vasilisa the Wise as well as the twists and turns of the crime genre. Ready-made structures (caricatured villains, seemingly impossible tasks) complemented the *detektiv*'s appeal to contemporaneity.

In this sense Marinina's novel *Chernyi spisok* (The Blacklist, 1995) followed a well-established plot: the transition from fleeting passion to emotional commitment. The shift implies that protagonist Stasov moves from one type of beauty (slender but cold ex-wife Rita) to another, more appropriate one (full-bodied, nurturing Tania). In a socialist realist work such romantic development would have accompanied an important leap in political consciousness. Stasov's feelings for Tania, however, reassert a deeper ideological attachment: the importance of the family.

Tania becomes the mother figure who, along with her friend Ira, looks after Stasov's daughter—whom Rita neglects.[75] This maternal master plot exemplifies how, in the transition period of the 1990s, political doctrine gave way to the "natural" importance of the nuclear family.

For their part readers experienced two different narratives when devouring these *detektivy*. On a superficial level, they surveyed the apparently unremarkable terrain of women's lives: sick children, overcrowded buses, and so forth. A deeper stratum, however, revealed how these obstacles can be overcome as the deserving reached the "happy end" Russians derided in Hollywood yet still demanded from their own popular literature.[76]

While clichéd characters and predictable plots paired *detektivy* with mass entertainment, the prominence of intertextuality and ekphrasis evoked elite literature. Representation—particularly the act of writing—is a common theme in a genre determined to create its own identity. Characters repeatedly—and with no apparent shame—devour the novels of other women crime authors. Liliia, Stasov's precocious eight-year-old daughter, reads her first crime novel, conveniently written by Tania. This coincidence brings the future lovers closer together and, more subtly, critiques the traditional image of the sentimental female reader. Indeed, Liliia is a miniature Kamenskaia: her powers of observation and logic are sharp and she is anything but emotional as she contributes to solving the celebrity murders in *Chernyi spisok*.[77]

Marinina's works conveyed the power of representation. *Posmertnyi obraz* (Posthumous Image, 1995) shows how the killing of actress Alina Vandis stems from the omnipotence of the image. Alina's life has been marred by Psycho, who stalks her for years and experiences orgasms after imagining attacking her. His victim became alienated and withdrawn, choosing the screen as a haven. For Alina self-image may either empower or destroy.

Highlighting the potency of representation solidified the cultural status of the female *detektiv* in two ways. First, the genre associated itself with elite literature by appropriating one of the favorite themes of modernist (and postmodernist) authors. On a more fundamental level, women crime authors used representation to assert that the genre, unlike most popular culture, was aware of its artifice and was even capable of self-irony.[78]

Critics, however, thought otherwise. Irina Savkina laments that opponents equated women's *detektivy* with a "profane" tendency arising from the "broads'" (*babskii*) mentality of the post-Soviet reader. As with earlier accusations that Grekova was a romance writer, associating Marinina with a middlebrow female readership instantly discredited the author. This argument also extended to the debate over the gender of the genre's readers.[79] Such acrimony shows that after 1992 women's culture continued to be opposed to its "worthier" elite/masculine counterpart.

Overgeneralizations elided the complex role of the quotidian. Women's *detektivy* as a part of popular culture offered the reader a bifurcated approach to *byt*. In the (unacknowledged) tradition of Grekova and Baranskaia, these novels depicted everyday life through the post-Stalinist appeal to documentation. This drive for verisimilitude, as Todorov notes concerning literature as a whole, was a ruse that masked artifice beneath a comfortably familiar view of the world.

However, many works also provided a wish-fulfillment scenario, in which the plot and its heroines enacted blatantly unrealistic reader desires. Wolfgang Iser, who has done much to restore the importance of the reader, provides a key to these moments in observing that "effects and responses are properties neither of the text nor of the reader; the text represents a potential effect that is realized in the reading process."[80] The documentary and wish-fulfillment functions of the women's mystery combined with reader expectations to create a multifaceted representation of everyday life. In this way the *detektiv*, an allegedly objective depiction of external reality, resembled the narratives of Trifonov, Baranskaia, and Grekova. It first convinced the reader of its scrupulous mimesis in general and then of its "truthful" representation of specific human transgressions.

Such *detektiv* strategies shaped readers' ideas of "us" and "them" in the chaos following the collapse of the USSR.[81] "Our" people in these works have unassuming apartments and modest incomes. The moneyed New Russians, unsurprisingly, are the alien force in these plots. Their fabulous wealth inevitably accompanies dubious or simply immoral ethics. In this sense Elena Baraban astutely notes that Marinina's Kamenskaia is an exemplary heroine: despite a pitiful salary, she stays on the police force out of love for her profession and her coworkers. Her values, like those of Ulitskaia's characters, showed the reader the possibility of preserving one's individual ethics in the midst of economic collapse.[82]

The various good and evil fates meted out to the genre's heroines and villains combined documentation with wish fulfillment. In this manner Ustinova's protagonist Natal'ia obtains her prince, the director of a transportation company (himself a former trucker). Following Natal'ia home, he "rescues" her from an overcrowded minibus, presumably whisking her away to a better life. Miraculous endings, of course, appeared in other post-Soviet genres. In Ol'ga Postnikova's short story "Tristan i Izol'da" (Tristan and Isolde) a philandering alcoholic husband suddenly returns to his wife, helping her battle the stress-induced cancer his behavior caused.[83] For *detektivy*, however, the wish-fulfillment scenario was a formative feature of the genre.

The popularity of these novels showed positive reader responses to clearly contrived but satisfying plot resolutions. Marinina took the importance of the ending a step further, observing that she had received letters from readers claiming that her works had saved them from depression and even suicide.[84] Such responses to the genre's representation of *byt* recall Iser's scenario of readers modifying a prefabricated reality—the novels' image of daily life—to gain what they wish from it.

Everyday life emerged as a realm of surprises in post-Soviet women's prose. Ulitskaia and Vasilenko used the quotidian to model how a family based on emotional or spiritual ties transcends history. Unlike the doomed repetition shaping Baranskaia's, Grekova's, and Petrushevskaia's sense of the past, Ulitskaia and Vasilenko showed that kinship creates a parallel yet alternate experience of events, providing hope amid the horrors of the Russian twentieth century. Their narratives likewise offered less rigid conceptions of both heterosexual and homosexual interactions. However, two types of characters—the saint and the disabled woman—conveyed traditional images of female suffering. As during perestroika, the interplay of innovative and conservative women characters suggested a critique of gender roles (whether or not they were explicitly framed as such) operating within a culture prizing "natural" differences between men and women as a source of stability during a time of change.

After 1991 reactions to female authors crystallized around relations to feminism and the widening gap between elite and popular literature. Following patterns inherited from the Thaw and Stagnation, critics of women's *detektivy* linked supposedly "lowbrow" content to a petty, female everydayness that was antithetical to the great mission of Russian literature. From this standpoint, *byt* impeded what the beleaguered intelligentsia saw as fiction's primary function, namely, to educate and improve readers. At the same time, however, critics and authors created several interrelated metaphors to address the artistic potential of the everyday. These images implied a need to envision the quotidian in a way that permitted author and reader to more freely interpret the formless yet variegated expanse of daily life.

Conclusion

Cultural Divides and the Future
of Women's Prose

The author remains in the middle, between the observer and
the observed. . . . One notices that the beauty of leaves and
stones, of the human face, of clouds, is formed by the same
master craftsman.

Liudmila Ulitskaia

The most deserving topic seems to be private life and, moreover,
in its most obnoxious manifestations.

Ol'ga Slavnikova

Women's writing after Stalinism coalesced around the quotidian,
first moving from select illustration to broadened critique and
then acceptance of the everyday as an artistic resource valuable
in its own right. Emphases on documenting *byt* and, by extension, gender combined within narratives using temporality to
focus on history and the family. Privileging daily life helped both
intellectual and "ordinary" readers identify with prose that dealt
with controversial subjects, which, from the 1960s onward, had a
significant presence in mainstream literature.[1]

The post-Soviet years, bringing the end of the intelligentsia's
dominance over literary production, showed women authors
adroitly adapting to the Russian Federation's new publishing

conditions. The general decline in sales of "high-culture" authors made this success all the more striking. Earlier Baranskaia and Grekova had appropriated their era's emphasis on documentation. A more imaginative interpretation of this mandate for mimesis unified the otherwise diverse prose of Petrushevskaia, Ulitskaia, and Tolstaia, attracting readers eager to examine their daily life on the printed page. This desire to see one's image reflected in literature is part of human nature. What was new was how a genre such as the female crime novel recast *byt*'s banal trials as a puzzle to be solved. In its fictional guise the everyday moved from crisis to artistry, allowing readers to conceive of their lives as something other than immutable. The grim chaos of the 1990s made this sense of control over the everyday a comfort to both male and female readers.

During the Yeltsin and Putin eras, images of everyday life and the literary genres reflecting them became more varied. Women's writing—and Russian literature generally—reflected the growing gap between the center and the provinces.[2] However, divergence between elite and popular writing after 1991 had an even larger impact on women's prose. The rise of heightened distinctions during a time of accelerated change is far from surprising. Andreas Huyssen observed that popular culture has long been considered urban, feminine, and disruptive. Such suspect associations had already crept into the allegedly gender-neutral Soviet criticism of the 1960s and 1970s, which itself inherited cultural assumptions linking *byt* to that which is female, common, and material. This pairing later became an explicit concern in debates over perestroika-era *chernukha* and the post-Soviet eclipse of high literature.[3]

The association between women's writing, the everyday, and non-elite literature will no doubt continue. After 1991 this prose was often reduced to two popular genres dominated by female authors: romance novels and *detektivy*. (Despite winning the Booker Prize, even Ulitskaia was the victim of such mistaken identity.) Many of these authors' works were serialized on television. Not withstanding the misgivings of various critics, such prominence in popular culture was far from detrimental. In fact, large print runs and media exposure awakened huge numbers of readers to the women's issues embedded in this prose. For

instance, female mystery authors greatly heightened the visibil-
ity of independent women characters and their daily lives.[4]

In the post-Soviet context, distinctions between elite and mass
culture relied on inherited arguments. To a striking degree these
assertions reflected earlier efforts to denigrate women's prose as
a supposedly substandard fictional product damned by its association with *byt*. Critics ascribed sophisticated analysis of everyday life to high literature, while its popular counterpart suffered
from a naive replication of the quotidian. Tat'iana Morozova exemplifies this sweeping claim, arguing that trivial pursuits and
their happy resolution defined the Russian romance novel, a
genre she envisioned as combining the feminine and the lowbrow. Such pronouncements, however, ignore Jim McGuigan's
comment that high/elite culture "has always refreshed itself
from the springs of popular culture." Without the appropriation
of folklore, peasant religion, and so forth, Russian belles lettres
would have been greatly impoverished.[5]

Conflating women's prose and popular writing recalls another
enduring axiom, namely, Iurii Tynianov's belief that in "true" art
representation shapes content, not vice versa. From this standpoint Viktoriia Tokareva's post-Soviet story "Perelom" (Breaking
Point) shows how *byt* limits the narrative as everyday life molds
the plot. The narrative relates how Tat'iana, a former figure
skater, breaks her leg after fighting with her unfaithful husband.
The narrative is closed within itself; details and events lead to
one another but do not extend beyond the diegesis. In a work
such as Ulitskaia's "Pikovaia dama," however, the realia of life
expand outward, hinting at the friendships and other opportunities implied in descriptions of Anna Fedorovna's books and
letters. For Tynianov mastery over the quotidian permits the author to transform the narrative into art, broadening its possibilities. Tokareva's reliance on the shocking raw material of life, on
the other hand, limits the resulting story.[6] While there is some validity to this schematic assessment of *byt*'s role, it encourages an
automatic and dismissive association between depictions of
everyday life and mass literature. More important, this divisive
drive to separate "worthy" from "worthless" prose ignores how
byt operates as a key commonality between these two writers.[7]

There are two other problems with conflating post-Soviet women's prose and a preformed view of popular literature. First, the gap between high and low genres was not new. Critics who bemoaned the decline of good reading dehistoricized the history of Russian and Soviet mass literature. For instance, there was a wave of enthusiasm for detective fiction, first in 1905–8 and then during the 1920s (the reign of the "Red Pinkerton") before vanishing under Stalinism, only to reappear during Thaw and Stagnation.[8] The thirst for popular literature was not conjured out of emptiness by the market economy or by the new prominence of women readers and authors.

Nor does gender influence narrative quality in any meaningful sense. Those who associated women authors only with popular (viz. second-rate) literature studiously ignored the success of an author such as Ulitskaia among both elite and mass readers. In the tellingly titled article "Ulitskaia Has Stopped Loving People," one critic's attack on "cheap melodrama" in *Iskrenne Vash Shurik* (Sincerely Yours, Shurik, 2004) obscures the privileged place of said melodrama in high culture by men and women authors. The insinuated link between the female, emotional, and middlebrow also elides what Louise McReynolds and Joan Neuberger see as melodrama's ability to connect everyday life to larger issues through "a uniquely accessible mode of analysis" binding politics and art to *byt*. While Shurik's tragicomic sexual entanglements do give Ulitskaia's plot an episodic quality, they are only one level of a novel that uses its protagonist's private life to point to the anomaly of the supportive male.[9] Misdiagnosing melodrama as a female malady calls to mind another accusation that shaped post-Soviet criticism: literature had given up its age-old duty to serious social commentary in favor of the titillations of everyday life.

Within this charged cultural atmosphere, Ulitskaia's success with readers had enormous implications for debates over high and low culture. There are four reasons for her popularity, a term whose quantitative connotations I am aware of but use without any qualitative reservation. First, her narratives subtly and unobtrusively engaged the past ("history by indirection"). Works such as *Kazus Kukotskogo* showed the cost of Stalinism reflected through the prism of the female body. The result was accessible themes, which accompanied stylistic sophistication as a part of the realist mode of representation with which Russian readers were most comfortable. In a similar vein, Ulitskaia's artistic treatment of everyday life was innovative yet resonated with those raised on documenting *byt* as a literary topic. Her novel *Daniel' Shtain, perevodchik* (Daniel Stein, Translator, 2006) used fictionalized letters and interviews to bring the horrors of the Holocaust down to a human scale for Russian readers, who were still relatively unfamiliar with this national tragedy. Finally, her protagonists' lives implied that we can live through difficult times while preserving ethical standards—a rare positive message in the fraught post-Soviet era. A character such as Medeia demonstrates how love creates a viable and nurturing alternative to the mass brutalities of Russian history.

Ulitskaia's literary career suggested that women writers need not worry about differences between elite and popular literature: talent—and clever marketing—resolved such issues. Ulitskaia's themes, style, and intellectual characters linked her to high culture, while the choice of Eksmo as a publisher grew out of a desire to reach a wider audience.[10] In short, her position illustrated that the putative gap between elite and popular literature was neither insurmountable nor a substitute for judging writers on their own merits.

Ulitskaia's remarkable success, along with the plethora of talented female writers appearing after 1991, augured well for the future of women's prose. Her novels and stories signaled an engagement with history, reduced idealism, and a focus on the body as locus of trauma.[11] These tendencies were not unique to this particular author. Ulitskaia redefined themes that began emerging in the 1960s and 1970s and were amplified during perestroika. Embedding this content in a rich and refreshing image of *byt* connected her to previous women's prose and provided a milieu made familiar by both male and female authors. However, the virtues of humanism—in its broadest ecumenical and ethical sense—set her works apart. Ulitskaia revealed women's writing to be an integrated part of Russian culture. Her prose shows how women's issues are both distinct from those of men yet inextricable from society as a whole.

Ulitskaia benefited from her predecessors while diversifying their legacy. Women authors first established the quotidian as a venue within which to legitimate women's issues, selectively depicting key moments within *byt* to highlight sharper social commentary conveyed through increasingly varied styles. This ability to adapt in a culture that had itself undergone dramatic changes provides a viable future for Russian female writers, one that will make literature more inclusive of both male and female experience.

Notes

Introduction

1. The opening epigraph, a typically dramatic assessment of everyday life in Russian culture, is from Roman Jakobson, "On a Generation That Squandered Its Poets," *Language in Literature*, ed. Krystyna Pomorska and Stephen Rudy (Cambridge: Belknap Press, 1987), 277. The second quotation is from the introduction to the anthology *Ne pomniashchaia zla* (She Who Remembers No Evil), ed. N. A. Ryl'nikova, comp. Larisa Vaneeva (Moscow: Moskovskii rabochii, 1990), 4. All translations are my own unless otherwise noted.

2. On Petrushevskaia's experience with *Novyi mir,* see Georgii Viren, "Takaia liubov'," *Oktiabr'*, no. 3 (1989): 205; quoted in Carol Adlam's study of women's alternative prose entitled *Women in Russian Literature after Glasnost: Female Alternatives* (London: Legenda, 2005), 104. Ol'ga Vronskaia mentions Grekova's failed attempt to publish her novel *Svezho predanie* (In Recent Memory). See Ol'ga Vronskaia, "Mama, ia zhid?" *Literaturnaia gazeta*, no. 27 (1997): 3. The only monograph devoted to Grekova appeared before the publication of *Svezho predanie.* See Elisabeth Menke's thorough albeit schematic study *Die Kultur der Weiblichkeit in der Prosa Irina Grekovas* (Munich: Otto Sagner, 1988).

3. For stylistic reasons I use *"byt,"* "everyday," "quotidian," and "daily life" synonymously. The second portion of the introduction, however, will show that Western and Russian conceptions of the everyday differ dramatically.

4. Vladimir Nabokov, "Philistines and Philistinism," in *Lectures on Russian Literature*, ed. Fredson Bowers (New York: Harcourt Brace Jovanovich, 1981), 309. Private life is one element of *byt*, but it has mainly avoided the negative associations of the latter, broader term. Conceiving

of *byt* as daily existence implies that everyday life encompasses the realm of the private. See Iurii Bessmertnyi, "Chastnaia zhizn': Stereotipnoe i individual'noe. V poiskakh novykh reshenii," in *Chelovek v krugu sem'i. Ocherki po istorii chastnoi zhizni v Evrope do nachala novogo vremeni*, ed. Iurii Bessmertnyi (Moscow: Rossiiskii gosudarstvennyi gumanitarnyi universitet, 1996), 11.

5. As Joan Scott has remarked, gender denotes the often problematic significance society attaches to biological distinctions between men and women: "Gender . . . means knowledge about sexual difference," where knowledge implies understanding that society produces. Knowledge reveals itself through everyday interaction, which women authors in turn reproduce in fictional form. Joan Scott, introduction to *Gender and the Politics of History* (New York: Columbia University Press, 1988), 2.

6. For a discussion of how these images appear in literature, see David Gillespie, "Textual Abuse: The (Mis)Treatment of the Body in Russian Literature," *Australian Slavonic and East European Studies* 12, no. 2 (1998): 5–6. Rolf Hellebust provides an intriguing and informative overview of the masculine, feminine, and machine body in his *Flesh to Metal: Soviet Literature and the Alchemy of Revolution* (Ithaca, N.Y.: Cornell University Press, 2003).

7. Eve Sedgwick, *Epistemology of the Closet* (Berkeley: University of California Press, 1990), 9–10. See also Jeannette Batz Cooperman, *The Broom Closet: Secret Meanings of Domesticity in Postfeminist Novels by Louise Erdrich, Mary Gordon, Toni Morrison, Marge Piercy, Jane Smiley, and Amy Tan* (New York: Peter Lang, 1999), 2. Helena Goscilo connects female authors to the image of domesticity in her short but pithy discussion of women's prose in "Coming a Long Way, Baby: A Quarter-Century of Russian Women's Fiction," *Harriman Institute Forum*, no. 1 (1992): 7. Lastly, see Iuliia Gradskova, *"Obychnaia" sovetskaia zhenshchina* (Moscow: Sputnik, 1999), 15–16.

8. Sandra Gilbert and Susan Gubar, *The Madwoman in the Attic: The Woman Writer and the Nineteenth-Century Literary Imagination*, 2nd ed. (New Haven, Conn.: Yale University Press, 2000), 11–13.

9. Alan Pollard, "The Russian Intelligentsia: The Mind of Russia," *California Slavic Papers*, no. 3 (1964): 19, 32.

10. See Vera Dunham, "The Changing Image of Women in Soviet Literature," in *The Role and Status of Women in the Soviet Union*, ed. D. R. Brown (New York: Columbia University Press, 1968), 63. See also Josephine Woll, *Real Images: Soviet Cinema and the Thaw* (London: I. B. Tauris, 2000), xiii.

11. Barbara Heldt, "Gynoglasnost: Writing the Feminine," in *Perestroika and Soviet Women*, ed. Mary Buckley (Cambridge: Cambridge University Press, 1992), 169.

12. Gilbert and Gubar, *The Madwoman in the Attic*, 17. See also Nancy Armstrong, *Desire and Domestic Fiction: A Political History of the Novel* (New York: Oxford University Press, 1987), 8.

13. Michel de Certeau, *The Practice of Everyday Life*, trans. Steven Rendall (Berkeley: University of California Press, 1984), xix.

14. Andreas Huyssen, *After the Great Divide: Modernism, Mass Culture, Postmodernism* (Bloomington: Indiana University Press, 1987), 53; Maurice Blanchot, "Everyday Speech," trans. Susan Hanson, *Yale French Studies*, no. 73 (1987): 13. Henri Lefebvre recasts the opposition quotidian/order as the divide between the everyday and "philosophy," where the latter tries to impose standardized truths based on an authority removed from the quotidian. See his study *Everyday Life in the Modern World*, trans. Sacha Rabinowitz (New York: Harper & Row, 1971), 12–13.

15. Oleg Kharkhordin maps the varying semantics of personal and private life in his perceptive article "Reveal and Dissimulate: A Genealogy of Private Life in Soviet Russia," in *Public and Private in Thought and Practice: Perspectives on a Grand Dichotomy*, ed. Jeff Weintraub and Krishan Kumar (Chicago: University of Chicago Press, 1997), 355. To avoid confusion, aside from this discussion I have translated both *lichnaia zhizn'* and *chastnaia zhizn'* as "private life," although the former term has romantic overtones that the latter lacks. Russian culture marks *lichnaia zhizn'* as women's discourse, while *chastnaia zhizn'* is more abstract, less colloquial, and not associated with a single gender.

16. For Stuart Hall, the most prominent figure of the Birmingham School, the interdisciplinarity inherent in studying the everyday promoted the "cultural change . . . at the very heart of social life." "The Emergence of Cultural Studies and the Crisis of the Humanities," *October* 53 (1990): 14. It is no coincidence that Western feminism also developed within institutional interstices around the same time. Both responded to perceived oversights in traditional fields of inquiry and were shaped by the New Left. On the development of US feminism as an academic field, see Ellen Messer-Davidow, *Disciplining Feminism: From Social Activism to Academic Discourse* (Durham, N.C.: Duke University Press, 2002).

17. Iurii Lotman, *Besedy o russkoi kul'ture: Byt i traditsii russkogo dvorianstva (XVIII–nachalo XIX veka)* (St. Petersburg: Iskusstvo-SPB, 1994), 10.

18. Huyssen, *After the Great Divide*, 47, 53.

19. Stephen Hutchings, *Russian Modernism: The Transfiguration of the Everyday* (Cambridge: Cambridge University Press, 1997), 38; italics in original. This well-reasoned study traces the division between *byt* and *bytie* to Orthodox concerns over the gap between the icon as religious image and the holy figures it depicts. As Hutchings notes, his commentary draws on Lotman and Boris Uspenskii's discussion of the absence

of purgatory in Russian medieval theology, which hinted at a cultural intolerance for any semiotically neutral space (i.e., *byt*). Iurii Lotman and Boris Uspenskii, "Binary Models in the Dynamics of Russian Culture (to the End of the Eighteenth Century)," in *The Semiotics of Russian Cultural History: Essays by Iurii M. Lotman, Lidiia Ia. Ginsburg, Boris A. Uspenskii*, ed. Alexander Nakhimovsky and Alice Nakhimovsky (Ithaca, N.Y.: Cornell University Press, 1985), 32.

20. Jakobson, "On a Generation That Squandered Its Poets," 277.

21. See Katerina Clark, *The Soviet Novel: History as Ritual* (Bloomington: Indiana University Press, 2000), 9–10.

22. Gary Saul Morson, "Prosaics and *Anna Karenina*," *Tolstoy Studies Journal*, no. 1 (1988): 7. See Andrei Sinyavsky, *Soviet Civilization: A Cultural History*, trans. Joanne Turnbull with Nikolai Formozov (New York: Arcade, 1990), 189; Nicolay Dobrolyubov, "What Is Oblomovitis?" in *Belinsky, Chernyshevsky, and Dobrolyubov: Selected Criticism*, ed. Ralph E. Matlaw (New York: Dutton, 1962), 135.

23. L. I. Skvortsov, "V zhanre damskoi povesti," *Russkaia rech'*, no. 1 (1968): 26; Svetlana Boym, *Common Places: Mythologies of Everyday Life in Russia* (Cambridge, Mass.: Harvard University Press, 1994), 168.

24. Boym, *Common Places*, 41. Boym's study remains one of the most imaginative and engaging discussions of how Russian culture envisions *byt*.

25. Edward P. Thompson, *The Making of the English Working Class* (New York: Vintage, 1963), 12. For a recent assessment of Lotman's contributions to Western and Russian cultural studies, including a discussion of post-Soviet issues, see the collection *Lotman and Cultural Studies: Encounters and Extensions*, ed. Andreas Schönle (Madison: University of Wisconsin Press, 2006).

26. Gary Saul Morson's description of the crucial yet overlooked role of *byt* in Leo Tolstoy's novels helped form the thinking that underlies my study (Gary Saul Morson, *Hidden in Plain View: Narrative and Creative Potentials in* War and Peace [Stanford: Stanford University Press, 1987]). Likewise, Morson and Caryl Emerson developed American investigations of Bakhtinian thought in a manner that illuminated this versatile thinker's love of the quotidian. In many ways discussions of heteroglossia and the novel's varied contexts were forerunners of everyday-life studies.

27. Joan Scott, "Women's History," in *Gender and the Politics of History* (New York: Columbia University Press, 1988), 27. On prerevolutionary attitudes toward the peasant woman as a signifier of Russian backwardness, see Xenia Gasiorowska's groundbreaking study *Women in Soviet Fiction, 1917–1964* (Madison: University of Wisconsin Press, 1968), 28.

28. Sheila Fitzpatrick, *The Cultural Front: Power and Culture in Revolutionary Russia* (Ithaca, N.Y.: Cornell University Press, 1992), 2. See also Lynne Attwood, *Creating the New Soviet Woman: Women's Magazines as Engineers of Female Identity, 1922-53* (New York: St. Martin's Press, 1999), 173.

29. Mikhail Bakhtin, "Epic and Novel," in *The Dialogic Imagination: Four Essays by M. M. Bakhtin*, ed. Michael Holquist, trans. Caryl Emerson and Michael Holquist (Austin: University of Texas Press, 1981), 31. See also Boym, *Common Places*, 34. On utopian schemes for housing, see Richard Stites, *Revolutionary Dreams: Utopian Vision and Experimental Life in the Russian Revolution* (New York: Oxford University Press, 1989), 190-222.

30. Blanchot, "Everyday Speech," 13. See also: Susan Reid, "Cold War in the Kitchen: Gender and the De-Stalinization of Consumer Taste in the Soviet Union under Khrushchev," *Slavic Review* 61, no. 2 (2002): 220; Attwood, *Creating the New Soviet Woman*, 171, 13; and Kharkhordin, "Reveal and Dissimulate," 343-44, 355.

31. See Beth Holmgren, "Writing the Female Body Politic, 1945-1985," in *A History of Women's Writing in Russia*, ed. Adele Barker and Jehanne Gheith (Cambridge: Cambridge University Press, 2002), 231.

32. Attwood, *Creating the New Soviet Woman*, 161.

33. Vera Panova, "Mal'chik i devochka," in *Povesti* (Leningrad: Sovetskii pisatel', 1969); Alexander Prokhorov, "Inherited Discourse: Soviet Tropes in Thaw Culture" (Ph.D. diss., University of Pittsburgh, 2002), 143; Woll, *Real Images*, 12.

34. Liubov' Kabo, *Ne veselo byt' meshchaninom!* (Moscow: Izdatel'stvo politicheskoi literatury, 1965), 2; Kharkhordin, "Reveal and Dissimulate," 357; Reid, "Cold War in the Kitchen," 217-18.

35. Previous Western studies of these two authors begin with Baranskaia's best-known work *Nedelia kak nedelia* (A Week Like Any Other, 1969). However, several earlier works laid the groundwork for this later publication, such as Baranskaia's story "Provody" (The Farewell Party, 1968) and Grekova's novella *Damskii master* (Ladies' Hairdresser, 1963).

36. Nicholas Žekulin, "Soviet Russian Women's Literature in the Early 1980s," in *Fruits of Her Plume: Essays on Contemporary Russian Women's Culture*, ed. Helena Goscilo (Armonk, N.Y.: M. E. Sharpe, 1993), 33-35; Adele Barker and Jehanne Gheith, introduction to *A History of Women's Writing in Russia* (Cambridge: Cambridge University Press, 2002), 13.

37. Dunham, "The Changing Image of Women in Soviet Literature," 84. See also Gasiorowska, *Women in Soviet Fiction, 1917-1964*, 185.

38. As the prose of Baranskaia and Grekova illustrates, from the 1950s through the 1980s layers of private life were determined by social convention more than by physical removal from public view. The main reason for intimacy's resulting opacity was the overcrowded communal apartments in which most Soviets lived. See Boym, *Common Places*, 74.

39. Bakhtin, "Epic and Novel," 23. See also Prokhorov, "Inherited Discourse," 215–16, 249.

40. Attwood, *Creating the New Soviet Woman*, 171. See also Susan Reid, "Women in the Home," in *Women in the Khrushchev Era*, ed. Melanie Ilič, Susan Reid, and Lynne Attwood (Hampshire, Engl.: Palgrave, 2004), 153; On the ambivalent prominence of the postwar woman, see Holmgren, "Writing the Female Body Politic, 1945–1985," 226–27; Susan Reid, "Gender Relations in the Visual Culture of the Khrushchev Thaw," in *Fenomen pola v kul'ture/Sex and Gender in Culture. Materialy mezhdunarodnoi nauchnoi konferentsii. Moskva, 15–17 ianvaria 1998 g.*, ed. G. A. Tkachenko (Moscow: Rossiiskii gosudarstvennyi gumanitarnyi universitet, 1998), 93; Xenia Gasiorowska, "Two Decades of Love and Marriage in Soviet Fiction," *Russian Review* 34, no. 1 (1975): 19; and Lynne Attwood, "Gender Angst in Russian Society and Cinema in the Post-Stalin Era," in *Russian Cultural Studies: An Introduction*, ed. Catriona Kelly and David Shepherd (Oxford: Oxford University Press, 1998), 353.

41. For a recent discussion of the "demographic crisis" and its even more disturbing post-Soviet instantiation, see Michele Rivkin-Fish, "From 'Demographic Crisis' to 'Dying Nation': The Politics of Language and Reproduction in Russia," in *Gender and National Identity in Twentieth-Century Russian Culture*, ed. Helena Goscilo and Andrea Lanoux (Dekalb: Northern Illinois University Press, 2006). See also: Mark Banting, Catriona Kelly, and James Riordan, "Sexuality," in *Russian Cultural Studies: An Introduction*, ed. Catriona Kelly and David Shepherd (Oxford: Oxford University Press, 1998), 338–39; Bernice Madison, "Social Services for Women: Problems and Priorities," in *Women in Russia*, ed. Dorothy Atkinson, Alexander Dallin, and Gail Lapidus (Stanford, Calif.: Stanford University Press, 1977), 313. Gail Lapidus discusses the demographic crisis and the state's pro-natalist response in "Sexual Equality in Soviet Policy: A Developmental Perspective," in *Women in Russia*, 129–36.

42. Gradskova, *"Obychnaia" sovetskaia zhenshchina*, 131. Marianne Liljeström surveys official fears during the 1970s of producing effeminate boys, suggesting that this anxiety was part of a set of gendered stereotypes. See "The Soviet Gender System: The Ideological Construction of Femininity and Masculinity in the 1970s," in *Gender Restructuring*

in Russian Studies, ed. Marianne Liljeström, Eila Mäntysaari, and Arya Rosenholm, Slavica Tamperensia 11 (Tampere: University of Tampere, 1993), 169–70. Indeed, one of the coauthors of a Soviet article contends that overbearing women may emasculate their sons. See "How Much Housework Should a Man Do?" *Current Digest of the Soviet Press* 34, no. 46 (1982): 11.

43. Reid, "Gender Relations in the Visual Culture of the Khrushchev Thaw," 93.

44. Anatoly Vishevsky, *Soviet Literary Culture in the 1970s: The Politics of Irony* (Gainesville: University Press of Florida, 1993), 5; Boym, *Common Places,* 25, 147–48.

45. See Anatolii Strelianyi, *Zhenskie pis'ma* (Moscow: Sovetskaia Rossiia, 1981), 33. Strelianyi collates readers' letters to an unnamed newspaper, commenting on the unfortunate imbalance in household chores. The shiftless husband's relation to the double burden is a favorite topic of Western Slavists as well—in this vein, see Susan Kay, "A Woman's Work," *Irish Slavonic Studies,* no. 8 (1987): 118; and Elsbeth Wolffheim, "Das Frauenbild bei Viktorija Tokareva," in *Frauenbilder und Weiblichkeitsentwürfe in der russischen Frauenprosa: Materialen des wissenschaftlichen Symposiums in Erfurt,* ed. Christina Parnell (Frankfurt: Peter Lang, 1996), 172.

46. For one of the most influential psychological discussions of the interactions between the self and others, see Erving Goffman, *The Presentation of Self in Everyday Life* (Garden City, N.Y.: Doubleday, 1959).

47. Tat'iana Klimenkova, "Perestroika kak gendernaia problema," in *Gender Restructuring in Russian Studies,* ed. Marianne Liljeström, Eila Mäntysaari, and Arya Rosenholm, Slavica Tamperensia 11 (Tampere: University of Tampere, 1993), 161. Gorbachev summarized his ambivalent but ultimately restrictive ideas on the role of women in his *Perestroika: New Thinking for Our Country and the World* (New York: Harper & Row, 1987), 116–18. For how feminists viewed these pronouncements, see Nadezhda Azhgikhina, "Zhenshchina kak ob"ekt i sub"ekt v sovremennoi rossiiskoi literature," in *Sila slova-2: Novyi evropeiskii poriadok: Prava cheloveka, polozhenie zhenshchin, i gendernaia tsenzura,* comp. Nadezhda Azhgikhina (Moscow: Zhenskii mir i Eslan, 2000), 60. For an overview of the (re)introduction of pornography to Russia, see Helena Goscilo, *Dehexing Sex: Russian Womanhood During and After Glasnost* (Ann Arbor: University of Michigan Press, 1996), 135–70.

48. Beth Holmgren, "Bug Inspectors and Beauty Queens: The Problems of Translating Feminism into Russian," in *Postcommunism and the Body Politic,* ed. Ellen Berry (New York: New York University Press, 1995), 15–17. See also Goscilo, *Dehexing Sex,* 12–13.

49. Holmgren, "Bug Inspectors and Beauty Queens," 25. Beginning in perestroika, women's job losses were much greater than men's. By 1994 68 percent of the registered unemployed were women, with women comprising 78.2 percent of the highly educated and unemployed. See Valerie Sperling, *Organizing Women in Contemporary Russia: Engendering Transition* (Cambridge: Cambridge University Press, 1999), 150; Natalia Rimashevskaia, "The New Women's Studies," in *Perestroika and Soviet Women,* ed. Mary Buckley (Cambridge: Cambridge University Press, 1992), 247). Finding reliable unemployment figures for most of the Gorbachev era is impossible since the USSR only began gathering such statistics in 1991. See Valentina Bodrova, "The Socioeconomic Transition in Post-Soviet Russia: The Impact on Women," in *Encyclopedia of Russian Women's Movements,* ed. Norma C. Noonan and Carol Nechemias (Westport, Conn.: Greenwood Press, 2001), 331; Azhgikhina, "Zhenshchina kak ob"ekt i sub"ekt v sovremennoi rossiiskoi literature," 61.

50. See Helena Goscilo, "Perestroika and Post-Soviet Prose: From Dazzle to Dispersal," in *A History of Women's Writing in Russia,* ed. Adele Barker and Jehanne Gheith (Cambridge: Cambridge University Press, 2002), 311.

51. Jane Harris, "Diversity of Discourse: Autobiographical Statements in Theory and Praxis," in *Autobiographical Statements in Twentieth-Century Russian Literature,* ed. Jane Harris (Princeton, N.J.: Princeton University Press, 1990), 19; M. Kuznetsov, "Gorizont romana," in *Zhanrovo-stilevye iskaniia sovremennoi sovetskoi prozy,* ed. Lidiia Poliak and Vadim Kovskii (Moscow: Nauka, 1971), 15. For a discussion of how documenting history putatively intersects with Lenin's biography, see Iakov Iavchunovskii, *Dokumental'nye zhanry: obraz, zhanr, struktura proizvedeniia* (Saratov: Izdatel'stvo Saratovskogo universiteta, 1974), 5.

52. In discussing the literature of fact, formalist critic Iurii Tynianov distinguished the artistic quotidian (*khudozhestvennyi byt*) from true art (*iskusstvo*): *byt* controls the first term through the process of representation. See "O literaturnom fakte," *Arkhaisty i novatory* (Munich: Wilhelm Fink, 1967), 19. Content dictates its own depiction, damning such literature to a liminal status Bakhtin finds enlivening but Tynianov deems threatening. See Mikhail Bakhtin, "Discourse in the Novel," in *The Dialogic Imagination: Four Essays by M. M. Bakhtin,* ed. Michael Holquist, trans. Caryl Emerson and Michael Holquist (Austin: University of Texas Press, 1992), 270, 338.

53. Nina Dikushina, "Nevydumannaia proza (o sovremennoi dokumental'noi literature)," in *Zhanrovo-stilivye iskaniia sovremennoi sovetskoi prozy,* ed. Lidiia Poliak and Vadim Kovskii (Moscow: Nauka, 1971), 154. See also Kuznetsov, "Gorizont romana," 41.

54. Irzhi Gaek [Jiří Hajek], "Literatura fakta," *Voprosy literatury,* no. 12 (1965): 102.
55. Kuznetsov, "Gorizont romana," 15.
56. Dikushina, "Nevydumannaia proza (o sovremennoi dokumental'noi literature)," 156. See also Iavchunovskii, *Dokumental'nye zhanry,* 19.
57. Tzvetan Todorov, *The Poetics of Prose,* trans. Richard Howard (Ithaca, N.Y.: Cornell University Press, 1977), 82. This theoretical piece, while not addressing Russian literature per se, convincingly argues for basic commonalities of mimetic fiction.
58. Mikhail Bakhtin, "Forms of Time and of the Chronotope in the Novel," in *The Dialogic Imagination: Four Essays by M. M. Bakhtin,* ed. Michael Holquist, trans. Caryl Emerson and Michael Holquist (Austin: University of Texas Press, 1981), 253.
59. For a recent example, see Adele Barker, "The Persistence of Memory: Women's Prose Since the Sixties," in *A History of Women's Writing in Russia,* ed. Adele Barker and Jehanne Gheith (Cambridge: Cambridge University Press, 2002), 287.

Chapter 1. Documenting Women's *Byt* during the Thaw and Stagnation

1 The first epigraph is from I. Grekova, "Za prokhodnoi," *Na ispytaniiakh. Povesti i rasskazy* (Moscow: Sovetskii pisatel', 1990), 403, while the second is from an interview by A. Bocharov of Iurii Trifonov, "V kratkom—beskonechnoe," *Voprosy literatury,* no. 8 (1974): 194. On Baranskaia's life and the events precipitating her early retirement, see Natal'ia Baranskaia, "Avtobiografiia bez umolchanii," *Grani,* no. 156 (1990): 135–36.
2. Nadya Peterson provides a good overview of Grekova's biography. See "Irina Grekova (Elena Sergeevna Venttsel')," in *Dictionary of Literary Biography,* vol. 302, *Russian Prose Writers after World War II,* ed. Christine Rydel (Detroit, Mich.: Thomson Gale, 2004).
3. N. Klado, "Prokrustovo lozhe byta," *Literaturnaia gazeta,* no. 19 (1976): 4.
4. For representative Western articles using this approach, see Kay, "A Woman's Work"; and Sigrid McLaughlin, introduction to *The Image of Women in Contemporary Soviet Fiction: Selected Short Stories from the USSR,* ed. and trans. Sigrid McLaughlin (New York: St. Martin's Press, 1989).
5. Madison, "Social Services for Women: Problems and Priorities," 311–12; Gradskova, *"Obychnaia" sovetskaia zhenshchina,* 93; Mikhail

Matskovsky and Tatyana Gurko, "Scholars Favor Marriages in Which Couples Share Housework, Child Rearing. (As Opposed to Traditional Male-Dominated Marriage and the 'Individualistic' Type, in Which Careers Come First and Children Last)," *Current Digest of the Soviet Press* 37, no. 5 (1984): 6.

6. McLaughlin, introduction, 3; Strelianyi, *Zhenskie pis'ma*, 24.

7. Natal'ia Baranskaia, *Nedelia kak nedelia, Zhenshchina s zontikom* (Moscow: Sovremennik, 1981), 20, 9.

8. See Igor Kon, *The Sexual Revolution in Russia: From the Age of the Czars to Today* (New York: Free Press, 1995), 211. See also Boris Segal, *The Drunken Society: Alcohol Abuse and Alcoholism in the Soviet Union: A Comparative Study* (New York: Hippocrene Books, 1990), 200–201.

9. Liljeström, "The Soviet Gender System," 165; Sergei Chuprinin, "Ladies' Tango," *Current Digest of the Soviet Press* 37, no. 11 (1985): 12.

10. Unlike male homosexuality, lesbianism was never illegal in the USSR. This incongruity does not reflect more tolerance toward same-sex relations between women. Instead, it signals a different type of state intervention: lesbianism was deemed a medical disorder and patients were placed under psychiatric care in an effort to "cure" them. See Dan Healey, *Homosexual Desire in Revolutionary Russia: The Regulation of Sexual and Gender Dissent* (Chicago: University of Chicago Press, 2001), 256. As one gay activist whose lover was murdered in 1991 lamented, "Gay life had been easier in the Brezhnev years, when it was not recognized: parents would not see anything wrong in a son sleeping with his best friend, assuming this to be ordinary male friendship." Quoted in Banting, Kelly, and Riordan, "Sexuality," 346.

11. See Niusa Mil'man, *Chitaia Petrushevskuiu: Vzgliad iz-za okeana* (St. Petersburg: Rosprint, 1997), 38.

12. Morson, "Prosaics and *Anna Karenina*," 2.

13. Boris Groys, *The Total Art of Stalinism: Avant-Garde, Aesthetic Dictatorship, and Beyond*, trans. Charles Rougle (Princeton, N.J.: Princeton University Press, 1992), 10.

14. I. Grekova, "Bez ulybok," *Na ispytaniiakh* (Moscow: Sovetskii pisatel', 1990). Such carefully crafted "objectivity" favorably influenced a work's reception. In Baranskaia's case, critics praised the intersection of document and fiction in the image of Goncharova. Use of a marginal genre mollified those who otherwise might have objected to Baranskaia's humanization of Goncharova, who is traditionally blamed for the poet's early death. See O. Murav'eva, "Vstrecha s poetom," *Neva*, no. 5 (1984): 164; V. Nepomniashchii, "Izbrannitsa poeta," *Nedelia*, no. 10 (1978): 11.

15. Roland Barthes, *Writing Degree Zero*, trans. Annette Lavers and Colin Smith (New York: Hill and Wang, 1968), 5. See I. Grekova, "Ne govoria lishnikh slov," *Literaturnaia gazeta*, no. 3 (1983): 6.

16. Rita Felski, *Beyond Feminist Aesthetics: Feminist Literature and Social Change* (Cambridge, Mass.: Harvard University Press, 1989), 7. Felski reacts against post-Lacanian "écriture féminine" and its supposed esotericism, which she believes hinders literature's mission to "influence individual and cultural self-understanding in the sphere of everyday life" and catalyze social change. The choice between "realist" and nonrealist expression, however, is a matter of personal taste, ultimately having little bearing on how effective the narrative is.

17. Natal'ia Baranskaia, "Provody," in *Zhenshchina s zontikom* (Moscow: Sovremennik, 1981).

18. Elena Kashkarova, "Zhenskaia tema v proze 60-kh godov: Natal'ia Baranskaia kak zerkalo russkogo feminizma," *Vse liudi sestry*, no. 5 (1996): 62–63, 59. See Felski, *Beyond Feminist Aesthetics*, 7.

19. Baranskaia, "Provody," 114–15.

20. Baranskaia, *Nedelia kak nedelia*, 29. Thomas Lahusen—one of the few critics to address Baranskaia on a sophisticated level that moves beyond the purely sociological—argues that the honeymoon flashback is an example of "epic time." This portion of the narrative recalls the epic temporality of Georg Lukács rather than that of Bakhtin: prelapsarian interconnectedness that opposes the fragmented time and numerous tasks overwhelming Ol'ga in the present-tense time frame. "'Leaving Paradise' and Perestroika: 'A Week Like Any Other' and 'Memorial Day' by Natal'ia Baranskaia," in *Fruits of Her Plume: Essays on Contemporary Russian Women's Culture*, ed. Helena Goscilo (Armonk, N.Y.: M. E. Sharpe, 1993), 212. See Georg Lukács, *The Theory of the Novel*, trans. Anna Bostock (Cambridge, Mass.: MIT Press, 1993), 29–30.

21. Natal'ia Baranskaia, *Den' pominoveniia. Roman, povest'* (Moscow: Sovetskii pisatel', 1989).

22. The designation "Great Patriotic War" is crucial. Baranskaia, like almost all published Soviet authors, elides the Soviet cooperation with Nazi forces in Eastern Europe from 1939 to 1941.

23. See Žekulin, "Soviet Russian Women's Literature in the Early 1980s," 36.

24. Natal'ia Baranskaia, interview by Pieta Monks, in *Writing Lives: Conversations between Women Writers*, ed. Mary Chamberlain (London: Virago, 1988), 34; Natal'ia Baranskaia, "Natalja Baranskaja zu einigen Aspekten ihres Werkes. Ein Interview [by S. Gressler]," *Osteuropa*, no. 7 (1990): 588. Baranskaia's complete disavowal of feminism upholds the

late-Soviet idea that this group of theories is an alien Western concept synonymous with hating men. For a partisan assessment of one of the few pre-1985 feminist networks, see Tatyana Mamonova, "The Feminist Movement in the Soviet Union," in *Women and Russia: Feminist Writings from the Soviet Union,* ed. Tatyana Mamonova (Boston: Beacon Press, 1984). For an overview of Soviet fears and dismissals of feminism, see Goscilo, *Dehexing Sex,* 11.

25. I. Grekova, "Zamysel: Zarozhdenie i voploshchenie," *Literaturnaia Rossiia,* no. 28 (1982): 11. Grekova never made any comments related to either feminism or women's prose per se. However, from her viewpoint any explicitly ideological approach to gender seemed alien and insincere. N. Naumova, "The Modern Heroine," *Soviet Studies in Literature,* no. 15 (1979): 99; Helena Goscilo, "Introduction," in *Present Imperfect: Stories by Russian Women,* ed. Ayesha Kagal and Natal'ia Perova (Boulder, Colo.: Westview Press, 1996), 1.

26. Viktoriia Tokareva, interview by author, Moscow, January 9, 2003; Grekova, "Ne govoria lishnikh slov," 6.

27. Nina Denisova, "Inertsiia nashikh priviazannostei," *Literaturnoe obozrenie,* no. 1 (1978): 67.

28. Georg Lukács, *Realism in Our Time: Literature and the Class Struggle,* trans. George Steiner (New York: Harper & Row, 1964), 122; Vladimir Rozanov, "Proza s zapakhom," *Molodaia gvardiia,* no. 1 (1968): 295; Dikushina, "Nevydumannaia proza," 161; Adele Barker, "Irina Grekova's 'Na ipsytaniiakh': The History of One Story," *Slavic Review* 43, no. 3 (1989): 399. The author's pseudonym comes from the Russian term for the mathematical variable "Y"—*igrek.* "Bez ulybok" evokes the atmosphere surrounding Grekova leaving the military academy. The story was published in 1975, eight years after the scandal surrounding the authorship of *Na ispytaniiakh.*

29. Vladimir Poremantsev began the Thaw discussion of sincerity in literature with his essay "Ob iskrennosti v literature," *Novyi mir,* no. 12 (1953). Svetlana Boym, however, notes that sincerity as a specifically "Russian" value marked the self-image of the intellectual long before 1917. See *Common Places,* 96–97.

30. Nadezhda Azhgikhina, interview by author, Moscow, May 11, 2003; Baranskaia, interview by Pieta Monks, 31.

31. Yuri Slezkine, "The USSR as a Communal Apartment, or How a Socialist State Promoted Ethnic Particularism," *Slavic Review* 53, no. 2 (1994): 415. As Slezkine notes, this analogy (a concept that has long circulated among Soviet and post-Soviet citizens) comes from I. Vareikis and I. Zelenskii, *Natsional'no-gosudarstvennoe razmezhevanie Srednei Azii* (Tashkent: Sredne-Aziatskoe gosudarstvennoe izdatel'stvo, 1924), 59.

32. I. Vladimirova, "Ne tol'ko byt," *Neva*, no. 8 (1981): 181–82.

33. Viacheslav Savateev, "Bogatstvo dushi i iasnosti tseli. O nekoto-rykh chertakh geroia sovremennoi prozy," *Oktiabr'*, no. 10 (1982): 175.

34. Maiia Ganina, "Uslysh' svoi chas," in *Sozvezdie bliznetsov. Povesti, rasskazy* (Moscow: Sovetskii pisatel', 1984); Klado, "Prokrustovo lozhe byta," 4.

35. Vladimir Stepanov, "Lzheromantika obshchikh mest," *Molodaia gvardiia*, no. 11 (1973): 307. V. Lysenko, "Filosofiia anekdota?" *Literaturnoe obozrenie*, no. 8 (1980): 103.

36. Ia. El'sberg, "Byt i dukhovnaia zhizn'," *Literaturnaia gazeta*, no. 51 (1968): 4. Kashkarova alleges that this remark by El'sberg, whom she links to the repression of the poet Osip Mandel'shtam and other literary figures of the 1930s, shows that the state was especially worried by the story. See "Zhenskaia tema v proze 60-kh godov," 60.

37. O. Novikova and V. Novikov, "Chestnaia igra," *Literaturnoe obozrenie*, no. 11 (1979): 56; Tokareva, interview by author.

38. Iuliia Govorukhina, "Proza I. Grekovoi v kontekste literaturnogo protsessa 1960–80-kh godov" (Ph.D. diss., Komsomol'sk-na-Amure State Pedagogical University, 2000), 29.

39. Grekova, "Za prokhodnoi," 403; Blanchot, "Everyday Speech," 12.

40. Trifonov, "V kratkom—beskonechnoe," 194.

41. L. Zhukhovitskii, "Neudachlivost'? Net—chelovechnost'!" *Znamia*, no. 1 (1980): 246.

42. Bakhtin, "Forms of Time and of the Chronotope in the Novel," 84.

43. Lotman, *Besedy o russkoi kul'ture*, 10; Bakhtin, "Forms of Time and of the Chronotope in the Novel," 248.

44. Vasilii Grossman, *Life and Fate*, trans. Robert Chandler (New York: Harper & Row, 1986); I. Grekova, *Malen'kii Garusov, Kafedra. Povesti* (Moscow: Sovetskii pisatel', 1980); Heldt, "Gynoglasnost," 169.

45. I. Grekova, *Damskii master, Pod fonarem* (Moscow: Sovetskaia Rossiia, 1966), 83.

46. I. Grekova, "Zamysel: Zarozhdenie i voploshchenie," *Literaturnaia Rossiia*, no. 28 (1982): 11; Goscilo, "Coming a Long Way, Baby," 4.

47. Baranskaia, *Nedelia kak nedelia*, 54; Goscilo, "Coming a Long Way, Baby," 6.

48. Natal'ia Baranskaia, "Krai sveta," in *Zhenshchina s zontikom* (Moscow: Sovremennik, 1981), 144.

49. Viktoriia Tokareva, "Iaponskii zontik," in *Banketnyi zal* (Moscow: AST, 2001), 139.

50. Novikova and Novikov, "Chestnaia igra," 57; Karl Marx, *Capital: A Critique of Political Economy*, trans. Ben Fowkes, 3 vols. (New York: Vintage, 1977), 1:209.

51. I. Grekova, *The Ship of Widows*, trans. Cathy Porter (Evanston, Ill.: Northwestern University Press, 1994), 45–46.

52. Clark, *The Soviet Novel*, 15.

53. Govorukhina, "Proza I. Grekovoi v kontekste literaturnogo protsessa 1960–80-kh godov," 19, 135. In the novel *Porogi* (The Rapids, 1981), set in the cybernetics department of a scientific institute, dialogue is a structural principle: the narrative contains a point of view that shifts from one researcher to another. I. Grekova, *Vdovii parokhod, Porogi. Roman, Povesti* (Moscow: Sovetskii pisatel', 1986).

54. I. Grekova, *Vdovii parokhod*, 331–32; Il'ia Utekhin, *Ocherki kommunal'nogo byta* (Moscow: OGI, 2001), 110–11.

55. Grekova, *Vdovii parokhod*, 313.

56. I. Grekova, *Perelom, Na ispytaniiakh. Povesti i rasskazy* (Moscow: Sovetskii pisatel', 1990), 150. See Helena Goscilo, "Women's Wards and Wardens: The Hospital in Contemporary Russian Women's Fiction," in "Soviet Women," special issue, *Canadian Women's Studies/Les Cahiers de la femme* 10, no. 4 (1989): 83–84.

57. Grekova, *Perelom*, 168.

58. Govorukhina, "Proza I. Grekovoi v kontekste literaturnogo protsessa 1960–80-kh godov," 169.

59. I. Grekova, "Letom v gorode," in *Na ispytaniiakh. Povesti i rasskazy* (Moscow: Sovetskii pisatel', 1990), 486–87; Nancy Armstrong, "Some Call It Fiction: On the Politics of Domesticity," in *Feminisms: An Anthology of Literary Theory and Criticism*, ed. Robyn R. Warhol and Diane Price Herndi (New Brunswick, N.J.: Rutgers University Press, 1997), 920; Liudmila Ulitskaia, *Kazus Kukotskogo* (Moscow: Eksmo, 2002). On the differences between government control over men and women, see Gradskova, *"Obychnaia" sovetskaia zhenshchina*, 92. This overlooked study outlines the conditions under which men and women experienced state power over their bodies. For males this was during wartime (or imprisonment) while female citizens felt this control in everyday life.

60. Govorukhina, "Proza I. Grekovoi v kontekste literaturnogo protsessa 1960–80-kh godov," 79; I. Grekova, *Svezho predanie* (Moscow: Eksmo, 2002), 50, 156, 242–45.

61. Baranskaia, interview by Pieta Monks, 33.

62. Beth Holmgren, "Writing the Female Body Politic, 1945–1985," 226–27; Birgit Fuchs, *Natal'ja Baranskaja als Zeitzeugin des Sowjetregimes* (Munich: Otto Sagner, 2005), 20.

63. Petrushevskaia's perestroika prose will attack the intelligentsia and its idea of the workplace as a surrogate family. The resulting void robs her characters of the support network provided by stable families

and amiable colleagues. See Monika Katz, "The Other Woman: Character Portrayal and the Narrative Voice in the Short Stories of Liudmila Petrushevskaia," trans. Nina Draganić, in *Women and Russian Culture: Projections and Self-Perceptions*, ed. Rosalind Marsh (New York: Berghahn Books, 1998), 190.

64. Vladimir Men'shov, *Moskva slezam ne verit* (Mosfil'm, 1979); Grekova, *Damskii master*, 82.

65. Tat'iana Rovenskaia, "Vinovata li ia . . . ? Ili fenomen gendernoi viny (na materiale zhenskoi prozy 80-kh—nachalo 90-kh godov)," *Gendernye issledovaniia*, no. 3 (1999): 221. See also Beate Jonscher, "Zu Tendenzen der Frauenliteratur in den 60er und 70er Jahren," in *Frauenbilder und Weiblichkeitsentwürfe in der russischen Frauenprosa: Materialen wissenschaftlichen Symposiums in Erfurt*, ed. Christina Parnell (Frankfurt: Peter Lang, 1996), 163.

66. I. Grekova, "Pod fonarem," in *Na ispytaniiakh. Povesti i rasskazy* (Moscow: Sovetskii pisatel', 1990), 539. In a similar case of gendered estrangement, Mar'ia Vladimirovna in *Damskii master* feels uneasy while at the hair salon—a female realm where the only person she identifies with is Vitalik (68). Baranskaia, interview by Pieta Monks, 34–35.

67. Nicholas Žekulin, "Soviet Russian Women's Literature in the Early 1980s," 43; I. Grekova, *Kafedra, Novyi mir*, no. 9 (1978): 23.

68. Boym, *Common Places*, 101.

69. See N. N. Shneidman, *Soviet Literature in the 1970s: Artistic Diversity and Ideological Conformity* (Toronto: University of Toronto Press, 1979), 31; E. Iukina, "Ispytaniia," *Literaturnoe obozrenie*, no. 4 (1986): 50.

70. Baranskaia, *Nedelia kak nedelia*, 10.

71. Gary Saul Morson and Caryl Emerson, *Mikhail Bakhtin: Creation of a Prosaics* (Stanford, Calif.: Stanford University Press, 1990), 25. I. Grekova, *Porogi, Porogi. Roman. Povesti* (Moscow: Sovetskii pisatel', 1986), 55.

72. I. Grekova, *Fazan, Na ispytaniiakh. Povesti i rasskazy* (Moscow: Sovetskii pisatel', 1990), 77–78, 89; Grekova, *Kafedra*, 50.

73. Natal'ia Baranskaia, "Muzhchiny, beregite zhenshchin!" *Literaturnaia gazeta*, no. 46 (1971): 13; I. Grekova, "Zastavit' zadumat'sia," *Literaturnaia gazeta*, no. 9 (1986): 36.

74. On the components of private life and their relationship to public morality, see Deborah Field's excellent study "Communist Morality and the Meaning of Private Life in Post-Stalinist Russia, 1953–1964" (Ph.D. diss., University of Michigan, 1996), 2.

75. Drinking resembles the Bakhtinian concept of the carnival in another respect. The chronotope of drunkenness is a unique combination of time and space, marked by narrowed temporal perception as past

and future collapse into a present moment existing (apparently) without consequences. Alternate crowning and decrowning join with loss of consciousness in the literal and metaphorical sense. See Mikhail Bakhtin, *Problems of Dostoevsky's Poetics*, ed. and trans. Caryl Emerson (Minneapolis: University of Minnesota Press, 1984), 162. This chronotope, episodic in Petrushevskaia's short works, structures Venichka's doomed reflections in Erofeev's "poem" *Moskva-Petushki*. For an exhaustive (and exhausting) commentary on drinking and Soviet realia, see Venedikt Erofeev, *Moskva-Petushki s kommentariiami Eduarda Vlasova* (Moscow: Vagrius, 2000).

76. Andrei Zorin has surveyed Stagnation-era desiderata for literature and perestroika's withering response in "Kruche, kruche, kruche . . . Istoriia pobedy: chernukha v kul'ture poslednikh let," *Znamia*, no. 10 (1992): 199. Baranskaia's and Grekova's peripheral male characters may drink, but their reproachable behavior serves as a foil for more virtuous personages. In *Nedelia kak nedelia* Shura's hard-drinking husband highlights the positive aspects of Ol'ga's apathetic but sober Dima. Selection of character types, which emphasizes morality, reaffirms representation as a mediated process in these works (e.g., see Baranskaia, *Nedelia kak nedelia*, 10).

77. Field, "Communist Morality and the Meaning of Private Life in Post-Stalinist Russia," 92.

78. Grekova, *Damskii master*, 96; Natal'ia Baranskaia, "Vstrecha," *Grani*, no. 168 (1993): 38–41.

79. I. Grekova, *Khoziaika gostinitsy*, *Kafedra. Povesti* (Moscow: Sovetskii pisatel', 1981), 281. See Naumova, "The Modern Heroine," 96.

80. Baranskaia, interview by Pieta Monks, 34. See "How Much Housework Should a Man Do?"; Barbara Heldt, *Terrible Perfection: Women and Russian Literature* (Bloomington: Indiana University Press, 1987), 12–13.

81. Grekova, *Kafedra*, 35–36; Baranskaia, *Nedelia kak nedelia*, 15.

82. Gradskova, *"Obychnaia" sovetskaia zhenshchina*, 92; Baranskaia, *Nedelia kak nedelia*, 41, 21, 49.

83. Baranskaia, "Fotografiia Zoiki na fone dvora," *Grani*, no. 168 (1993): 108.

84. Grekova, *The Ship of Widows*, 53; Grekova, *Vdovii parokhod*, 369; Helena Goscilo, foreword to *The Ship of Widows*, trans. Cathy Porter (Evanston, Ill.: Northwestern University Press, 1994), xxiv–xxv.

85. Elena Goshchilo [Helena Goscilo], "Vdovstvo kak zhanr i professiia à la Russe," *Preobrazhenie*, no. 3 (1995): 28; Holmgren, "Writing the Female Body Politic (1945–1985)," 228.

86. Goscilo, "Vdovstvo kak zhanr i professiia à la Russe," 30; "O povesti N. Baranskoi 'Tsvet temnogo medu,'" *Sibir'*, no. 2 (1979): 99; Natal'ia Baranskaia, *Tsvet temnogo medu, Portret, podarennyi drugu. Ocherki i rasskazy o Pushkine. Povest'* (Leningrad: Lenizdat, 1982), 216, 222.

87. Transporting Goncharova from one polarized image of femininity to another recalls the whore/madonna complex in Russian culture: much like the everyday she inhabits, a woman cannot be neutral in value. Whether sinner or saint, it is her (im)proper adherence to gender roles that determines character. See David Gillespie's survey of Baranskaia's and Grekova's characters in his "Whore or Madonna: Perceptions of Women in Modern Russian Literature," *Soviet Literature*, no. 2 (1990): 143–57. This article originally appeared in *Irish Slavonic Studies*, no. 9 (1988).

Chapter 2. Perestroika and the Emergence of Women's Prose

1. The epigraphs are by critic Marina Abasheva and author Tat'iana Tolstaia, respectively. Marina Abasheva, "Chisten'kaia zhizn' ne pomniashchaia zla," *Literaturnoe obozrenie*, nos. 5–6 (1992): 11; Tat'iana Tolstaia, "Nepal'tsy i miumziki: Interv'iu zhurnalu 'Afisha,'" in *Kys'* (Moscow: Eksmo, 2005), 328. On the meeting between Vasilenko and Vaneeva, see Svetlana Vasilenko, "'Novye amazonki'. Ob istorii pervoi literaturnoi zhenskoi pisatel'skoi gruppy. Postsovetskoe vremia," in *Zhenshchina: Svoboda slova i svoboda tvorchestva. Sbornik statei*, ed. Valentina Kizilo, comp. Svetlana Vasilenko (Moscow: Eslan, 2001), 81–82.

2. Helena Goscilo provides a good assessment of the trends that remade Soviet literature and society. See her introduction to *Glasnost: An Anthology of Russian Literature under Gorbachev*, ed. Helena Goscilo and Byron Lindsey (Ann Arbor, Mich.: Ardis, 1990), xxxi.

3. Mikhail Zolotonosov, "'Kakotopiia': Zhanr antiutopii v sovremennoi literature," *Oktiabr'*, no. 7 (1990): 192. Zolotonosov appropriated this term from the dystopian author (and Slavist) Anthony Burgess, who in turn borrowed it from Jeremy Bentham. See also Groys, *The Total Art of Stalinism*, 51.

4. Goscilo, "Coming a Long Way, Baby," 12; "Priniaty v Soiuz pisatelei," *Literaturnaia Rossiia*, no. 22 (1977): 11; Zorin, "Kruche, kruche, kruche," 200.

5. See Helena Goscilo, "Speaking Bodies: Erotic Zones Rhetoricized," in *Fruits of Her Plume: Essays on Contemporary Russian Women's Culture*, ed. Helena Goscilo (Armonk, N.Y.: M. E. Sharpe, 1993), 141. In

his discussion of *chernukha*, Mark Lipovetskii argues that Viktor Astaf'ev's *Pechal'nyi detektiv* (A Sad Detective Story, 1986) exemplifies this tendency by focusing on alcoholism and hopelessness. In a broader sense *chernukha* rejects the intelligentsia's axiom that mind triumphs over matter and that literature enriches the soul. Mark Lipovetsky, "Strategies of Wastefulness, or the Metamorphoses of *Chernukha*," *Russian Studies in Literature* 38, no. 2 (2002): 61.

6. In *Vremia noch'* naive Alena loses her virginity to classmate Sasha in a chance encounter that leaves her pregnant and echoes her mother's fate. The story "Detskii prazdnik" (A Children's Vacation) describes how a sixteen-year-old on vacation is raped and impregnated, while teenage Tan'ka in "Otets i mat'" (Father and Mother) has a miscarriage after allegedly having had sex with her father. Liudmila Petrushevskaia, *Vremia noch', Dom devushek. Povesti i rasskazy* (Moscow: Vagrius, 1998), 362–63, 386–87; Liudmila Petrushevskaia, "Detskii prazdnik," in *Naidi menia, son. Rasskazy* (Moscow: Vagrius, 2000), 129, 131; Liudmila Petrushevskaia, "Otets i mat'," in *Naidi menia, son*, 256.

7. Alka's fate unmasks the nefarious values of the same political system that produced her politically privileged corrupters. This implication undermines the intelligentsia's axiom that private life opposed the cynical opportunism of the late-Soviet public sphere. Petrushevskaia conclusively shattered this assumption as well as the sacrosanct image of the intelligentsia itself. See Gasiorowska, "Working Mothers in Recent Soviet Fiction," 61.

8. P. Spivak, "V sne i naiavu . . . ," *Oktiabr'*, no. 2 (1988): 202.

9. Tatyana Tolstaya, "The Poet and the Muse," in *Sleepwalker in a Fog*, trans. Jamey Gambrell (New York: Alfred A. Knopf, 1992), 117. See Helena Goscilo, *The Explosive World of Tatyana N. Tolstaya's Fiction* (Armonk, N.Y.: M. E. Sharpe, 1996), 88.

10. Tat'iana Tolstaia, "Poet i muza," in *Reka Okkervil'. Sbornik rasskazov* (Moscow: Podkova, 2004), 250; Alexandra Smith, "Carnivalising the Canon: The Grotesque and the Subversive in Contemporary Russian Women's Prose (Petrushevskaia, Sadur, Tolstaia, Narbikova)," in *Russian Literature in Transition*, ed. Ian Lilly and Henriette Mondry (Nottingham, Engl.: Astra, 1999), 44. The ending signals Nina's astounding lack of guilt over her husband's death, an absence not masked by the thin veneer of her "cultured" interest in interior design.

11. Liudmila Petrushevskaia, *Vremia noch'*, 368; "Batsilla," in *Dom devushek* (Moscow: Vagrius, 1998), 180; "Gripp," in *Dom devushek*, 214. See Sally Dalton-Brown, *Voices from the Void: The Genres of Liudmila Petrushevskaia* (New York: Berghahn Books, 2001), vii.

12. See Goscilo, "Coming a Long Way, Baby," 12. The heroine's

attempted hanging in the story "Dama s sobakami" (The Lady with the Dogs) revises the fate of Anton Chekhov's Anna Sergeevna, while the spendthrift son Vovik in "Chudo" (A Miracle) survives only thanks to the questionable beneficence of maternal love. Liudmila Petrushevskaia, "Dama s sobakami," in *Dom devushek* (Moscow: Vagrius, 1998), 201; Liudmila Petrushevskaia, "Chudo," in *Gde ia byla. Rasskazy iz inoi real'nosti* (Moscow: Vagrius, 2002), 172.

13. Natal'ia Ivanova, "Bakhtin's Concept of the Grotesque and the Art of Petrushevskaia and Tolstaia," trans. Helena Goscilo, in *Fruits of Her Plume: Essays on Contemporary Russian Women's Culture*, ed. Helena Goscilo (Armonk, N.Y.: M. E. Sharpe, 1993), 23–24. Occasionally altruism motivates such dramatic actions. The anonymous narrator in *Svoi krug* exploits the poetics of public display when beating her son, Alesha, in front of her friends, correctly assuming that they will take the boy away and thus care for him (however ineptly) following her impending death. Liudmila Petrushevskaia, *Svoi krug*, *Dom devushek* (Moscow: Vagrius, 1998), 347–48.

14. Liudmila Petrushevskaia, *Nomer Odin, ili V sadakh drugikh vozmozhnostei. Roman* (Moscow: Eksmo, 2006), 61. See Elena Goshchilo [Helena Goscilo], "Khudozhestvennaia optika Petrushevskoi: Ni odnogo 'lucha sveta v temnom tsarstve'," in *Russkaia literatura XX veka: napravleniia i techeniia*, ed. N. L. Leiderman, N. V. Barkovskaia, and M. N. Lipovetskii (Ekaterinburg: Ural'skii gosudarstvennyi pedagogicheskii universitet, 1996), 3:110–11.

15. Tat'iana Tolstaia, "Sonia," in *Reka Okkervil'* (Moscow: Podkova, 2004), 14. See Svetlana Boym, "The Poetics of Banality: Tat'iana Tolstaia, Larisa Gogoberidze, and Larisa Zvezdochetova," in *Fruits of Her Plume: Essays on Contemporary Russian Women's Culture*, ed. Helena Goscilo (Armonk, N.Y.: M. E. Sharpe, 1993), 71.

16. Tatyana Tolstaya, "The Circle," in *On the Golden Porch*, trans. Antonina Bouis (New York: Alfred A. Knopf, 1989), 65; emphasis in original.

17. Tolstaia offers a short material history of the modern woman in "Lilit" (Lilith), which traces changes in self-perception along with hat styles. The story is part of the collection *Reka Okkervil'* (Moscow: Podkova, 2004), 289. The author's complicated relationship with objects is one commonality uniting her fiction and essays, an often contradictory pair that has frustrated critics searching for unitary meaning. See Goscilo, *The Explosive World of Tatyana N. Tolstaya's Fiction*, 96.

18. I. Grekova, "Rastochitel'nost' talanta," *Novyi mir*, no. 1 (1988): 254. See also Goscilo, *The Explosive World of Tatyana N. Tolstaya's Fiction*, 143.

19. Liudmila Petrushevskaia, "Kredo," in *Izmenennoe vremia. Rasskazy i p'esy* (Moscow: Eksmo, 2005), 27–28.

20. Karla Hielscher, "Sozialpathologie oder Russische Alltags-mythen: Zur Prosa der Ljudmila Petruschewskaja," *Neue Gesellschaft*, Frankfurter Hefte 42, no. 4 (1995): 349–50. See also Goscilo, "Coming a Long Way, Baby," 13. Nobel laureate Toni Morrison also depicts victims of incest, rape, abject poverty, and maternal rage. Dana Heller makes an intriguing if problematic connection between Morrison's and Petru-shevskaia's dysfunctional families in her article "Engendering History: A Cross-Cultural Reading of Ludmila Petrushevskaya and Toni Morri-son," in *Fenomen pola v kul'ture/Sex and Gender in Culture. Materialy mezhdunarodnoi nauchnoi konferentsii. Moskva 15–17 ianvaria 1998 g.*, ed. G. A. Tkachenko (Moscow: Rossiiskii gosudarstvennyi gumanitarnyi universitet, 1998), 162–63.

21. Tat'iana Tolstaia, "Krug," in *Reka Okkervil'* (Moscow: Podkova, 2004), 62.

22. Tat'iana Tolstaia, "Okhota na mamonta," in *Reka Okkervil'* (Mos-cow: Podkova, 2004), 185. For an early and perceptive discussion of how Tolstaia uses folklore, see S. Piskunova and V. Piskunov, "Uroki zazerkal'ia," *Oktiabr'*, no. 8 (1988): 196.

23. Liudmila Petrushevskaia, "Lektsiia o zhanrakh. Prochitana 25.05.1998 g. (s pozdneishimi vstavkami)," in *Deviatyi tom* (Moscow: Eksmo, 2003), 322.

24. Liudmila Petrushevskaia, "Interview with Lyudmila Petru-shevskaya," in *Voices of Russian Literature: Interviews with Ten Contempo-rary Russian Writers*, ed. Sally Laird (Oxford: Oxford University Press, 1999), 41. See also Mil'man, *Chitaia Petrushevskuiu*, 51. Using darkly humorous depictions of *byt* as social and even spiritual commentary recalls the nineteenth-century author and playwright Nikolai Gogol. Petrushevskaia herself notes a childhood obsession with *Portret* (The Portrait, 1835), a Gogol novella emphasizing the dangers of representa-tion and the power of the gaze. See "Desiat' let spustia," in *Deviatyi tom* (Moscow: Eksmo), 312.

25. Liudmila Petrushevskaia, "Ioko Ono," in *Dom devushek* (Mos-cow: Vagrius, 1998), 145; Liudmila Petrushevskaia, "Teshcha Edipa," *Novyi mir*, no. 3 (1995): 18–21; Mark Lipovetskii, "Tragediia i malo li chto eshche," *Novyi mir*, no. 10 (1994): 232. In a slightly different vein, the story "Zhizn' eto teatr" (Life Is Theatre) details director Sasha's problems with lovers and apartments, with the third-person narrator voicing the dramatist's idea that her life is a play not fit for the stage. This narratorial comment is a Petrushevskaian ruse, masking the com-pulsion to watch and display others' shortcomings. The story appears in *Dom devushek* (Moscow: Vagrius, 1998), 150.

26. Liudmila Petrushevskaia, "Novye Gamlety," in *Naidi menia, son*.

Rasskazy (Moscow: Vagrius, 2000), 144. See also Ivanova, "Bakhtin's Concept of the Grotesque and the Art of Petrushevskaia and Tolstaia," 28, 32n.The *kommunalka* also influences time: in the story "Mest'" (Revenge), Raia's retribution against jealous neighbor Zina shapes temporality and narrative. While Hielscher reads this work as a Shakespearean story of guilt and innocence, she forgets the bard's ominous intersection of space and time in the doomed quotidian of Hamlet and others. The story appears in *Gde ia byla. Rasskazy iz inoi real'nosti* (Moscow: Vagrius, 2002), 213–14. See Hielscher, "Sozialpathologie oder Russische Alltagsmythen," 352.

27. Petrushevskaia, "Desiat' let spustia," 309.

28. Petrushevskaia, "Interview with Lyudmila Petrushevskaya," 35. Petrushevskaia mentions the term "positive hero" in a 1988 Bulgarian-language interview; see "Pisha za onova, koego obicham," interview by Rada Balareva, *Literaturen front*, no. 38 (1988): 7. See also Sigrid McLaughlin, "Lyudmila Petrushevskaya: Nets and Traps (1974)," in *The Image of Women in Contemporary Soviet Fiction: Selected Short Stories from the USSR*, ed. and trans. Sigrid McLaughlin (New York: St. Martin's Press, 1989), 98; quoted in Dalton-Brown, *Voices from the Void*, 176.

29. Mariia Remizova, "Teoriia katastrof, ili neskol'ko slov v zashchitu noch'," *Literaturnaia gazeta*, no. 11 (1996): 4.

30. Adlam, *Women in Russian Literature After Glasnost*, 75.

31. See Lyudmila Parts, "Down the Intertextual Lane: Petrushevskaia, Chekhov, Tolstoy," *Russian Review* 64, no. 1 (2005): 85.

32. A. Nitochkina, "Tat'iana Tolstaia: V bol'sheviki by ne poshla . . . ," *Stolitsa*, no. 33 (1991): 12; quoted in Nina Efimova, "Motiv igri v proizvedeniiakh L. Petrushevskoi i T. Tolstoi," *Vestnik Moskovskogo universiteta* seriia 9, *Filologiia*, no. 3 (1998): 61.

33. Language as the hero in Tolstaia's narrative has become a critical commonplace, albeit one that is accurate. See Goscilo, *The Explosive World of Tatyana N. Tolstaya's Fiction*, 28. Grekova, "Rastochitel'nost' talanta," 256, 252.

34. Liui Tsziiun, "Poetiko-filosofskoe svoebrazie rasskazov Tat'iany Tolstoi (na materiale sbornika Noch')" (Ph.D. diss., Tambov State Technical University, 2005), 3. See also Karen Smith, "Recollecting Wondrous Moments: Father Pushkin, Mother Russia, and Intertextual Memory in Tatyana Tolstaya's 'Night' and 'Limpopo,'" *Studies in Twentieth and Twenty-First Century Literature* 28, no. 2 (2004): 479.

35. Mikhail Zolotonosov, "Mechty i fantomy," *Literaturnoe obozrenie*, no. 4 (1987): 59; Tat'iana Tolstaia, "Ten' na zakate: Beseda za rabochim stolom," interview by S. Taroshchina, *Literaturnaia gazeta*, no. 30 (1986): 7.

36. Tat'iana Tolstaia, "Ogon' i pyl'," in *Chisten'kaia zhizn'*, comp. Anatolii Shavkuta (Moscow: Molodaia gvardiia, 1990), 267, 263, 268.

37. See Goscilo, *The Explosive World of Tatyana N. Tolstaya's Fiction*, 120. The rambling story "Limpopo" creates an analogous narrative. The protagonists suffer through a provincial Party enthusiast's hair-raising account of his descent into hell (e.g., a trip to Italy, an impossible dream for all but the elect). Walking along sidewalks slippery with the tubercular sputum of exploited workers, the loyal Soviet pities the poor Italians and eyes the Vatican's guards, who consider "a step to the left or right" an attempt on the pope's life and shoot without warning. This last detail resembles life in the labor camps, hinting that this phantasmagoric (and totally fictitious) Italy is a darkly humorous reworking of the story's main locale, the USSR during Stagnation. Tat'iana Tolstaia, "Limpopo," in *Reka Okkervil'. Sbornik rasskazov* (Moscow: Podkova, 2004), 346–47.

38. Liudmila Petrushevskaia, "Nagaina," in *Izmenennoe vremia. Rasskazy i p'esy* (Moscow: Eksmo, 2005), 115, 123–24.

39. Sergei Zalygin, "Trifonov, Shukshin i my," *Novyi mir*, no. 11 (1991): 226. Petrushevskaia, *Svoi krug*, 329–30; Liudmila Petrushevskaia, "Ali-Baba," in *Dom devushek* (Moscow: Vagrius, 1998), 66.

40. Tolstaia, "Poet i muza," 245.

41. Boym, "The Poetics of Banality," 60.

42. Baranskaia, interview by Pieta Monks, 30; Holmgren, "Writing the Female Body Politic, 1945–1985," 239–40.

43. Elena Tarasova, "Ne pomniashchaia zla," in *Ne pomniashchaia zla*, ed. N. A. Ryl'nikova, comp. Larisa Vaneeva (Moscow: Moskovskii rabochii, 1990), 195. For an original reading of this story, see Elizabeth Skomp, "Russian Women's Publishing at the Beginning of the 1990s: The Case of the New Amazons," in "Russian Women and Publishing," special issue, *Soviet and Post-Soviet Review* 1 (2006): 87.

44. Goscilo, "Coming a Long Way, Baby," 13. See also Elena Gessen, "Pobeg iz sotsrealizma, ili drugaia proza," *Strana i mir*, nos. 11–12 (1989): 177.

45. Natal'ia Doroshko, "Dvadtsat' piatoe fevralia," in *Abstinentki*, ed. Ol'ga Sokolova (Moscow: Seriia andergraund, Gumanitarnyi fond im. A. S. Pushkina, 1991); Grekova, *Svezho predanie*, 130.

46. Tolstaia, "Nepal'tsy i miumziki: Interv'iu zhurnalu 'Afisha,'" 328; Grekova, "Rastochitel'nost' talanta," 254.

47. Tat'iana Tolstaia, "Samaia liubimaia," in *Reka Okkervil'. Sbornik rasskazov* (Moscow: Podkova, 2004), 144; Tat'iana Tolstaia, "Belye steny," in *Den'. Lichnoe* (Moscow: Eksmo, 2004), 19–20.

48. Elena Gessen, "Esse o zhenskoi proze," *Vremia i my*, no. 114 (1991): 208. For two instances of critics conflating Petrushevskaia and her characters, see Leonid Kostiukov, "Iskliuchitel'naia mera," *Literaturnaia gazeta*, no. 11 (1996): 4; and Evgenii Ovenasian, "Tvortsy raspada (tupiki i anomalii 'drugoi prozy')," *Molodaia gvardiia*, no. 3 (1992): 249.

49. See Evgenii Bulin, "Otkroite knigi molodykh!" *Molodaia gvardiia*, no. 3 (1989): 240; Andrei Vasilevskii, "Nochi kholodny," *Druzhba narodov*, no. 7 (1988): 256.

50. Liudmila Petrushevskaia, "Pchelka," in *Naidi menia, son. Rasskazy* (Moscow: Vagrius, 2000), 143–44; Viktoriia Tokareva, *Piat' figur na postamente, Vse normal'no, vse khorosho* (Moscow: AST, 2002), 439; Petrushevskaia, *Nomer Odin, ili V sadakh drugikh vozmozhnostei*, 333.

51. Lina Tarkhova cites these letters in her article "Kto vernet silu sil'nomu polu?" *Sputnik*, no. 3 (1987): 123–24.

52. Petrushevskaia, *Vremia noch'*, 410; Liudmila Petrushevskaia, "Medeia," in *Dom devushek* (Moscow: Vagrius, 1998), 224. For other variants of this story, see Anja Grothe, "Medusa, Cassandra, Medea: Reinscribing Myth in Contemporary German and Russian Women's Writing" (Ph.D. diss., City University of New York, 2000), 234–35n.Tat'iana Tolstaia, "Svidanie s ptitsei," in *Reka Okkervil'. Sbornik rasskazov* (Moscow: Podkova, 2004), 76.

53. Mar'a-Leena Raunio, "Kak ia ne stala pisatel'nitsei," in *Mariia. Literaturnyi al'manakh*, comp. Galina Skvortsova (Petrozavodsk: Kareliia, 1990), 1:272.

54. Tarkhova, "Kto vernet silu sil'nomu polu?" 124–25. See also Vera Dunham, "The Strong Woman Motif," in *The Transformation of Russian Society*, ed. Cyril Black (Cambridge, Mass.: Harvard University Press, 1960), 479. Gorbachev, *Perestroika*, 117.

55. Nina Sadur, "Worm-Eaten Sonny," trans. Wendi Fornoff, in *Lives in Transit: A Collection of Recent Russian Women's Writing*, ed. Helena Goscilo (Dana Point, Calif.: Ardis, 1995), 203–4; italics in original.

56. Elena Tarasova, "Ty khorosho nauchilsia est', Adam," in *Ne pomniashchaia zla*, ed. N. A. Ryl'nikova, comp. Larisa Vaneeva (Moscow: Moskovskii rabochii, 1990).

57. Goscilo, *The Explosive World of Tatyana N. Tolstaya's Fiction*, 82; Oleg Dark, "Zhenskie antinomii," *Druzhba narodov*, no. 4 (1991): 261; Abasheva, "Chisten'kaia zhizn' ne pomniashchaia zla," 11.

58. I. Grekova, *Damskii master, Pod fonarem* (Moscow: Sovetskaia Rossiia, 1966), 79; Petrushevskaia, *Vremia noch'*, 436.

59. Gessen, "Pobeg iz sotsrealizma, ili drugaia proza," 176–77; I. Vladimirova, "Svoi golos," *Neva*, no. 3 (1977): 162.

60. Petrushevskaia, *Vremia noch'*, 408–9.

61. Petrushevskaia, *Vremia noch'*, 445–47. Reliance on orality privileges a present tense that, in turn, intensifies feeling. In this respect the stream-of-consciousness conclusion heightens the crisis surrounding Anna Andrianovna as the reader drowns in her maelstrom of anxiety. See Karla Hielscher, "Gerede—Gerüchte—Klatsch: Mündlichkeit als Form weiblichen Schreibens bei Ljudmila Petruševskaja," in *Frauenbilder und Weiblichkeitsentwürfe in der russischen Frauenprosa: Materialen des wissenschaftlichen Symposiums in Erfurt*, ed. Christina Parnell (Frankfurt: Peter Lang, 1996), 185; E. Nevzgliadova, "Siuzhet dlia nebol'shego rasskaza," *Novyi mir*, no. 4 (1988): 259.

62. Tat'iana Meleshko, *Sovremennaia otechestvennaia zhenskaia proza: Problemy poetiki v gendernom aspekte. Uchebnoe posobie po spetskursu* (Kemerovo: Kemerovskii gosudarstvennyi universitet, 2001), 84–85. The *durochka* exists outside accepted social conventions yet is endowed with a divine right to critique them, while the *urodina* is a physically deformed person who may or may not possess a special spiritual status. See Vladimir Dal', *Tol'kovyi slovar' zhivogo velikorusskogo iazyka*, 4 vols. (Moscow: Russkii iazyk, 1989), 1:501, 4:508.

63. Yelena Tarasova, "She Who Bears No Ill," in *Half a Revolution: Contemporary Fiction by Russian Women*, ed. and trans. Masha Gessen (Pittsburgh, Pa.: Cleis, 1995), 99.

64. Tarasova, *Ne pomniashchaia zla*, 190. Petrushevskaia's mannish alcoholic Nad'ka in the story of the same name seems almost spiritual compared to Tarasova's character. When the hairdressers Svetochka and Natashka go to find her after a long absence, a relative tells them that Nad'ka waited for their visit to die. Here, too, there is no redeeming conclusion. Only the prick of their temporarily awakened consciences will remind the two of Nad'ka's suffering. Liudmila Petrushevskaia, "Nad'ka," in *Naidi menia, son. Rasskazy* (Moscow: Vagrius, 2000), 32.

65. Polina Slutskina, "Studen'," in *Abstinentki*, ed. Ol'ga Sokolova (Moscow: Seriia andergraund, Gumanitarnyi fond im. A. S. Pushkina, 1991), 84–85; Tolstaia, "Poet i muza," 249–50.

66. Liudmila Petrushevskaia, "Gimn sem'e," in *Dom devushek* (Moscow: Vagrius, 1998), 105–6; Liudmila Petrushevskaia, "Vasen'ki," *Novyi mir*, no. 3 (1995).

67. *Vremia noch'* is the best example of doomed repetition in the families Petrushevskaia portrays. The hypocritically self-righteous Anna Andrianovna gave birth to Alena after having sex with a man she never saw again, later losing her job because of an affair with a married supervisor. Alena has already repeated these missteps, and Tima and the

other grandchildren will probably have similar fates. Petrushevskaia, *Vremia noch'*, 387.

68. Josephine Woll, "The Minotaur in the Maze: On Lyudmila Petrushevskaya," *World Literature Today* 67, no. 1 (1993): 129; Petrushevskaia, *Svoi krug*, 328.

69. Valentina Solov'eva, "U vsekh deti kak deti," in *Chisten'kaia zhizn'*, comp. Anatolii Shavkuta (Moscow: Molodaia gvardiia, 1990), 223. See also Dalton-Brown, *Voices from the Void*, 185. Liudmila's thought reflects the quiet moments of domestic epiphany that are part of Bakhtin's prosaic ethics. These reassuring visions of everyday life, upheld as models for family happiness in Tolstoy's *Anna Karenina* and *Voina i mir*, are exceptions in perestroika women's prose. In general, authors depict the Dostoevskian rather than the Tolstoyan model of the family, i.e., not the linear progression of generations in *Voina i mir* but the degenerative repetition of *Besy* (The Possessed, 1872).

70. Tolstaia, "Svidanie s ptitsei," 76; Tat'iana Tolstaia, "Liubish'—ne liubish'," in *Reka Okkervil'. Sbornik rasskazov* (Moscow: Podkova, 2004), 17–18.

71. Tat'iana Tolstaia, "Perevodnye kartinki," in *Kys'* (Moscow: Eksmo, 2005), 345.

72. Tatyana Tolstaya, "On the Golden Porch," in *On the Golden Porch*, trans. Antonina Bouis (New York: Alfred A. Knopf, 1989), 41.

73. Petrushevskaia has also written a number of works focusing on the dacha. In her early and perestroika prose, the stories "Cherez polia" (Across the Fields), "Diadia Grisha" (Uncle Grisha), and "Milaia dama" (A Dear Lady) use rural locales as a continuation of problems bred in the overcrowded city, now exacerbated by often hostile local neighbors. Liudmila Petrushevskaia, *Naidi menia, son. Rasskazy* (Moscow: Vagrius, 1998). Later Petrushevskaia stories such as "Boginia Parka" (The Goddess Parka) envision the dacha as a backdrop for mystical events revealing the meaning of life. Liudmila Petrushevskaia, *Boginia Parka. Povesti i rasskazy* (Moscow: Eksmo, 2006).

74. See Leona Toker, *Return from the Archipelago: Narratives of Gulag Survivors* (Bloomington: Indiana University Press, 2000), 48–49. This magisterial study of camp prose includes the significant contributions of women authors.

75. Helena Goscilo, *Dehexing Sex: Russian Womanhood During and After Glasnost* (Ann Arbor: University of Michigan Press, 1996), 119–20; Aleksandr Solzhenitsyn, *The First Circle*, trans. Thomas P. Whitney (New York: Harper & Row, 1968); Liudmila Petrushevskaia, *Malen'kaia Groznaia, Dom devushek* (Moscow: Vagrius, 1998).

76. Tat'iana Tolstaia, "Spi spokoino, synok," in *Reka Okkervil'. Sbornik rasskazov* (Moscow: Podkova, 2004), 91, 96–97.

77. Nina Gorlanova, "Istoriia ozera Veselogo," in *Ne pomniashchaia zla*, ed. N. A. Ryl'nikova, comp. Larisa Vaneeva (Moscow: Moskovskii rabochii, 1990), 52, 56.

78. Marina Palei, "The Bloody Women's Ward," in *Women's View*, ed. Natasha Perova and Andrew Bromfield (Moscow: Glas, 1992), 74–91; Rovenskaia, "Vinovata li ia . . . ?" 217.

79. Svetlana Vasilenko, "Suslik," in *Zhenskaia logika*, ed. L. V. Stepanenko and A. V. Fomenko (Moscow: Sovremennik, 1989), 100–101; Svetlana Vasilenko, *Shamara*, trans. Daria Kirjanov and Benjamin Sutcliffe, in *"Shamara" and Other Stories*, ed. Helena Goscilo (Evanston, Ill.: Northwestern University Press, 1999), 3; Svetlana Vasilenko, *Shamara*, in *Ne pomniashchaia zla*, ed. N. A. Ryl'nikova, comp. Larisa Vaneeva (Moscow: Moskovskii rabochii, 1990), 100–101.

80. This scene foreshadows Ustin's account of how he and seven others raped his future wife in the snow, for which he was imprisoned by Maks, who is driving one of the vehicles on the riverbank. Maks handcuffs Shamara and later has sex with her in exchange for his agreeing to Ustin's release, thus reifying Iuliia Gradskova's idea of the female body controlled by the state in *byt*. Here, however, the narrative shows that women participate in their own victimization; Shamara sleeps with Maks for Ustin's sake. Vasilenko, *Shamara*, in *Ne pomniashchaia zla*, 89, 112–14.

81. Vasilenko, "'Novye amazonki," 89.

82. Marina Karpova, "Lovlia maiskikh zhukov," in *Chisten'kaia zhizn'*, comp. Anatolii Shavkuta (Moscow: Molodaia gvardiia, 1990), 68, 72, 78, 79.

83. This discussion of Glinka and Khava Volovich is adapted from my article "Documenting Women's Voices in Perestroika Gulag Narratives," *Toronto Slavic Quarterly*, winter 2002–3, http://www.utoronto.ca/tsq/03/sutcliffe.shtml.

84. Elena Trofimova, "Elena Glinka," trans. Jill Roese, in *Dictionary of Russian Women Writers*, ed. Marina Ledkovsky, Charlotte Rosenthal, and Mary Zirin (Westport, Conn.: Greenwood Press, 1994), 215; Elena Glinka, "'Kolymskii tramvai' srednei tiazhesti," *Neva*, no. 10 (1989): 112–13. See also Elena Glinka, "The Hold," trans. Natalie Rey, in *Strange Soviet Practices* (Moscow: Glas, 2004), 111–32.

85. Khava Volovich, "O proshlom," in *Dodnes' tiagoteet*, vol. 1, *Zapiski vashei sovremennitsy*, ed. Semen Vilenskii (Moscow: Sovetskii pisatel', 1989), 477.

86. Liudmila Petrushevskaia, "Peregrev," in *Boginia Parka. Povesti i*

rasskazy (Moscow: Eksmo, 2006), 62–63. Although this story was published after 1991, it contains the gender roles, generational conflict, and voyeurism that run throughout the author's oeuvre.

87. Petrushevskaia, *Vremia noch'*, 370; Liudmila Petrushevskaia, "Shato," in *Naidi menia, son. Rasskazy* (Moscow: Vagrius, 2000), 94. Such attitudes are not unique to Petrushevskaia. The editors of *Abstinentki* planned to publish anthologies of gay and feminist prose, but the typesetters refused to help produce them. Nadezhda Azhgikhina, interview by author, Moscow, May 11, 2003.

88. Liudmila Petrushevskaia, "Muzyka ada," in *Dom devushek* (Moscow: Vagrius, 1998), 85; Liudmila Petrushevskaia, "Muzhestvennost' i zhenstvennost'," in *Dom devushek* (Moscow: Vagrius, 1998), 187.

89. Sedgwick, *Epistemology of the Closet*, 9–10.

90. Irina Sliusareva, "Opravdanie zhiteiskogo: Irina Sliusareva predstavliaet 'novuiu zhenskuiu prozu,'" *Znamia*, no. 11 (1991): 238. See also Heldt, *Terrible Perfection*, 2.

91. Anon., "Ot avtorov," in *Ne pomniashchaia zla*, ed. N. A. Ryl'nikova, comp. Larisa Vaneeva (Moscow: Moskovskii rabochii, 1990), 3, 4. This paradoxical formulation brings to mind both the boundlessness Bakhtinian prosaics ascribes to ordinary life and Trifonov's task for the writer, namely, to make the ephemeral endure.

92. Baranskaia, interview by Pieta Monks, 34. Grekova never commented on her attitude toward women's writing as a phenomenon. However, her antipathy to literature as instruction certainly distanced her from a literary manifesto such as the one introducing *Ne pomniashchaia zla*. See Grekova, "Zamysel: Zarozhdenie i voploshchenie," 11. See also the following: Rosalind Marsh, "Introduction: New Perspectives on Women and Gender in Russian Literature," in *Gender and Russian Literature*, ed. and trans. Rosalind Marsh (Cambridge: Cambridge University Press, 1996), 2–4; Catriona Kelly, "Missing Links: Russian Women Writers as Critics of Women Writers," in *Russian Writers on Russian Writers*, ed. Faith Wigzell (Oxford: Berg, 1994), 68; Elaine Showalter, *A Literature of Their Own: British Women Novelists from Brontë to Lessing* (Princeton, N.J.: Princeton University Press, 1977), 11–12.

93. Raunio "Kak ia ne stala pisatel'nitsei," 269; Natal'ia Perova, interview by author, Moscow, May 29, 2003.

94. Goscilo, *Dehexing Sex*, 12; *Gendernye issledovaniia v Rossii i SNG: kto est' kto. Spravochnik*, ed. Zoia Khotkina (Moscow: Tsentr dokumentatsii "Zhenskii arkhiv," 2000), viii. In 1988 Lipovskaia began publishing *Zhenskoe chtenie* (Women's Reading), a periodical with articles by Russian feminists and translations of the works of such prominent Westerners as Adrienne Rich. In addition to *Zhenskoe chtenie*, the journal

Preobrazhenie (Transfiguration) appeared in 1993. On the little-known Federation of Women Writers, see Larisa Vasil'eva, "Zhenshchina. Zhizn'. Literatura," *Literaturnaia gazeta,* no. 51 (1989): 7.

95. Nadezhda Azhgikhina, interview by author, Moscow, May 11, 2003. One critic worried that women's involvement in the workplace would make them give up childbirth, a fear most likely centered on ethnic Russians. See Natal'ia Startseva, "Damy s sobakami i bez," *Literaturnaia gazeta,* no. 30 (1988): 4; Klimenkova, "Perestroika kak gendernaia problema," 156–57.

96. Little research has been done on the connection between women's prose and the *derevenshchiki.* For a sense of their common literary history, see Goscilo's "Coming a Long Way, Baby," 8–9. In great part this oversight is due to Moscow/Leningrad/Saint Petersburg publishers and journals assuming all provincial writers to be both marginal and second-rate. Women authors from the regions face the additional burden of sexism, as Tat'iana Meshko and others observe in *Mariia* (1990). On alternative prose, see Oleg Dark, "Mir mozhet byt' liuboi," *Druzhba narodov,* no. 6 (1990): 223–35. See also Adlam, *Women in Russian Literature After Glasnost.*

97. Dark, "Mir mozhet byt' liuboi," 223; Tat'iana Rovenskaia, "K voprosu o periodizatsii istorii russkoi zhenskoi literatury 1980-kh— 1990-kh godov XX veka," *Zhenshchiny v istorii: vozmozhnost' byt' uvidennymi* 2 (2002): 292; Adlam, *Women in Russian Literature After Glasnost,* 17.

98. In chapter 3 I discuss the several collections that appeared from 1992 to 2002, including the second volume of *Mariia* (1995) and two other anthologies from northwest Russia. An expanded discussion of late- and post-Soviet women's provincial anthologies appears in Benjamin Sutcliffe, "Publishing the Russian Soul? Women's Provincial Literary Anthologies, 1990–1995"; Skomp, "Russian Women's Publishing at the Beginning of the 1990s."

99. Rovenskaia, "K voprosu o periodizatsii istorii russkoi zhenskoi literatury 1980-kh—1990-kh godov XX veka," 293. In 1979 Tat'iana Mamonova edited *Zhenshchina i Rossiia,* which served as one of the sources for the English-language volume *Women and Russia.* This volume ascribed the birth of Soviet-era feminism to the allegedly broad-based work of Mamonova's organization. However, Natasha Kolchevska notes that KGB intimidation, internal dissension, and lack of broad support prevented Mamonova's group from attaining lasting influence. The fictional and documentary works by Iuliia Voznesenskaia, one of the group's members, were more successful. Her *Zhenskii dekameron* (Women's Decameron, 1987) and *Zvezda Chernobyl'* (The Star Chernobyl,

1987) effectively used prose to convey women's experiences. Vozne-senskaia broke away from Mamonova's group Zhenshchina i Rossiia (Women and Russia) in 1980, helping to found a more religious women's group in Leningrad. See Natasha Kolchevska, "Woman and Russia," in *Encyclopedia of Russian Women's Movements*, ed. Norma C. Noonan and Carol Nechemias (Westport, Conn.: Greenwood Press, 2001), 182; Natasha Kolchevska, "Voznesenskaia, Iuliia Nikolaevna," in *Encyclopedia of Russian Women's Movements*, 177–78.

100. Vasilenko, "Novye Amazonki," 80; "Vmesto vstupleniia," in *Mariia. Literaturnyi al'manakh*, comp. Galina Skvortsova (Petrozavodsk: Kareliia, 1990), 1:5.

101. Irina Savkina, "Zhenskaia proza—bez kavychek," *Literaturnaia ucheba*, no. 3 (1997): 72; Vasilenko, "Novye amazonki," 81–82.

102. *Novye amazonki*, comp. Svetlana Vasilenko (Moscow: Moskov-skii rabochii, 1991), 4. Sometimes these authors focus on the self-reflexive subject of women's experiences in literature. While Raunio offers a Russian revision of *A Room of One's Own*, Tat'iana Meshko's "Grafomanka iz provintsii" (A Scribbler from the Provinces) describes a writer who is nearly raped while visiting Moscow. The would-be rapist editor, who praises village prose, conflates the woman's presumed inability to write with her status as sex object. Gorlanova's "Protokol" (The Minutes) records the thoughts of male writers, who decide not to publish an author who did not sleep with enough of them. See Tat'iana Meshko, "Grafomanka iz provintsii," in *Mariia. Literaturnyi al'manakh*, comp. Galina Skvortsova (Petrozavodsk: Kareliia, 1990), 1:209, 199; Nina Gorlanova, "Protokol," in *Abstinentki*, ed. Ol'ga Sokolova (Moscow: Se-riia andergraund, Gumanitarnyi fond im. A. S. Pushkina, 1991), 6.

103. Rovenskaia, "Vinovata li ia . . . ?" 215; Irina Savkina, "Da, zhenshchina dolzhna v teni svetit'sia," in *Zhena, kotoraia umela letat': Proza russkikh i finskikh pisatel'nits*, ed. Galina Skvortsova (Petroza-vodsk: INKA, 1993), 389.

104. Rovenskaia, "K voprosu o periodizatsii istorii russkoi zhenskoi literatury 1980-kh—1990-kh godov XX veka," 291, 293; Elena Trofi-mova, "Zhenskaia literatura i knigoizdanie v sovremennoi Rossii," *Obshchestvennye nauki i sovremennost'*, no. 5 (1998): 147; Nina Gabrielian, "Eva—eto znachit 'zhizn' '": Problema prostranstva v sovremennoi rus-skoi zhenskoi proze," *Voprosy literatury*, nos. 7–8 (1996): 31; Adlam, *Women in Russian Literature After Glasnost*, 109.

105. Pavel Basinskii, "Pozabyvshie dobro? Zametki na poliakh 'novoi zhenskoi prozy,'" *Literaturnaia gazeta*, no. 7 (1991): 10; Vasilenko, "Novye amazonki," 81.

106. "Vmesto vstupleniia," 5. Gulag survivor Glinka concisely links women's lives and the written word when describing the difficulty of publishing her story about women in the camps: "My whole life has been crushed and nobody wants to listen." Quoted by Natal'ia Perova, interview by author, Moscow, May 29, 2003.

107. Basinskii, "Pozabyvshie dobro?" 10; Evgeniia Shcheglova, "V svoem krugu. Polemicheskie zametki o 'zhurnal'noi proze,'" *Literaturnoe obozrenie*, no. 3 (1990): 23.

108. A. Kuralekh, "Byt i bytie v proze Liudmily Petrushevskoi," *Literaturnoe obozrenie*, no. 5 (1993): 67; Vasilevskii, "Nochi kholodny," 257; N. Medvedeva, "Povestvovanie i geroi v rasskazakh T. Tolstoi," in *Problemy tipologii russkoi literatury XX veka: Mezhvuzovskii sbornik nauchnikh trudov*, ed. N. E. Vasil'eva et al. (Perm: Permskii gosudarstvennyi universitet, 1991), 139.

109. Lipovetsky, "Strategies of Wastefulness, or the Metamorphoses of *Chernukha*," 60–62, 70.

110. Ovenasian, "Tvortsy raspada," 249; Evgenii Ovenasian "Raspada venok," *Literaturnaia Rossiia*, no. 36 (1991): 23.

111. Vladimir Bondarenko, "Ocherki literaturnikh nravov: polemicheskie zametki," *Moskva*, no. 12 (1987): 181. The increasingly contentious nature of literature's division into liberal and conservative camps appeared in titles foregrounding the rhetoric of dissent and need for morality, as Bondarenko's article shows.

112. V. Bushin, "S vysoty svoego kurgana: Neskol'ko nravstvennykh nabliudenii v sviazi s odnim literaturnym debiutom," *Nash sovremennik*, no. 8 (1987): 185.

113. Rovenskaia, "K voprosu o periodizatsii istorii russkoi zhenskoi literatury 1980-kh—1990-kh godov XX veka," 301. Various critics have voiced this argument, describing women's prose as rooted less in literature than in social awareness: because women's daily lives dictate women's writing, female familiarity with *byt* justifies its prominence. See Mil'man, *Chitaia Petrushevskuiu*, 53; and Bulin, "Otkroite knigi molodykh!" 238.

114. Adlam, *Women in Russian Literature After Glasnost*, 73.

Chapter 3. The Artistry of Everyday Life

1. The first epigraph is from Svetlana Vasilenko, "Novye amazonki iziashchnoi slovesnosti," in *Bryzgi shampanskogo. Novaia zhenskaia proza. Sbornik rasskazov*, ed. Svetlana Vasilenko (Moscow: AST/Olimp, 2002), 7. The second epigraph is from Liudmila Ulitskaia, "Liudmila Ulitskaia: I Accept Everything That Is Given," interview by Anastasiia Gosteva,

Russian Studies in Literature 38, no. 2 (2002): 72. See also Liudmila Ulits-kaia, "Liudmila Ulitskaia: Ne mogli by vyzhit', esli by . . . ," interview by Vladimir Prikhod'ko, *Moskovskaia pravda*, no. 17 (2001): 6.

2. Stephen Lovell argues that two crucial trends marked literature from 1986 to 1995. First, Russian readers lost their mythic gloss, moving from rhetorical emblem ("the most avid readers in the world") to a mere "socio-economic reality." At the same time, the book trade was exposed to a market hungry for Western-style mass genres often marginalized during the Soviet era. However, diminished interest in elite literature should be seen in relative terms: in the 1990s fiction was still more popular in Russia than in France, the United States, or the United Kingdom. Stephen Lovell, *The Russian Reading Revolution: Print Culture in the Soviet and Post-Soviet Eras* (New York: St. Martin's Press, 2000), 158. See also Vladimir Korobov, "So Many Books, Yet So Few, or the New Publishing Crisis," ed. Deming Brown, trans. Marian Schwartz, *Russian Social Science Review* 38, no. 1 (1997): 84; Mikhail Morozovskii, "Rynok khudozhestvennoi literatury," *Knizhnoe delo*, no. 6 (1994): 2.

3. Print runs show that publishers found this prose profitable: a 2006 hardback novel by Ulitskaia was issued in 150,000 copies. Both her works and those of Tolstaia and Petrushevskaia regularly appear in paperback. See Liudmila Ulitskaia, *Daniel' Shtain, perevodchik* (Moscow: Eksmo, 2006).

4. Liudmila Ulitskaia, *Medeia i ee deti* (Moscow: Eksmo, 2002), 5–6, 78.

5. Ludmila Ulitskaya, *Medea and Her Children*, trans. Arch Tait (New York: Schocken Books, 2002), 312.

6. Ulitskaia's novel *Veselye pokhorony* (The Funeral Party, 1997), about Russian emigrants in New York, provides an urban counterpart to Medeia's beautiful Crimea, focusing on friends as a surrogate community brought together by loss. Following Alik's death and the ensuing informal wake, his friends Dzhoika and Valentina both have sexual experiences unlike anything they have known before. This juxtaposition recalls the grotesque and its cyclical interchange of life and death, a natural alternation shaping both *Veselye pokhorony* and *Medeia i ee deti*. See Liudmila Ulitskaia, *Veselye pokhorony* (Moscow: Eksmo, 2006), 275, 283.

7. On family as common ethical response, see Svetlana Timina, "Ritmy vechnosti. Roman Liudmily Ulitskoi *Medeia i ee deti*," in *Perom i prelest'iu: Zhenshchiny v panteone russkoi literatury. Sbornik statei*, ed. Wanda Laszczak and Daria Ambroziak (Opole, Poland: Wydawca Dariusz Karbowiak, 1999), 147. The symbolic families of Judaism and Christianity are a central theme in Ulitskaia's heterogeneous novel *Daniel' Shtain, perevodchik* (Daniel Stein, Translator, 2006). For a discussion of Ulitskaia's own experiences as a Christian and a Jew, see the

autobiographical short story "Moi liubimyi arab" (My Favorite Arab) collected in *Liudi nashego tsaria* (Moscow: Eksmo, 2005), 269. For a discussion of Judaism and Christianity in *Daniel' Shtain*, see Livdmila Ulitskaia, "Imenno eto propovedoval Iiusus," interview with Vladimir Volodarskii, December 8, 2007, http://www.bigbook.ru/smi/detail .php?ID=3825 (last accessed August 3, 2008).

8. Fernand Braudel, *On History*, trans. Sarah Matthews (Chicago: University of Chicago Press, 1980), 27–28. See also Tat'iana Rovenskaia, "Arkhetip doma v novoi zhenskoi proze, ili Kommunal'noe zhitie i kommunal'nye tela," *Inoi vzgliad*, no. 3 (2001): 26.

9. Tat'iana Kazarina, "Bednye rodstvenniki," *Preobrazhenie*, no. 4 (1996): 171. In this sense one critic misreads *Medeia i ee deti* when he claims it is not a family chronicle. On the contrary, kinship structures temporality despite the subjective narration and nonlinear plot distinguishing the novel from nineteenth-century family chronicles. See Leonid Bakhnov, "Genio loci," *Druzhba narodov*, no. 8 (1996): 179. Ulitskaia's play, *Moi vnuk Veniamin* (My Grandson Veniamin, 2008) subordinates ethnicity to tolerance in its image of the Jewish family. See Liudmila Ulitskaia, *Moi vnuk Veniamin*, in *Russkoe varen'e i drugoe* (Moscow: Eksmo, 2008).

10. Bakhtin, "Epic and Novel," 27; Ulitskaia, *Medeia i ee deti*, 252; Liudmila Ulitskaia, e-mail to author dated July 30, 2005.

11. Svetlana Vasilenko, *Durochka* (Moscow: Vagrius, 2000), 16, 105, 125–26. Nad'ka-Ganna is compared to both the Mongol princess giving the southern Akhtuba River its name and, less directly, to pagan Mother Damp Earth, who influenced Russian culture's appropriation of the Mother of God. See Vasilenko, *Durochka*, 73; Tat'iana Taiganova, "Roman v rubishche: O romane Svetlany Vasilenko 'Durochka'," *Druzhba narodov*, no. 6 (2000): 188.

12. Jerome Beaty, "History by Indirection: The Era of Reform in *Middlemarch*," in *Middlemarch: An Authoritative Text, Backgrounds, Reviews and Criticism*, ed. Bert Hornback (New York: Norton, 1977), 706. For Anja Grothe Medeia's life combines mythological elements with the quotidian and "a kind of parallel documentation to the [twentieth] century." History and myth in the novel are complementary, reflecting Ulitskaia's refusal to isolate modes of thought or find a single way of interpreting the past. This shunning of simple solutions is at the heart of *Daniel' Shtain, perevodchik*, where the protagonist's quest for meaning leads him from Zionism to Catholicism. See Anja Grothe, "Medusa, Cassandra, Medea," 266. Vasilenko, *Durochka*, 39; Ulitskaia, *Medeia i ee deti*, 11.

13. Liudmila Ulitskaia, *Kazus Kukotskogo* (Moscow: Eksmo, 2002), 165.

14. Ulitskaia, *Kazus Kukotskogo*, 140.

15. Vasilenko, "'Novye amazonki'," 89. Traktorina Petrovna has another opposite in the earthy Aunt Kharyta, who is deeply religious and humane. Not surprisingly, she is eventually destroyed by the Stalinist juggernaut and its human personification. Aunt Kharyta is based on one of Vasilenko's relatives, who was killed by the Nazis. The fictional substitution of German occupier by the Stalinist state underscores these parallel misfortunes befalling the Russian people. See Svetlana Vasilenko, "Otvet na dva voprosa," *Znamia*, no. 5 (1995): 188.

16. Tat'iana Tolstaia, *Kys'* (Moscow: Eksmo, 2005), 233, 63, 313. See also Tat'iana Tolstaia, "Miumziki i Nostradamus (Interv'iu gazete *Moskovskie novosti*)," in *Kys'*, 331.

17. Ulitskaya, *Medea and Her Children*, 94; Ulitskaia, *Medeia i ee deti*, 164. This lighthearted discussion of sexuality also obscures the fact that Sandra's adventures involved Medeia's husband. Unlike her murderous namesake, after discovering the affair Medeia chooses incomprehension and silence instead of revenge.

18. Petrushevskaia's post-Soviet fictional works do, however, provide a more diverse treatment of sexuality. While a short story such as "Vasen'ki" links the erotic to physiology, the autobiographical "Nezrelye iagody kryzhovnika" (Ripening Gooseberries) subordinates it to the female protagonist's growing sense of independence. Petrushevskaia, "Vasen'ki," 7; Liudmila Petrushevskaia, "Nezrelye iagody kryzhovnika," in *Naidi menia, son. Rasskazy* (Moscow: Vagrius, 2000), 20.

19. Liudmila Ulitskaia, "Vetrianaia ospa," in *Bednye, zlye, liubimye. Povesti i rasskazy* (Moscow: Eksmo, 2002), 194; Helena Goscilo, introduction to *Present Imperfect: Stories by Russian Women*, ed. Ayesha Kagal and Natal'ia Perova (Boulder, Colo.: Westview Press, 1996), 6. This story highlights interactions between girls and women; men have marginal roles. In the cycle *Devochki* (Girls) Plishkina and Chelysheva are surrounded by female friends, implying that de facto sexual segregation promotes a less traumatic path to maturity.

20. Ol'ga Tatarinova, "Seksopatologiia," in *Chego khochet zhenshchina . . . Sbornik zhenskikh rasskazov* (Moscow: Linor, 1993), 245.

21. Liudmila Ulitskaia, "Bron'ka," in *Bednye, zlye, liubimye. Povesti i rasskazy* (Moscow: Eksmo, 2002), 36.

22. Ol'ga Lobova, "Lëniny sny," in *Chego khochet zhenshchina . . . Sbornik zhenskikh rasskazov* (Moscow: Linor, 1993), 291–92. In a more imaginative reworking of this theme, Ulitskaia's Gulia in the eponymous story seduces the much younger San Sanych. However, unlike Baranskaia's "Potselui" (The Kiss), this atypical scenario is not the focus of the story (although Gulia subsequently brags about her conquest).

Indeed, unlike the works by Baranskaia and Lobova, Ulitskaia's narrative stresses sexuality between an older woman and younger man as only one part of an interaction promoting emotional stability for both. Liudmila Ulitskaia, "Gulia," in *Bednye, zlye, liubimye. Povesti i rasskazy* (Moscow: Eksmo, 2002), 93; Natal'ia Baranskaia, "Potselui," in *Zhenshchina s zontikom* (Moscow: Sovremennik, 1981). See also Helena Goscilo, "Introduction: Squaring the Circle," in *Lives in Transit: Recent Russian Women's Writing*, ed. Helena Goscilo (Dana Point, Calif.: Ardis, 1995), xv.

23. Liudmila Ulitskaia, *Sonechka, Medeia i ee deti* (Moscow: Vagrius, 1997), 303–4, 319.

24. Galina Skvortsova, "Russkaia dusha," in *Russkaia dusha. Sbornik poezii i prozy sovremennykh pisatel'nits russkoi provintsii*, Frauenliteraturgeschichte: Texte und Materialen zur russischen Frauenliteratur 3, ed. Galina Skvortsova-Akbulatova (Wilhelmshorst, Ger.: F. K. Göpfert, 1995), 172, 176, 173–74.

25. In one of the anthology's introductory articles, Elena Markova notes that this choice shows that Ol'ga has changed from mother to courtesan. The story also warns against "xenophilia," suggesting a clear distinction between Russian/pure and alien/impure that "Russkaia dusha" challenges. Elena Markova, "Nitki rvutsia—ia viazhu . . . ," in *Russkaia dusha. Sbornik poezii i prozy sovremennykh pisatel'nits russkoi provintsii*, Frauenliteraturgeschichte: Texte und Materialen zur russischen Frauenliteratur 3, ed. Galina Skvortsova-Akbulatova (Wilhelmshorst, Ger.: F. K. Göpfert, 1995), 18.

26. Viktoriia Tokareva, "Lilovyi kostium," in *Vse normal'no, vse khorosho* (Moscow: AST, 2002), 34–36. By contrast, Ulitskaia's "Zhenshchiny russkikh selenii . . ." (Dauntless Women of the Russian Steppe) links homoerotic activity to a crucial discovery: Margo finds a cancerous lump in Vera's breasts while massaging them. It is significant that this scene occurs while both women are drunk. As with Plishkina's and Chelysheva's game, there are mitigating circumstances "explaining" such controversial behavior. Liudmila Ulitskaia, "Zhenshchiny russkikh selenii . . . ," in *Skvoznaia liniia. Povest', rasskazy* (Moscow: Eksmo, 2002), 131–32.

27. Liudmila Ulitskaia, "Golubchik," in *Skvoznaia liniia. Povest', rasskazy* (Moscow: Eksmo, 2002), 240; Ludmila Ulitskaya, "Angel," in *Sonechka: A Novella and Stories*, trans. Arch Tait (New York: Schocken Books, 2005), 190.

28. Ulitskaia, "Golubchik," 243–45. In "Zatychka" (The Plug) the autobiographical narrator meets Nikita, an old friend imprisoned under Soviet anti-sodomy laws, who is probably the prototype for

Slava. Liudmila Ulitskaia, "Zatychka," in *Liudi nashego tsaria* (Moscow: Eksmo, 2005), 259.

29. Ulitskaia, "Liudmila Ulitskaia: I Accept Everything That Is Given," interview by Anastasiia Gosteva, 80.

30. Rovenskaia, "Arkhetip doma v novoi zhenskoi proze," 26.

31. Vasilenko, *Durochka*, 103–4, 119.

32. Ibid., 23–24, 19. While she does not speak per se, Nad'ka-Ganna's outbursts and songs recall what Vasilenko notes was the alternate title for the *Ne pomniashchaia zla* anthology: *Velikaia nemaia zagovorila* (The Great Silent Woman Has Spoken). Vasilenko joins this silence to women's opinions, which, she argues, female authors could more fully express only during perestroika. Vasilenko, "Novye amazonki," 85.

33. Ulitskaia, *Kazus Kukotskogo*, 184–87. In the short story "Chuzhie deti" (A Stranger's Children) Margarita falls into a catatonic state after her husband, Sergo, accuses her of giving birth to another man's children. Her helplessness is the result of his unjustified suspicions. While Sergo is in the room she often talks to the (imaginary) spouse who still loves her. Liudmila Ulitskaia, "Chuzhie deti," in *Bednye, zlye, liubimye. Povesti i rasskazy* (Moscow: Eksmo, 2002), 132.

34. Liudmila Ulitskaia, "Lialin dom," in *Bednye, zlye, liubimye. Povesti i rasskazy* (Moscow: Eksmo, 2002), 75, 78, 69.

35. The jury included novelists, prominent critics (Zoia Boguslavskaia, Lev Rubinshtein, Galina Belaia, Mariia Mikhailova, Elena Trofimova), and two US professors (Goscilo, Marina Ledkovsky). See Elena Trofimova, introduction to *Chego khochet zhenshchina . . . Sbornik zhenskikh rasskazov* (Moscow: Linor, 1993), 6. The ten-thousand-copy print run of this anthology was fairly large for a "serious" literary work published in the early 1990s. However, a number were never sold: in 2000 I discovered that one Moscow bookstore was simply giving away remainder copies!

36. Diana Medman, "Na vzgliad feministicheskogo zhiuri," in *Chego khochet zhenshchina . . . Sbornik zhenskikh rasskazov* (Moscow: Linor, 1993), 286, 287.

37. Liudmila Ulitskaia, "Koridornaia sistema," in *Liudi nashego tsaria* (Moscow: Eksmo, 2005), 34.

38. Vasilenko, *Novye amazonki*, 83–85. The anthology *Bryzgi shampanskogo* (Splashes of Champagne, 2002), compiled by Vasilenko, continued this trend. Other than Tokareva, Tat'iana Nabatnikova, and Nina Katerli, no authors who were highly visible in the late 1980s participated in the collection. However, the works of such well-known newer writers as Marina Vishnevetskaia and 2006 Booker winner Ol'ga Slavnikova did appear.

39. Meleshko, *Sovremennaia otechestvennaia zhenskaia proza,* 80–86.

40. Elaine Showalter, "The Feminist Critical Revolution," in *The New Feminist Criticism: Essays on Women, Literature, and Theory,* ed. Elaine Showalter (New York: Pantheon Books, 1985), 8.

41. Gabrielian, "Eva—eto znachit 'zhizn'," 43.

42. Irina Savkina, "Kto i kak pishet istoriiu russkoi zhenskoi literatury," *Novoe literaturnoe obozrenie,* no. 2 (1997): 364; Showalter, "The Feminist Critical Revolution," 5–6. Gabrielian's third stage would seem to describe the prose of an author such as Tolstaia, who emphasizes language as a medium for increasing possibilities. However, Tolstaia's earlier stories have many aspects of the rebellion Gabrielian critiques, as when they explicitly challenge gender stereotypes by means of the author's scathing parodies of clichéd romantic discourse. In a similar manner, naive Benedikt in *Kys'* recounts how on Fedor Kuz'mych's "new" holiday, Women's Day, women will continue to do all the cooking and cleaning but men cannot beat them. Tolstaia, *Kys',* 111–12. See also Goscilo, *The Explosive World of Tatyana N. Tolstaya's Fiction,* 82.

43. Ulitskaia's artistic depictions of the mundane (sexuality, family life, etc.) are liberating: they reject the binarism of the *byt/bytie* relationship by suggesting that the ideal can be found within the physical.

44. Rovenskaia, "K voprosu o periodizatsii istorii russkoi zhenskoi literatury 1980-kh—1990-kh godov XX veka," 294–309. Natal'ia Perova, editor of the English-language literary journal *Glas,* also implicitly envisioned a three-part development of women's prose. In the first groundbreaking issue devoted to female authors (*Women's View*), Perova maintains that the characters created by the authors (Glinka, Galina Shcherbakova, and others) do not know that they are oppressed, while in the second and third volumes (*A Will and a Way; Nine of Russia's Foremost Women Writers*) an awareness of this injustice is evident and attempts are made to struggle against it. Natal'ia Perova, interview by author, Moscow, May 29, 2003.

45. Abasheva, "Chisten'kaia zhizn' ne pomniashchaia zla," 13–14; Tat'iana Rovenskaia, "Zhenskaia proza serediny 1980-kh—nachala 1990-kh godov. (Problematika, mental'nost', identifikatsiia") (Ph.D. diss., Moscow State University, 2000), 82.

46. Trofimova, "Zhenskaia literatura i knigoizdanie v sovremennoi Rossii," 147; Ol'ga Slavnikova, "Zhenskii pocherk. A takzhe portret," *Vremia MN,* no. 124 (2000): 7. Vagrius was careful to distinguish the series from other, presumably less worthy types of writing by women: "This is not 'women's novels' in a middlebrow sense. This is real literature." See http://www.vagrius.ru/series/.

47. Iurii Tynianov, "O literaturnom fakte," 19; Valentina Fedotova, "Informatsionnoe obshchestvo i knigi dlia elit i mass," in *Obshchestvo i kniga: Ot Gutenberga do Interneta,* ed. A. P. Koroleva (Moscow: Traditsiia, 2000), 222.

48. Tolstaia, *Kys',* 212–15, 270–71, 44; Natal'ia Ivanova, "Grind the Peacack into *Burkers:* On Tatyana Tolstaya's *The Slynx,*" trans. Liv Bliss, *Russian Studies in Literature* 39, no. 4 (2003): 77. Molly Thomasy makes an insightful connection between *Kys'* and the story "Siuzhet" (Plot), which heretically and hilariously revises the Pushkin myth. See "Rewriting Pushkin's Death: Tat'iana Tolstaia's 'Siuzhet' in Literary and Cultural Context," paper presented at the National Convention of the American Association for the Advancement of Slavic Studies, New Orleans, November 16, 2007.

49. Tolstaia, *Kys',* 77–79, 322.

50. Slavnikova, "Zhenskii pocherk. A takzhe portret," 7; Natal'ia Perova, interview by author, Moscow, May 29, 2003.

51. Such innovation outstripped the staid work of Baranskaia and Grekova, who began to lose readers during perestroika and were all but forgotten by the late 1990s. Eksmo reissued Grekova's works in 2002–3. Several months earlier, however, I noticed that even salespeople in central Moscow bookstores rarely recognized the author's name.

52. Nadezhda Azhgikhina, interview by author, Moscow, May 11, 2003. These publication figures are double those of Grekova, whose *Svezho predanie* was reissued in a print run of five thousand.

53. Vasilenko, "Novye amazonki iziashchnoi slovesnosti," 7; Mikhail Zolotonosov, "Damskoe schast'e," *Moskovskie novosti,* January 21, 2003.

54. Nina Gorlanova, "Kak napisat' rasskaz," in *Russkaia dusha. Sbornik poezii i prozy sovremennykh pisatel'nits russkoi provintsii,* Frauenliteraturgeschichte: Texte und Materialen zur russischen Frauenliteratur 3, ed. Galina Skvortsova-Akbulatova (Wilhelmshorst, Ger.: F. K. Göpfert, 1995), 198.

55. Rovenskaia, "Zhenskaia proza serediny 1980-kh—nachala 1990-kh godov," 115; Tolstaia, *Kys',* 29, 83.

56. Taiganova, "Roman v rubishche," 189.

57. Nadezhda Azhgikhina, interview by author, Moscow, May 11, 2003. For a tragicomic discussion of post-Soviet *byt,* see Tolstaia's "Polzet" (It's Crawling!) and "Chastnaia godovshchina" (A Private Anniversary), in *Den'. Lichnoe* (Moscow: Eksmo, 2004).

58. Ulitskaia, "Liudmila Ulitskaia: I Accept Everything That Is Given," interview by Anastasiia Gosteva, 82, 74, 80–81; Ulitskaia, "Liudmila Ulitskaia: Ne mogli by vyzhit', esli by . . . ," 6.

59. Nina Malygina, "Zdes' i seichas: poetika ischeznoveniia," *Oktiabr'*, no. 9 (2000): 157.

60. Ludmila Ulitskaya, "The Queen of Spades," in *Sonechka: A Novella and Stories*, trans. Arch Tait (New York: Schocken Books, 2005), 76.

61. Such tranquility contrasts sharply with the depiction of Anna Andrianovna's free time in *Vremia noch'*. In a flashback she begins her maternal mantra: "Night. The kid's asleep. I keep up my defences." *Vremia noch'* lacks the liberating digressions of "Pikovaia dama." Anna Andrianovna allows nothing to escape from her overprotective grasp. Ludmila Petrushevskaya, *The Time: Night*, trans. Sally Laird (Evanston, Ill.: Northwestern University Press, 2000), 30.

62. Aleksandr Prokhanov's assessment of Vasilenko's story "Za saigakami" (Going After Goat-Antelopes) was made as part of the author's work on her undergraduate thesis but describes her oeuvre as a whole. See "Studenty Literaturnogo instituta I. Agafanov, S. Kaznacheev, A. Talybov i rukovoditel' seminara A. Prokhanov o rasskaze Svetlany Vasilenko 'Za saigakami,'" *Literaturnaia ucheba*, no. 5 (1982): 23; Ol'ga Slavnikova, "Taina neprochitanoi zapiski," in *Bryzgi shampanskogo. Novaia zhenskaia proza. Sbornik rasskazov*, ed. Svetlana Vasilenko (Moscow: AST/Olimp, 2002), 297.

63. *Detektiv* is the catchall term for any novel that focuses on solving a crime. In Anglo-American literature, a plethora of subgenres exists, depending on the function of the protagonist (e.g., police procedural, hard-boiled). My discussion uses *detektivy* to avoid confusing English genre terms, which are irrelevant to post-Soviet readers. For an overview of Anglo-American mystery subgenres and their female protagonists, see Kathleen Klein, *The Woman Detective: Gender and Genre* (Urbana: University of Illinois Press, 1995), 5–6.

64. See Lovell, *The Russian Reading Revolution*, 132.

65. On *detektivy* see: Ol'ga Kostiukova, "Detektiv. Zhenskaia dolia," *Itogi*, no. 24 (2001): 57; Elena Baraban, "Detektivy Aleksandry Marininoi, ili 'Starye motivy—novye pesni'," in *Tvorchestvo Aleksandry Marininoi kak otrazhenie sovremennoi rossiiskoi mental'nosti*, ed. Elena Trofimova (Moscow: Institut nauchnoi informatsii po obshchestvennym naukam, 2002), 93; Leonid Geller, "'Kogda zhenshchiny smeiutsia poslednimi': Zamechaniia o zhenskom detective," in *Tvorchestvo Aleksandry Marininoi kak otrazhenie sovremennoi rossiiskoi mental'nosti*, 63. On the peculiarities of verisimilitude in the mystery novel, see Todorov, *The Poetics of Prose*, 84.

66. Aleksandra Marinina, *Posmertnyi obraz, Chernyi spisok. Posmertnyi obraz. Romany* (Moscow: Eksmo, 2005), 258

67. Marinina, *Posmertnyi obraz*, 324. Kamenskaia's "inappropriate" female profession and her disdain for domestic tasks are mainstays of Russian masculinity. This redrawing of gender lines is another factor in Marinina's prose. For a more detailed analysis, see Catharine Nepomnyashchy, "Markets, Mirror, and Mayhem: Aleksandra Marinina and the Rise of the New Russian *Detektiv*," in *Consuming Russia: Popular Culture, Sex, and Society since Gorbachev*, ed. Adele Barker (Durham, N.C.: Duke University Press, 1999), 171.

68. Dar'ia Dontsova, *Figovyi listochek ot kutiur* (Moscow: Eksmo, 2005), 325; Elen Mela [Hélène Melat], "'Rozovoe i chernoe': Ob odnom romane Aleksandry Marininoi," in *Tvorchestvo Aleksandry Marininoi kak otrazhenie sovremennoi rossiiskoi mental'nosti*, ed. Elena Trofimova (Moscow: Institut nauchnoi informatsii po obshchestvennym naukam, 2002), 158.

69. Aleksandra Marinina, *Chernyi spisok, Chernyi spisok. Posmertnyi obraz. Romany* (Moscow: Eksmo, 2005), 210.

70. Dar'ia Dontsova, *Mukha v samolete* (Moscow: Eksmo, 2005), 39; Dar'ia Dontsova, *Dollary Tsaria Gorokha* (Moscow: Eksmo, 2005), 11.

71. See Geller, "'Kogda zhenshchiny smeiutsia poslednimi'," 55; Mela, "'Rozovoe i chernoe'," 4; Brian Baer, "Engendering Suspicion: Homosexual Panic in the Post-Soviet *Detektiv*," *Slavic Review* 64, no. 1 (2005): 28. Dissecting homophobic motifs in *detektivy*, Baer observed that the 1990s were a period of blurred gender lines, when fears about a new society of "hard" women and "soft" men accompanied the plummeting standard of living. This scenario recalls the Gorbachev years, with their heightened anxiety over the fate of Russian masculinity and femininity.

72. See Klein, *The Woman Detective*, 1–3, 7.

73. The women's *detektiv* encompassed elements of the romance novel, the adventure novel, and literary depictions of *byt*. This variegated structure recalls the Bakhtinian novel—an omnivorous form assimilating a wide range of nonliterary contexts. See Mariia Cherniak, "'Nashe vse' Aleksandra Marinina v zerkale sovremennogo ironicheskogo detektiva," in *Tvorchestvo Aleksandry Marininoi kak otrazhenie sovremennoi rossiiskoi mental'nosti*, ed. Elena Trofimova (Moscow: Institut nauchnoi informatsii po obshchestvennym naukam, 2002), 72.

74. *Mukha v samolete*, 252; *Figovyi listochek ot kutiur*, 9; Elena Trofimova, "Fenomen detektivnykh romanov Aleksandry Marininoi v kul'ture sovremennoi Rossii," in *Tvorchestvo Aleksandry Marininoi kak otrazhenie sovremennoi rossiiskoi mental'nosti*, ed. Elena Trofimova (Moscow: Institut nauchnoi informatsii po obshchestvennym naukam, 2002), 22.

75. Mela, "'Rozovoe i chernoe'," 156; Marinina, *Chernyi spisok*, 14. Stasov's description of having sex with Tania is telling. The first-person narration depicts intercourse from a female point of view. "Arousal came slowly. . . . I floated among the waves, quietly rocking back and forth, and I felt as good as I had in the recent dream [about Tania]" (109, 11). This scene, along with Stasov's status as a single parent, marks him as a nontraditional masculine character, while the simultaneous affairs he had after his divorce confirm his "manliness."

76. The promise of an upbeat conclusion unites *detektivy* with the romance novel. The reader expects this happy ending in any work, yet it is the individual variations of a given narrative that make the reading experience worthwhile. For an early discussion of how this interplay of expectation/variation shapes American romances, see Janice Radway's "Reading the Romance," in *The Communication Theory Reader*, ed. Paul Cobley (London: Routledge, 1996), 458.

77. Marinina, *Chernyi spisok*, 28. Dontsova's works go one step further, alerting the reader to the authors' other books that address important events in her heroines' lives. Sometimes the footnotes do not give much credit to the implied reader: one explains the role of the KGB, an organization that was presumably still familiar to Russians. See, e.g., Dontsova, *Mukha v samolete*, 296; Dontsova, *Dollary Tsaria Gorokha*, 175.

78. In addition to the numerous references to characters confusing themselves with "real" detectives, some works actually mock their own convoluted plots. After two crimes have been solved due to a series of particularly unlikely coincidences, Tat'iana Ustinova's heroine Anfisa admits that even she finds this unbelievable. Tat'iana Ustinova, *Zakon obratnogo volshebstva* (Moscow: Eksmo, 2005), 347.

79. Irina Savkina, "'Gliazhus' v tebia, kak v zerkalo . . . '. Tvorchestvo Aleksandry Marininoi v sovremennoi russkoi kritike: gendernyi aspekt," in *Tvorchestvo Aleksandry Marininoi kak otrazhenie sovremennoi rossiiskoi mental'nosti*, ed. Elena Trofimova (Moscow: Institut nauchnoi informatsii po obshchestvennym naukam, 2002), 6, 11. Critics, authors, and their characters have pondered the gender of their genre's readers. One of Dontsova's female protagonists snidely remarks that (presumably male) intellectuals devour the novels in secret, a claim echoed by Marinina. In the introduction to *Chernyi spisok* one critic revealed the hidden subtext of such assertions: men read Marinina for the plot, while their female counterparts appreciated the details taken from women's *byt*. From this viewpoint Marinina was a universal genius, whose multivalent talents elicited the "natural" differences between male and female readers. Dontsova, *Dollary Tsaria*

Gorokha, 201; Kostiukova, "Detektiv. Zhenskaia dolia," 57; Natal'ia Tat'ianina, "Ne tol'ko Kamenskaia," in *Chernyi spisok. Posmertnyi obraz. Romany* (Moscow: Eksmo, 2005), 7.

80. Wolfgang Iser, *The Act of Reading* (Baltimore, Md.: Johns Hopkins University Press, 1978), ix.

81. This documentation is not unique to *detektivy*. In Ol'ga Postnikova's story "Kazino" (Casino) middle-aged Inessa encounters the shock of *byt* in extraordinary times. Desperate for a stable salary, she finds work renovating a casino, where the immorality and evil she is prepared to encounter never materialize. Instead, she realizes that her fellow workers are simply individuals struggling to survive. Ol'ga Postnikova, "Kazino," in *Bryzgi shampanskogo. Novaia zhenskaia proza. Sbornik rasskazov,* ed. Svetlana Vasilenko (Moscow: AST/Olimp, 2002), 79.

82. Baraban, "Detektivy Aleksandry Marininoi, ili 'Starye motivy — novye pesni'," 93–94. Kamenskaia's antithesis is a villain such as Ustinova's Valerii Pevtsov, a wealthy intellectual and incompetent criminal. He scorns ordinary Russians, who read *detektivy* as they suffer in the overcrowded subway. The heavy-handed irony with which the narrator eviscerates Pevtsov confirms that such people oppose "our" values, which presumably include honesty, fidelity, and modesty. Ustinova, *Zakon obratnogo volshebstva*, 125.

83. Ustinova, *Zakon obratnogo volshebstva*, 328; Ol'ga Postnikova, "Tristan i Izol'da," in *Bryzgi shampanskogo. Novaia zhenskaia proza. Sbornik rasskazov,* ed. Svetlana Vasilenko (Moscow: AST/Olimp, 2002), 85.

84. Melat, "'Rozovoe i chernoe'," 160n.

Conclusion

1. The first epigraph is from Liudmila Ulitskaia, introduction to *Liudi nashego tsaria* (Moscow: Eksmo, 2005), 8; the second epigraph is from Ol'ga Slavnikova, "Petrushevskaia and Emptiness," trans. Vladimir Talmy, *Russian Studies in Literature* 37, no. 2 (2001): 57.

2. My analysis of provincial writing is based on materials found in several anthologies published in northwestern Russia after 1991: *Zhena, kotoraia umela letat', Mariia* (1995), and *Russkaia dusha. Chego khochet zhenshchina . . .* also contains several authors from outside the "center" (Nina Gorlanova, Alla Sel'ianova, and Mariia Kirpichnikova). The collections highlight a few talented authors against a backdrop of repetitive stories chronicling disappointed love, shattered families, and crushing poverty. These anthologies, however, are atypical because of their availability in Moscow. As critics have bemoaned, many provincial publications do not reach the capital. See, e.g., Ivan Kuz'michev,

"Marginal'nye zametki o sovremennoi russkoi literature," *Nizhnii Novgorod*, no. 12 (1998): 224.

3. Huyssen, *After the Great Divide*, 47, 53.

4. Slavnikova, "Zhenskii pocherk. A takzhe portret," 7; Rovenskaia, "Zhenskaia proza serediny 1980-kh—nachala 1990-kh godov," 64; Azhgikhina, "Zhenshchina kak ob"ekt i sub"ekt v sovremennoi rossiiskoi literature," 63. Ulitskaia's *Kazus Kukotskogo* appeared on Russian television in 2005 and, thanks to the booming pirated films business, was simultaneously available for sale on DVD (Iurii Grymov, dir., *Kazus Kukotskogo* [NTV, 2005]).

5. Jim McGuigan, *Cultural Populism* (London: Routledge, 1993), 3. Tat'iana Morozova, "Posle dolgogo vozderzhaniia," *Druzhba narodov*, no. 9 (1997): 181. Of course, in Russia after 1991 male genres (e.g., the thriller and pornography) played an equally prominent role in mass literature.

6. Viktoriia Tokareva, "Perelom," in *Malo li chto byvaet . . .* (Moscow: AST, 1999), 187. In 1992 Richard Chapple accurately observed that the author was producing lower-quality, mainstream work, a shift illustrated by the major publishing house AST, which eventually issued her books with gaudy flowers on the covers. Richard Chapple, "A Note on Viktoria Tokareva and Anton Chekhov," *Australian Slavonic and East European Studies* 6, no. 1 (1992): 119–20.

7. The form of literature is another feature of post-Soviet literature erroneously linked to perceived quality. There were several prominent Web sites that either reissued existing literature online or published directly through the Internet. One such site (*NaStoiashchaia literatura: Zhenskii rod* [Real Literature: Feminine Gender], http://www.lit women.ru/letter.html?pg=2) was specifically designated for female authors. Many women's works also appeared on the two leading online literature sites: *Vavilon* (Babylon), http://www.vavilon.ru and *Biblioteka Maksima Moshkova* (Maksim Moshkov's Library), http://www.lib.ru. Western Slavists have thus far neglected the important role played by online writing, which is faster and cheaper to publish and provides a globally accessible venue for authors from the provinces.

8. Morozova, "Posle dolgogo vozderzhaniia," 178; Kuz'michev, "Marginal'nye zametki o sovremennoi russkoi literature," 223; Fedotova, "Informatsionnoe obshchestvo i knigi dlia elit i mass," 234; Nepomnyashchy, "Markets, Mirrors, and Mayhem," 162–63, 165.

9. Anna Orlova, "Ulitskaia razliubila liudei," *Komsomol'skaia pravda*, no. 74 (2004): 12. On how melodrama illuminates the connections between high and low culture, see Louise McReynolds and Joan Neuberger, introduction to *Imitations of Life: Two Centuries of Melodrama in*

Russia, ed. Louise McReynolds and Joan Neuberger (Durham, N.C.: Duke University Press, 2002), 5. Shurik is an eroticized version of Grekova's nurturing and exploited Garusov. This coincidence of character types reveals the caring male to be a continuing rarity worth displaying in Russian literature.

10. Liudmila Ulitskaia, "'Tvorets znal, chto on delal . . .' Besedu vela Inessa Tsiporkina," *Knizhnoe obozrenie,* no. 33 (2000): 5.

11. Goscilo, "Perestroika and Post-Soviet Prose: From Dazzle to Dispersal," 309.

Bibliography

Abasheva, Marina. "Chisten'kaia zhizn' ne pomniashchaia zla." *Litera-turnoe obozrenie*, nos. 5–6 (1992): 9–14.

Adlam, Carol. *Women in Russian Literature after Glasnost: Female Alternatives*. London: Legenda, 2005.

Althusser, Louis. *"Lenin and Philosophy" and Other Essays*. Trans. Ben Brewster. New York: Monthly Review Press, 1971.

Armstrong, Nancy. *Desire and Domestic Fiction: A Political History of the Novel*. New York: Oxford University Press, 1987.

———. "Some Call It Fiction: On the Politics of Domesticity." In *Feminisms: An Anthology of Literary Theory and Criticism*, ed. Robyn R. Warhol and Diane Price Herndi, 921–30. New Brunswick, N.J.: Rutgers University Press, 1997.

Astaf'ev, Viktor. *Pechal'nyi detektiv: povesti, roman, rasskaz*. Kishinev: Literatura Artistike, 1988.

Attwood, Lynne. *Creating the New Soviet Woman: Women's Magazines as Engineers of Female Identity, 1922–53*. New York: St. Martin's Press, 1999.

———. "Gender Angst in Russian Society and Cinema in the Post-Stalin Era." In *Russian Cultural Studies: An Introduction*, ed. Catriona Kelly and David Shepherd, 352–67. Oxford: Oxford University Press, 1998.

Azhgikhina, Nadezhda. "Zhenshchina kak ob"ekt i sub"ekt v sovremennoi rossiiskoi literature." In *Sila slova-2: Novyi evropeiskii poriadok: prava cheloveka, polozhenie zhenshchin, gendernaia tsenzura*, comp. Nadezhda Azhgikhina, 57–63. Moscow: Zhenskii mir i Eslan, 2000.

Baer, Brian. "Engendering Suspicion: Homosexual Panic in the Post-Soviet *Detektiv*." *Slavic Review* 64, no. 1 (2005): 24–42.

Bakhnov, Leonid. "Genio loci." *Druzhba narodov*, no. 8 (1996): 178–80.

Bakhtin, Mikhail. *The Dialogic Imagination. Four Essays by M. M. Bakhtin*.

Ed. Michael Holquist. Trans. Caryl Emerson and Michael Holquist. Austin: University of Texas Press, 1992.

———. *Problems of Dostoevsky's Poetics.* Ed. and trans. Caryl Emerson. Minneapolis: University of Minnesota Press, 1999.

Banting, Mark, Catriona Kelly, and James Riordan. "Sexuality." In *Russian Cultural Studies: An Introduction,* ed. Catriona Kelly and David Shepherd, 311–51. Oxford: Oxford University Press, 1998.

Baraban, Elena. "Detektivy Aleksandry Marininoi, ili 'Starye motivy— novye pesni.'" In *Tvorchestvo Aleksandry Marininoi kak otrazhenie sovremennoi rossiiskoi mental'nosti,* ed. Elena Trofimova, 83–101. Moscow: Institut nauchnoi informatsii po obshchestvennym naukam, 2002.

Baranskaia, Natal'ia. *Den' pominoveniia. Roman, povest'.* Moscow: Sovetskii pisatel', 1989.

———. Interview by Pieta Monks. In *Writing Lives: Conversations between Women Writers,* ed. Mary Chamberlain, 26–36. London: Virago, 1988.

———. "Muzhchiny, beregite zhenshchin!" *Literaturnaia gazeta,* no. 46 (1971): 13.

———. "Natalja Baranskaja zu einigen Aspekten ihres Werkes. Ein Interview [with S. Gressler]." *Osteuropa,* no. 7 (1990): 588–92.

———. *Portret, podarennyi drugu. Ocherki i rasskazy o Pushkine.* Leningrad: Lenizdat, 1982.

———. "Portret Zoiki na fone dvora." *Grani,* no. 168 (1993): 86–113.

———. *Stranstvie bezdomnykh. Zhizneopisanie: Semeinyi arkhiv. Starye al'bomy. Pis'ma raznykh let. Dokumenty. Vospominaniia moikh roditelei, ikh druzei. Moi sobstvennye vospominaniia.* Moscow: n.p., 1999.

———. "Vstrecha." *Grani,* no. 168 (1993): 38–41.

———. *Zhenshchina s zontikom.* Moscow: Sovremennik, 1981.

Barker, Adele. "Ginzburg, Evgeniia Semenovna." In *Dictionary of Russian Women Writers,* ed. Marina Ledkovsky, Charlotte Rosenthal, and Mary Zirin, 205–6. Westport, Conn.: Greenwood Press, 1994.

———. "Irina Grekova's 'Na ipsytaniiakh': The History of One Story." *Slavic Review* 43, no. 3 (1989): 399–412.

———. "The Persistence of Memory: Women's Prose Since the Sixties." In *A History of Women's Writing in Russia,* ed. Adele Barker and Jehanne Gheith, 277–96. Cambridge: Cambridge University Press, 2002.

Barker, Adele, and Jehanne Gheith. Introduction to *A History of Women's Writing in Russia,* ed. Adele Barker and Jehanne Gheith, 1–15. Cambridge: Cambridge University Press, 2002.

Barthes, Roland. *Writing Degree Zero.* Trans. Annette Lavers and Colin Smith. New York: Hill and Wang, 1968.

Basinskii, Pavel. "Pozabyvshie dobro? Zametki na poliakh 'novoi zhenskoi prozy.'" *Literaturnaia gazeta,* no. 7 (1991): 10.

Beaty, Jerome. "History by Indirection: The Era of Reform in *Middle-march.*" In *Middlemarch: An Authoritative Text, Backgrounds, Reviews and Criticism,* ed. Bert Hornback, 700–706. New York: Norton, 1977.

Bessmertnyi, Iurii. "Chastnaia zhizn': Stereotipnoe i individual'noe. V poiskakh novykh reshenii." In *Chelovek v krugu sem'i. Ocherki po istorii chastnoi zhizni v Evrope do nachala novogo vremeni,* ed. Iurii Bessmertnyi, 11–19. Moscow: Rossiiskii gosudarstvennyi gumani-tarnyi universitet, 1996.

Biblioteka Maksima Moshkova. http://www.lib.ru.

Blanchot, Maurice. "Everyday Speech." Trans. Susan Hanson. *Yale French Studies,* no. 73 (1987): 12–20.

Bodrova, Valentina. "The Socioeconomic Transition in Post-Soviet Rus-sia: The Impact on Women." In *Encyclopedia of Russian Women's Movements,* ed. Norma C. Noonan and Carol Nechemias, 331–32. Westport, Conn.: Greenwood Press, 2001.

Bondarenko, Vladimir. "Ocherki literaturnykh nravov: polemicheskie zametki." *Moskva,* no. 12 (1987): 179–99.

Boym, Svetlana. *Common Places: Mythologies of Everyday Life in Russia.* Cambridge, Mass.: Harvard University Press, 1994.

———. "The Poetics of Banality: Tat'iana Tolstaia, Larisa Gogoberidze, and Larisa Zvezdochetova." In *Fruits of Her Plume: Essays on Contem-porary Russian Women's Culture,* ed. Helena Goscilo, 59–83. Armonk, N.Y.: M. E. Sharpe, 1993.

Braudel, Fernand. *On History.* Trans. Sarah Matthews. Chicago: Univer-sity of Chicago Press, 1980.

Bryzgi shampanskogo. Novaia zhenskaia proza. Sbornik rasskazov. Comp. Svetlana Vasilenko. Moscow: AST/Olimp, 2002.

Bulgakov, Mikhail. *Belaia gvardiia. Teatral'nyi roman. Master i Margarita. Romany.* Moscow: Khudozhestvennaia literatura, 1973.

Bulin, Evgenii. "Otkroite knigi molodykh!" *Molodaia gvardiia,* no. 3 (1989): 237–48.

Bushin, V. "S vysoty svoego kurgana: Neskol'ko nravstvennykh nabliu-denii v sviazi s odnim literaturnym debiutom." *Nash sovremennik,* no. 8 (1987): 182–85.

Certeau, Michel de. *The Practice of Everyday Life.* Trans. Steven Rendall. Berkeley: University of California Press, 1984.

Chapple, Richard. "A Note on Viktoria Tokareva and Anton Chekhov." *Australian Slavonic and East European Studies* 6, no. 1 (1992): 115–24.

Chego khochet zhenshchina . . . Sbornik zhenskikh rasskazov. Moscow: Linor, 1993.

Cherniak, Mariia. "'Nashe vse' Aleksandra Marinina v zerkale sov-remennogo ironicheskogo detektiva." In *Tvorchestvo Aleksandry*

Marininoi kak otrazhenie sovremennoi rossiiskoi mental'nosti, ed. Elena Trofimova, 69–82. Moscow: Institut nauchnoi informatsii po ob-shchestvennym naukam, 2002.

Chisten'kaia zhizn'. Comp. Anatolii Shavkuta. Moscow: Molodaia gvardiia, 1990.

Chukovskaia, Lidiia. *Sof'ia Petrovna. Spusk pod vodu.* Moscow: Moskovskii rabochii, 1988.

Chuprinin, Sergei. "Ladies' Tango." *Current Digest of the Soviet Press* 37, no. 11 (1985): 12.

Clark, Katerina. *The Soviet Novel: History as Ritual.* Bloomington: Indiana University Press, 2000.

Cooperman, Jeannette Batz. *The Broom Closet: Secret Meanings of Domesticity in Postfeminist Novels by Louise Erdrich, Mary Gordon, Toni Morrison, Marge Piercy, Jane Smiley, and Amy Tan.* New York: Peter Lang, 1999.

Dal', Vladimir. *Tolkovyi slovar' zhivogo velikorusskogo iazyka.* 4 vols. Moscow: Russkii iazyk, 1989.

Dalton-Brown, Sally. *Voices from the Void: The Genres of Liudmila Petrushevskaia.* New York: Berghahn Books, 2001.

Dark, Oleg. "Mir mozhet byt' liuboi." *Druzhba narodov,* no. 6 (1990): 223–35.

———. "Zhenskie antinomii." *Druzhba narodov,* no. 4 (1991): 257–69.

Denisova, Nina. "Inertsiia nashikh priviazannostei." *Literaturnoe obozrenie,* no. 1 (1978): 65–67.

Dikushina, Nina. "Nevydumannaia proza (o sovremennoi dokumental'noi literature)." In *Zhanrovo-stilevye iskaniia sovremennoi sovetskoi prozy,* ed. Lidiia Poliak and Vadim Kovskii, 149–74. Moscow: Nauka, 1971.

Dobrolyubov, Nicolay. "What Is Oblomovitis?" In *Belinsky, Chernyshevsky, and Dobrolyubov: Selected Criticism,* ed. Ralph E. Matlaw, 133–75. New York: Dutton, 1962.

Dontsova, Dar'ia. *Dollary Tsaria Gorokha.* Moscow: Eksmo, 2005.

———. *Figovyi listochek ot kutiur.* Moscow: Eksmo, 2005.

———. *Mukha v samolete.* Moscow: Eksmo, 2005.

Dostoevskii, Fedor. *Besy.* 2 vols. Moscow: Moskovskii rabochii, 1993.

———. *Crime and Punishment.* Trans. Constance Garnett. New York: Dutton, 1958.

———. *Notes from Underground: An Authoritative Translation, Backgrounds, Reviews and Sources, Responses, Criticism.* Ed. and trans. Michael Katz. 2nd ed. New York: Norton, 2001.

Dunham, Vera. "The Changing Image of Women in Soviet Literature."

In *The Role and Status of Women in the Soviet Union*, ed. D. R. Brown, 60–97. New York: Columbia University Press, 1968.

———. *In Stalin's Time: Middleclass Values in Soviet Fiction*. New York: Cambridge University Press, 1976.

———. "The Strong Woman Motif." In *The Transformation of Russian Society*, ed. Cyril Black, 459–83. Cambridge, Mass.: Harvard University Press, 1960.

Efimova, Nina. "Motiv igri v proizvedeniiakh L. Petrushevskoi i T. Tolstoi." *Vestnik Moskovskogo universiteta* seriia 9, *Filologiia*, no. 3 (1998): 60–71.

El'sberg, Ia. "Byt i dukhovnaia zhizn'." *Literaturnaia gazeta*, no. 51 (1968): 4.

Emerson, Caryl. "Bakhtin and Women: A Nontopic with Immense Implications." In *Fruits of Her Plume: Essays on Contemporary Russian Women's Culture*, ed. Helena Goscilo, 3–20. Armonk, N.Y.: M. E. Sharpe, 1993.

Erofeev, Venedikt. *Moskva-Petushki s kommentariiami Eduarda Vlasova*. Moscow: Vagrius, 2000.

Erofeev, Viktor. *Russian Beauty*. Trans. Andrew Reynolds. New York: Viking, 1993.

Evtushenko, Evgenii. *Stikhotvoreniia i poemy*. 3 vols. Moscow: Sovetskaia Rossiia, 1987.

Fedotova, Valentina. "Informatsionnoe obshchestvo i knigi dlia elit i mass." In *Obshchestvo i kniga: Ot Gutenberga do Interneta*, ed. A. P. Koroleva, 222–34. Moscow: Traditsiia, 2000.

Felski. Rita. *Beyond Feminist Aesthetics: Feminist Literature and Social Change*. Cambridge, Mass.: Harvard University Press, 1989.

Field, Deborah Ann. "Communist Morality and the Meaning of Private Life in Post-Stalinist Russia, 1953–1964." Ph.D. diss., University of Michigan, 1996.

Fitzpatrick, Sheila. *The Cultural Front: Power and Culture in Revolutionary Russia*. Ithaca, N.Y.: Cornell University Press, 1992.

Foucault, Michel. *Discipline and Punish: The Birth of the Prison*. Trans. Alan Sheridan. New York: Vintage, 1995.

Fuchs, Birgit. *Natal'ja Baranskaja als Zeitzeugin des Sowjetregimes*. Munich: Otto Sagner, 2005.

Gabrielian, Nina. "Eva—eto znachit 'zhizn'.' Problema prostranstva v sovremennoi russkoi zhenskoi proze." *Voprosy literatury*, nos. 7–8 (1996): 31–71.

Gaek, Irzhi [Jiří Hajek]. "Literatura fakta." *Voprosy literatury*, no. 12 (1965): 100–110.

Ganina, Maiia. *Sozvezdie bliznetsov. Povesti, rasskazy.* Moscow: Sovetskii pisatel', 1984.

Gasiorowska, Xenia. "Two Decades of Love and Marriage in Soviet Fiction." *Russian Review* 34, no. 1 (1975): 10–21.

———. *Women in Soviet Fiction, 1917–1964.* Madison: University of Wisconsin Press, 1968.

———. "Working Mothers in Recent Soviet Fiction." *Slavic and East European Journal* 25, no. 2 (1981): 56–63.

Geller, Leonid. "'Kogda zhenshchiny smeiutsia poslednimi': Zamechaniia o zhenskom detektive." In *Tvorchestvo Aleksandry Marininoi kak otrazhenie sovremennoi rossiiskoi mental'nosti*, ed. Elena Trofimova, 54–68. Moscow: Institut nauchnoi informatsii po obshchestvennym naukam, 2002.

Gendernye issledovaniia v Rossii i SNG: kto est' kto. Spravochnik. Ed. Zoia Khotkina. Moscow: Tsentr dokumentatsii "Zhenskii arkiv," 2000.

Gessen, Elena. "Esse o zhenskoi proze." *Vremia i my*, no. 114 (1991): 203–17.

———. "Pobeg iz sotsrealizma, ili drugaia proza." *Strana i mir*, nos. 11–12 (1989): 174–81.

Gilbert, Sandra M., and Susan Gubar. *The Madwoman in the Attic: The Woman Writer and the Nineteenth-Century Literary Imagination.* 2nd ed. New Haven, Conn.: Yale Nota Bene, 2000.

Gillespie, David. "Textual Abuse: The (Mis)Treatment of the Body in Russian Literature." *Australian Slavonic and East European Studies* 12, no. 2 (1998): 1–14.

———. "Whore or Madonna: Perceptions of Women in Modern Russian Literature." *Soviet Literature*, no. 2 (1990): 143–57.

Glinka, Elena. "The Hold." Translated by Natalie Rey. In *Strange Soviet Practices*, New Russian Writing 34, 111–32. Moscow: Glas, 2004.

———. "'Kolymskii tramvai' srednei tiazhesti." *Neva*, no. 10 (1989): 111–13.

Goffman, Erving. *The Presentation of Self in Everyday Life.* Garden City, N.Y.: Doubleday, 1959.

Gorbachev, Mikhail. *Perestroika: New Thinking for Our Country and the World.* New York: Harper & Row, 1987.

Goscilo, Helena. "Coming a Long Way, Baby: A Quarter-Century of Russian Women's Fiction." *Harriman Institute Forum*, no. 1 (1992): 1–17.

———. *Dehexing Sex: Russian Womanhood During and After Glasnost.* Ann Arbor: University of Michigan Press, 1996.

———. *The Explosive World of Tatyana N. Tolstaya's Fiction.* Armonk, N.Y.: M. E. Sharpe, 1996.

————. Foreword to *The Ship of Widows* by I. Grekova, trans. Cathy Porter, vii–xxvi. Evanston, Ill.: Northwestern University Press, 1994.

————. Introduction to *Glasnost: An Anthology of Russian Literature under Gorbachev*, ed. Helena Goscilo and Byron Lindsey, xv–xlv. Ann Arbor, Mich.: Ardis, 1990.

————. Introduction to *Present Imperfect: Stories by Russian Women*, ed. Ayesha Kagal and Natal'ia Perova, 1–10. Boulder, Colo.: Westview Press, 1996.

————. "Introduction: Squaring the Circle." In *Lives in Transit: Recent Russian Women's Writing*, ed. Helena Goscilo, xi–xx. Dana Point, Calif.: Ardis, 1995.

————. "Khudozhestvennaia optika Petrushevskoi: Ni odnogo 'lucha sveta v temnom tsarstve.'" In *Russkaia literatura XX veka: napravleniia i techeniia*, ed. N. L. Leiderman, N. V. Barkovskaia, and M. N. Lipovetskii, 3:109–19. Ekaterinburg: Ural'skii gosudarstvennyi pedagogicheskii universitet, 1996.

————. "Paradigm Lost? Contemporary Women's Fiction." In *Women Writers in Russian Literature*, ed. Toby W. Clyman and Diana Greene, 205–28. Westport, Conn.: Greenwood Press, 1994.

————. "Perestroika and Post-Soviet Prose: From Dazzle to Dispersal." In *A History of Women's Writing in Russia*, ed. Adele Barker and Jehanne Gheith, 297–312. Cambridge: Cambridge University Press, 2002.

————. "Speaking Bodies: Erotic Zones Rhetoricized." In *Fruits of Her Plume: Essays on Contemporary Russian Women's Culture*, ed. Helena Goscilo, 135–63. Armonk, N.Y.: M. E. Sharpe, 1993.

————. "Vdovstvo kak zhanr i professiia à la Russe." *Preobrazhenie*, no. 3 (1995): 28–32.

————. "Women's Wards and Wardens: The Hospital in Contemporary Russian Women's Fiction." In "Soviet Women," special issue, *Canadian Women's Studies/Les Cahiers de la femme* 10, no. 4 (1989): 83–86.

Govorukhina, Iuliia. "Proza I. Grekovoi v kontekste literaturnogo protsessa 1960–80-kh godov." Ph.D. diss., Komsomol'sk-na-Amure State Pedagogical University, 2000.

Gradskova, Iuliia. *"Obychnaia" sovetskaia zhenshchina*. Moscow: Sputnik, 1999.

Grekova, I. *Kafedra*. *Novyi mir*, no. 9 (1978): 10–168.

————. *Kafedra*. *Povesti*. Moscow: Sovetskii pisatel', 1981.

————. *Na ispytaniiakh*. *Povesti i rasskazy*. Moscow: Sovetskii pisatel', 1990.

————. "Ne govoria lishnikh slov." *Literaturnaia gazeta*, no. 3 (1983): 6.

————. *Pod fonarem*. Moscow: Sovetskaia Rossiia, 1966.

————. *Porogi*. *Roman, povesti*. Moscow: Sovetskii pisatel', 1986.

————. "Rastochitel'nost' talanta." *Novyi mir*, no. 1 (1988): 252–56.

———. *The Ship of Widows*. Trans. Cathy Porter. Evanston, Ill.: North-western University Press, 1994.

———. *Svezho predanie*. Moscow: Eksmo, 2002.

———. "Zamysel: Zarozhdenie i voploshchenie." *Literaturnaia Rossiia*, no. 28 (1982): 11.

———. "Zastavit' zadumat'sia." *Literaturnaia gazeta*, no. 9 (1986): 36–37.

Grossman, Vasilii. *Life and Fate*. Trans. Robert Chandler. New York: Harper & Row, 1986.

Grothe, Anja. "Medusa, Cassandra, Medea: Re-inscribing Myth in Contemporary German and Russian Women's Writing." Ph.D. diss., City University of New York, 2000.

Groys, Boris. *The Total Art of Stalinism: Avant-Garde, Aesthetic Dictatorship, and Beyond*. Trans. Charles Rougle. Princeton, N.J.: Princeton University Press, 1992.

Hall, Stuart. "The Emergence of Cultural Studies and the Crisis of the Humanities." *October* 53 (1990): 11–23.

Harris, Jane. "Diversity of Discourse: Autobiographical Statements in Theory and Praxis." In *Autobiographical Statements in Twentieth-Century Russian Literature*, ed. Jane Harris, 3–35. Princeton, N.J.: Princeton University Press, 1990.

Healey, Dan. *Homosexual Desire in Revolutionary Russia: The Regulation of Sexual and Gender Dissent*. Chicago: University of Chicago Press, 2001.

Heldt, Barbara. "Gynoglasnost: Writing the Feminine." In *Perestroika and Soviet Women*, ed. Mary Buckley, 160–75. Cambridge: Cambridge University Press, 1992.

———. *Terrible Perfection: Women and Russian Literature*. Bloomington: Indiana University Press, 1987.

Hellebust, Rolf. *Flesh to Metal: Soviet Literature and the Alchemy of Revolution*. Ithaca, N.Y.: Cornell University Press, 2003.

Heller, Dana. "Engendering History: A Cross-Cultural Reading of Ludmila Petrushevskaya and Toni Morrison." In *Fenomen pola v kul'ture/ Sex and Gender in Culture. Materialy mezhdunarodnoi nauchnoi konferentsii. Moskva 15–17 ianvaria 1998 g.*, ed. G. A. Tkachenko, 162–70. Moscow: Rossiiskii gosudarstvennyi gumanitarnyi universitet, 1998.

Hielscher, Karla. "Gerede–Gerüchte–Klatsch: Mündlichkeit als Form weiblichen Schreibens bei Ljudmila Petruševskaja." In *Frauenbilder und Weiblichkeitsentwürfe in der russischen Frauenprosa: Materialen des wissenschaftlichen Symposiums in Erfurt*, ed. Christina Parnell, 183–91. Frankfurt: Peter Lang, 1996.

———. "Sozialpathologie oder Russische Alltagsmythen: Zur Prosa der Ljudmila Petruschewskaja." *Neue Gesellschaft*, Frankfurter Hefte 42, no. 4 (1995): 348–53.

Holmgren, Beth. "Bug Inspectors and Beauty Queens: The Problems of Translating Feminism into Russian." In *Postcommunism and the Body Politic,* ed. Ellen Berry, 15–31. New York: New York University Press, 1995.

———. "For the Good of the Cause: Russian Women's Autobiography in the Twentieth Century." In *Women Writers in Russian Literature,* ed. Toby W. Clyman and Diana Greene, 127–48. Westport, Conn.: Greenwood Press, 1994.

———. "Writing the Female Body Politic, 1945–1985." In *A History of Women's Writing in Russia,* ed. Adele Barker and Jehanne Gheith, 225–42. Cambridge: Cambridge University Press, 2002.

"How Much Housework Should a Man Do?" *Current Digest of the Soviet Press* 34, no. 46 (1982): 11–12.

Hutchings, Stephen. *Russian Modernism: The Transfiguration of the Everyday.* Cambridge: Cambridge University Press, 1997.

Huyssen, Andreas. *After the Great Divide: Modernism, Mass Culture, Postmodernism.* Bloomington: Indiana University Press, 1987.

Iavchunovskii, Iakov. *Dokumental'nye zhanry: obraz, zhanry, struktura proizvedeniia.* Saratov: Izdatel'stvo Saratovskogo universiteta, 1974.

Iser, Wolfgang. *The Act of Reading.* Baltimore, Md.: Johns Hopkins University Press, 1978.

Iukina, E. "Ispytaniia." *Literaturnoe obozrenie,* no. 4 (1986): 48–50.

Ivanova, Natal'ia. "Bakhtin's Concept of the Grotesque and the Art of Petrushevskaia and Tolstaia." Trans. Helena Goscilo. In *Fruits of Her Plume: Essays on Contemporary Russian Women's Culture,* ed. Helena Goscilo, 21–31. Armonk, N.Y.: M. E. Sharpe, 1993.

———. "Grind the *Peacack* into *Burkers:* On Tatyana Tolstaya's *The Slynx.*" Trans. Liv Bliss. *Russian Studies in Literature* 39, no. 4 (2003): 72–77.

Jakobson, Roman. "On a Generation That Squandered Its Poets." In *Language in Literature,* ed. Krystyna Pomorska and Stephen Rudy, 273–300. Cambridge, Mass.: Belknap Press, 1987.

Jonscher, Beate. "Zu Tendenzen der Frauenliteratur in den 6oer und 7oer Jahren." In *Frauenbilder und Weiblichkeitsentwürfe in der russischen Frauenprosa: Materialen wissenschaftlichen Symposiums in Erfurt,* ed. Christina Parnell, 159–69. Frankfurt: Peter Lang, 1996.

Kabo, Liubov'. *Ne veselo byt' meshchaninom!* Moscow: Izdatel'stvo politicheskoi literatury, 1965.

Kashkarova, Elena. "Zhenskaia tema v proze 6o-kh godov: Natal'ia Baranskaia kak zerkalo russkogo feminizma." *Vse liudi sestry,* no. 5 (1996) 57–69.

Katz, Monika. "Ljudmila Petruševskajas Erzählung "Svoi krug." In *Russland aus der Feder seiner Frauen. Zum femininen Diskurs in der russichen Literatur. Materialen des am 21/22 Mai 1992 im Fachbereich Slavistik der Universität Potsdam durchgeführten Kolloquiums,* ed. Frank Göpfert, 95–101. Munich: Otto Sagner, 1992.

———. "The Other Woman: Character Portrayal and the Narrative Voice in the Short Stories of Liudmila Petrushevskaia." Trans. Nina Draganić. In *Women and Russian Culture: Projections and Self-Perceptions,* ed. Rosalind Marsh, 188–97. New York: Berghahn Books, 1998.

Kay, Susan. "A Woman's Work." *Irish Slavonic Studies,* no. 8 (1987): 115–26.

Kazarina, Tat'iana. "Bednye rodstvenniki." *Preobrazhenie,* no. 4 (1996): 169–71.

Kelly, Catriona. *A History of Russian Women's Writing, 1820–1992.* New York: Oxford University Press, 1994.

———. "Missing Links: Russian Women Writers as Critics of Women Writers." In *Russian Writers on Russian Writers,* ed. Faith Wigzell, 67–79. Oxford: Berg, 1994.

Kharkhordin, Oleg. "Reveal and Dissimulate: A Genealogy of Private Life in Soviet Russia." In *Public and Private in Thought and Practice: Perspectives on a Grand Dichotomy,* ed. Jeff Weintraub and Krishan Kumar, 333–63. Chicago: University of Chicago Press, 1997.

Klado, N. "Prokrustovo lozhe byta." *Literaturnaia gazeta,* no. 19 (1976): 4.

Klein, Kathleen. *The Woman Detective: Gender and Genre.* Urbana: University of Illinois Press, 1995.

Klimenkova, Tat'iana. "Perestroika kak gendernaia problema." In *Gender Restructuring in Russian Studies,* Slavica Tamperensia 11, ed. Marianne Liljeström, Eila Mäntysaari, and Arya Rosenholm, 155–62. Tampere: [University of Tampere], 1993.

Knizhnye serii izdatel'stvo "Vagrius." http://www.vagrius.ru/series/.

Kolchevska, Natasha. "Voznesenskaia, Iuliia Nikolaevna." In *Encyclopedia of Russian Women's Movements,* ed. Norma C. Noonan and Carol Nechemias, 177–79. Westport, Conn.: Greenwood Press, 2001.

———. "Woman and Russia." In *Encyclopedia of Russian Women's Movements,* ed. Norma C. Noonan and Carol Nechemias, 180–82. Westport, Conn.: Greenwood Press, 2001.

Kon, Igor. *The Sexual Revolution in Russia: From the Age of the Czars to Today.* New York: Free Press, 1995.

Korobov, Vladimir. "So Many Books, Yet So Few, or the New Publishing Crisis." Ed. Deming Brown. Trans. Marian Schwartz. *Russian Social Science Review* 38, no. 1 (1997): 82–89.

Kostiukov, Leonid. "Iskliuchitel'naia mera." *Literaturnaia gazeta,* no. 11 (1996): 4.

Kostiukova, Ol'ga. "Detektiv. Zhenskaia dolia." *Itogi,* no. 24 (2001): 54–57.

Kuralekh, A. "Byt i bytie v proze Liudmily Petrushevskoi." *Literaturnoe obozrenie,* no. 5 (1993): 63–67.

Kuz'michev, Ivan. "Marginal'nye zametki o sovremennoi russkoi literature." *Nizhnii Novgorod,* no. 12 (1998): 223–36.

Kuznetsov, M. "Gorizont romana." In *Zhanrovo-stilevye iskaniia sovremennoi sovetskoi prozy,* ed. Lidiia Poliak and Vadim Kovskii, 7–42. Moscow: Nauka, 1971.

Lahusen, Thomas. "'Leaving Paradise' and Perestroika: 'A Week Like Any Other' and 'Memorial Day' by Natal'ia Baranskaia." In *Fruits of Her Plume: Essays on Contemporary Russian Women's Culture,* ed. Helena Goscilo, 205–24. Armonk, N.Y.: M. E. Sharpe, 1993.

Lapidus, Gail. "Sexual Equality in Soviet Policy: A Developmental Perspective." In *Women in Russia,* ed. Dorothy Atkinson, Alexander Dallin, and Gail Lapidus, 115–38. Stanford, Calif.: Stanford University Press, 1977.

Lefebvre, Henri. *Everyday Life in the Modern World.* Trans. Sacha Rabinowitz. New York: Harper & Row, 1971.

Lesin, Evgenii. "Sto let liubvi." http://www.newsru.com.

Liljeström, Marianne. "The Soviet Gender System: The Ideological Construction of Femininity and Masculinity in the 1970s." In *Gender Restructuring in Russian Studies,* Slavica Tamperensia 11, ed. Marianne Liljeström, Eila Mäntysaari, and Arya Rosenholm, 163–74. Tampere: [University of Tampere], 1993.

Lipovetsky, Mark. "Strategies of Wastefulness, or the Metamorphoses of *Chernukha.*" *Russian Studies in Literature* 38, no. 2 (2002): 59–84.

———. "Tragediia i malo li chto eshche." *Novyi mir,* no. 10 (1994): 229–32.

Lobanov, M. "Vnutrennyi i vneshnyi chelovek." *Molodaia gvardiia,* no. 5 (1966): 286–302.

Lotman, Iurii. *Besedy o russkoi kul'ture: byt i traditsii russkogo dvorianstva (XVIII—nachalo XIX veka).* St. Petersburg: Iskusstvo-SPB, 1994.

Lotman, Iurii, and Boris Uspenskii. "Binary Models in the Dynamics of Russian Culture (to the End of the Eighteenth Century)." In *The Semiotics of Russian Cultural History: Essays by Iurii M. Lotman, Lidiia Ia. Ginsburg, Boris A. Uspenskii,* ed. Alexander Nakhimovsky and Alice Nakhimovsky, 30–66. Ithaca, N.Y.: Cornell University Press, 1985.

Lovell, Stephen. *The Russian Reading Revolution: Print Culture in the Soviet and Post-Soviet Eras.* New York: St. Martin's Press, 2000.

Lukács, Georg. *Realism in Our Time: Literature and the Class Struggle.* Trans. George Steiner. New York: Harper & Row, 1964.

———. *The Theory of the Novel.* Trans. Anna Bostock. Cambridge, Mass.: MIT Press, 1993.

Lysenko, V. "Filosofiia anekdota?" *Literaturnoe obozrenie,* no. 8 (1980): 103–4.

Madison, Bernice. "Social Services for Women: Problems and Priorities." In *Women in Russia,* ed. Dorothy Atkinson, Alexander Dallin, and Gail Lapidus, 307–32. Stanford, Calif.: Stanford University Press, 1977.

Maiakovskii, Vladimir. *Polnoe sobranie sochinenii v 13 tomakh.* 13 vols. Moscow: Khudozhestvennaia literatura, 1961.

Mamonova, Tatyana, ed. *Women and Russia: Feminist Writings from the Soviet Union.* Trans. Rebecca Park and Catherine A. Fitzgerald. Boston: Beacon Press, 1984.

Mariia. Literaturnyi al'manakh. Vol. 1. Comp. Galina Skvortsova. Petrozavodsk: Kareliia, 1990.

Mariia. Literaturnyi al'manakh. Vol. 2. Comp. Galina Skvortsova. Petrozavodsk: Izdatel'stvo Petrozavodskogo universiteta, 1995.

Marinina, Aleksandra. *Chernyi spisok. Posmertnyi obraz. Romany.* Moscow: Eksmo, 2005.

Marsh, Rosalind. "Introduction: New Perspectives on Women and Gender in Russian Literature." In *Gender and Russian Literature,* ed. and trans. Rosalind Marsh, 1–37. Cambridge: Cambridge University Press, 1996.

Marx, Karl. *Capital: A Critique of Political Economy.* 3 vols. Trans. Ben Fowkes. New York: Vintage, 1977.

Matskovsky, Mikhail, and Tatyana Gurko. "Scholars Favor Marriages in Which Couples Share Housework, Child Rearing. (As Opposed to Traditional Male-Dominated Marriage and the 'Individualistic' Type, in Which Careers Come First and Children Last)." *Current Digest of the Soviet Press* 37, no. 5 (1984): 5–6.

Malygina, Nina. "Zdes' i seichas: poetika ischeznoveniia." *Oktiabr',* no. 9 (2000): 152–59.

McGuigan, Jim. *Cultural Populism.* London: Routledge, 1993.

McLaughlin, Sigrid. Introduction to *The Image of Women in Contemporary Soviet Fiction: Selected Short Stories from the USSR,* ed. and trans. Sigrid McLaughlin, 1–17. New York: St. Martin's Press, 1989.

———. "Lyudmila Petrushevskaya: Nets and Traps (1974)." In *The Image of Women in Contemporary Soviet Fiction: Selected Short Stories from the USSR,* ed. and trans. Sigrid McLaughlin, 98–100. New York: St. Martin's Press, 1989.

McReynolds, Louise, and Joan Neuberger. Introduction to *Imitations of Life: Two Centuries of Melodrama in Russia,* ed. Louise McReynolds and Joan Neuberger, 1–24. Durham, N.C.: Duke University Press, 2002.

Medvedeva, N, "Povestvovanie i geroi v rasskazakh T. Tolstoi." In *Problemy tipologii russkoi literatury XX veka: Mezhvuzovskii sbornik nauchnikh trudov,* ed. N. E. Vasil'eva et al., 137–47. Perm: Permskii gosudarstvennyi universitet, 1991.

Medvedeva, Nataliia. *A u nikh byla strast'.* Moscow: Vagrius, 1997.

Mela, Elen [Hélène Melat]. "'Rozovoe i chernoe': Ob odnom romane Aleksandry Marininoi." In *Tvorchestvo Aleksandry Marininoi kak otrazhenie sovremennoi rossiiskoi mental'nosti,* ed. Elena Trofimova, 153–66. Moscow: Institut nauchnoi informatsii po obshchestvennym naukam, 2002.

Meleshko, Tat'iana. *Sovremennaia otechestvennaia zhenskaia proza: Problemy poetiki v gendernom aspekte. Uchebnoe posobie po spetskursu.* Kemerovo: Kemerovskii gosudarstvennyi universitet, 2001.

Menke, Elisabeth. *Die Kultur der Weiblichkeit in der Prosa Irina Grekovas.* Munich: Otto Sagner, 1988.

Messer-Davidow, Ellen. *Disciplining Feminism: From Social Activism to Academic Discourse.* Durham, N.C.: Duke University Press, 2002.

Mil'man, Niusia. *Chitaia Petrushevskuiu. Vzgliad iz-za okeana.* St. Petersburg: Rosprint, 1997.

Morozova, Tat'iana. "Posle dolgogo vozderzhaniia." *Druzhba narodov,* no. 9 (1997): 177–84.

Morozovskii, Mikhail. "Rynok khudozhestvennoi literatury." *Knizhnoe delo,* no. 6 (1994): 2–11.

Morrison, Toni. *Beloved.* New York: Knopf, 1987.

Morson, Gary Saul. *Hidden in Plain View: Narrative and Creative Potentials in* War and Peace. Stanford, Calif.: Stanford University Press, 1987.

———. "Prosaics and *Anna Karenina.*" *Tolstoy Studies Journal,* no. 1 (1988): 1–12.

Morson, Gary Saul, and Caryl Emerson. *Mikhail Bakhtin: Creation of a Prosaics.* Stanford, Calif.: Stanford University Press, 1990.

Murav'eva, O. "Vstrecha s poetom." *Neva,* no. 5 (1984): 164–65.

Nabokov, Vladimir. "Philistines and Philistinism." In *Lectures on Russian Literature,* ed. Fredson Bowers, 309–14. New York: Harcourt Brace Jovanovich, 1981.

NaStoiashchaia literatura: zhenskii rod. http://www.litwomen.ru/letter .html?pg=2.

Naumova, N. "The Modern Heroine." *Soviet Studies in Literature,* no. 15 (1979): 80–102.

Nepomniashchii, V. "Izbrannitsa poeta." *Nedelia,* no. 10 (1978): 10–11.

Nepomnyashchy, Catharine. "Markets, Mirrors, and Mayhem: Aleksandra Marinina and the Rise of the New Russian *Detektiv.*" In

Consuming Russia: Popular Culture, Sex, and Society Since Gorbachev,
ed. Adele Barker, 161–91. Durham, N.C.: Duke University Press, 1999.
Nevzgliadova, E. "Siuzhet dlia nebol'shego rasskaza." *Novyi mir,* no. 4
(1988): 256–60.
Nitochkina, A. "Tat'iana Tolstaia: V bol'sheviki by ne poshla . . ." *Sto-
litsa,* no. 33 (1991): 12.
Novikova, O. and V. Novikov. "Chestnaia igra." *Literaturnoe obozrenie,*
no. 11 (1979): 55–57.
"O povesti N. Baranskoi 'Tsvet temnogo medu.'" *Sibir',* no. 2 (1979):
98–99.
Orlova, Anna. "Ulitskaia razliubila liudei." *Komsomol'skaia pravda,* no.
74 (2004): 12.
Ostrovsky, Nikolai. *How the Steel was Tempered.* Trans. R. Profokieva.
Moscow: Progress, 1964.
Ovenasian, E. "Raspada venok." *Literaturnaia Rossiia,* no. 36 (1991):
22–23.
———. "Tvortsy raspada (tupiki i anomalii 'drugoi prozy')." *Molodaia
gvardiia,* no. 3 (1992): 249–62.
Palei, Marina. "The Bloody Women's Ward." Trans. Arch Tait. In
Women's View, New Russian Writing 3, ed. Natasha Perova and An-
drew Bromfield, 74–91. Moscow: Glas, 1992.
Panova, Vera. *Povesti.* Leningrad: Sovetskii pisatel', 1969.
Parts, Lyudmila. "Down the Intertextual Lane: Petrushevskaia, Che-
khov, Tolstoy." *Russian Review* 64, no. 1 (2005): 77–89.
Perova, Natasha, Arch Tait, and Joanne Turnbull, eds. *Nine of Russia's
Foremost Women Writers.* New Russian Writing 30. Moscow: Glas,
2003.
Perova, Natasha, and Arch Tait, eds. *A Will and a Way.* New Russian
Writing 13. Moscow: Glas, 1996.
Perova, Natasha, and Andrew Bromfield, eds. *Women's View.* New Rus-
sian Writing 3. Moscow: Glas, 1992.
Peterson, Nadya. "Irina Grekova (Elena Sergeevna Venttsel')." In *Dic-
tionary of Literary Biography,* vol. 302, *Russian Prose Writers after World
War II,* ed. Christine Rydel, 115–19. Detroit, Mich.: Thomson Gale,
2004.
Petrushevskaia, Liudmila. *Boginia Parka. Povesti i rasskazy.* Moscow:
Eksmo, 2006.
———. *Deviatyi tom.* Moscow: Eksmo, 2003.
———. *Dom devushek. Povesti i rasskazy.* Moscow: Vagrius, 1998.
———. *Gde ia byla. Rasskazy iz inoi real'nosti.* Moscow: Vagrius, 2002.
———. "Interview with Lyudmila Petrushevskaya." In *Voices of Russian*

Literature: Interviews with Ten Contemporary Russian Writers, ed. Sally Laird, 23–48. Oxford: Oxford University Press, 1999.

———. *Izmenennoe vremia. Rasskazy i p'esy*. Moscow: Eksmo, 2005.

———. "Most Vaterloo. Rasskazy. 'Vasen'ki.' 'Most Vaterloo.' 'Ustroit' zhizn'.' 'Teshcha Edipa.' 'Niura Prekrasnaia.' 'Mil'grom.' 'O, schast'e.'" *Novyi mir*, no. 3 (1995): 7–26.

———. *Naidi menia, son. Rasskazy*. Moscow: Vagrius, 2000.

———. *Nomer Odin, ili V sadakh drugikh vozmozhnostei. Roman*. Moscow: Eksmo, 2006.

———. "Pisha za onova, koeto obicham" [interview by Rada Balareva]. *Literaturen front*, no. 38 (1988): 7.

———. *The Time: Night*. Trans. Sally Laird. Evanston, Ill.: Northwestern University Press, 2000.

Piskunova, S., and V. Piskunov. "Uroki zazerkal'ia." *Oktiabr'*, no. 8 (1988): 188–98.

Pollard, Alan. "The Russian Intelligentsia: The Mind of Russia." *California Slavic Papers*, no. 3 (1964): 1–32.

Pomerantsev, Vladimir. "Ob iskrennosti v literature." *Novyi mir*, no. 12 (1953): 218–45.

"Priniaty v Soiuz pisatelei." *Literaturnaia Rossiia*, no. 22 (1977): 11

Prokhanov, Aleksandr. "Studenty Literaturnogo instituta I. Agafanov, S. Kaznacheev, A. Talybov i rukovoditel' seminara A. Prokhanov o rasskaze Svetlany Vasilenko 'Za saigakami.'" *Literaturnaia ucheba*, no. 5 (1982): 21–23.

Prokhorov, Alexander. "Inherited Discourse: Soviet Tropes in Thaw Culture." Ph.D. diss., University of Pittsburgh, 2002.

Radway, Janice. "Reading the Romance." In *The Communication Theory Reader*, ed. Paul Cobley, 448–65. London: Routledge, 1996.

Rasputin, Valentin. "Cherchez la femme." *Nash sovremennik*, no. 3 (1990): 168–72.

Reid, Susan. "Cold War in the Kitchen: Gender and the De-Stalinization of Consumer Taste in the Soviet Union under Khrushchev." *Slavic Review* 61, no. 2 (2002): 211–52.

———. "Gender Relations in the Visual Culture of the Khrushchev Thaw." In *Fenomen pola v kul'ture/Sex and Gender in Culture. Materialy mezhdunarodnoi nauchnoi konferentsii. Moskva 15–17 ianvaria 1998 g.*, ed. G. A. Tkachenko, 93–106. Moscow: Rossiiskii gosudarstvennyi gumanitarnyi universitet, 1998.

———. "Women in the Home." In *Women in the Khrushchev Era*, ed. Melanie Ilič, Susan Reid, and Lynne Attwood, 149–76. Hampshire, Engl.: Palgrave, 2004.

Remizova, Mariia. "Teoriia katastrof, ili neskol'ko slov v zashchitu nochi." *Literaturnaia gazeta*, no. 11 (1996): 4.

Rimashevskaia, Natalia. "The New Women's Studies." In *Perestroika and Soviet Women*, ed. Mary Buckley, 118–22. Cambridge: Cambridge University Press, 1992.

Rivkin-Fish, Michele. "From 'Demographic Crisis' to 'Dying Nation': The Politics of Language and Reproduction in Russia." In *Gender and National Identity in Twentieth-Century Russian Culture*, ed. Helena Goscilo and Andrea Lanoux, 151–73. Dekalb: Northern Illinois University Press, 2006.

Rovenskaia, Tat'iana. "Arkhetip doma v novoi zhenskoi proze, ili Kommunal'noe zhitie i kommunal'nye tela." *Inoi vzgliad*, no. 3 (2001): 24–26.

———. "K voprosu o periodizatsii istorii russkoi zhenskoi literatury 1980-kh—1990-kh godov XX veka." *Zhenshchiny v istorii: vozmozhnost' byt' uvidennymi* 2 (2002): 290–310.

———. "Vinovata li ia . . . ? Ili fenomen gendernoi viny (na materiale zhenskoi prozy 80-kh—nachalo 90-kh godov)." *Gendernye issledovaniia*, no. 3 (1999): 214–24.

———. "Zhenskaia proza serediny 1980-kh—nachala 1990-kh godov. (Problematika, mental'nost', identifikatsiia)." Ph.D. diss., Moscow State University, 2000.

Rozanov, Vladimir. "Proza s zapakhom." *Molodaia gvardiia*, no. 1 (1968): 293–95.

Ryl'nikova, N. A., ed. *Ne pomniashchaia zla*. Comp. Larisa Vaneeva. Moscow: Moskovskii rabochii, 1990.

Sadur, Nina. "Worm-Eaten Sonny." Trans. Wendi Fornoff. In *Lives in Transit: A Collection of Recent Russian Women's Writing*, ed. Helena Goscilo, 203–4. Dana Point, Calif.: Ardis, 1995.

Savateev, Viacheslav. "Bogatstvo dushi i iasnosti tseli. O nekotorykh chertakh geroia sovremennoi prozy." *Oktiabr'*, no. 10 (1982): 174–78.

Savkina, Irina. "'Gliazhus'' v tebia, kak v zerkalo . . .' Tvorchestvo Aleksandry Marininoi v sovremennoi russkoi kritike: gendernyi aspekt." In *Tvorchestvo Aleksandry Marininoi kak otrazhenie sovremennoi rossiiskoi mental'nosti*, ed. Elena Trofimova, 1–8. Moscow: Institut nauchnoi informatsii po obshchestvennym naukam, 2002.

———. "Kto i kak pishet istoriiu russkoi zhenskoi literatury." *Novoe literaturnoe obozrenie*, no. 2 (1997): 359–72.

———. "Zhenskaia proza—bez kavychek," *Literaturnaia ucheba*, no. 3 (1997): 71–75.

Scherbakova, Galina. "The Three Loves of Masha Peredreeva." Trans.

Rachel Osorio. In *Women's View,* New Russian Writing 3, ed. Natasha Perova and Andrew Bromfield, 94–147. Moscow: Glas, 1992.

Schönle, Andreas, ed. *Lotman and Cultural Studies: Encounters and Extensions.* Madison: University of Wisconsin Press, 2006.

Scott, Joan. *Gender and the Politics of History.* New York: Columbia University Press, 1988.

Sedgwick, Eve. *Epistemology of the Closet.* Berkeley: University of California Press, 1990.

Segal, Boris. *The Drunken Society: Alcohol Abuse and Alcoholism in the Soviet Union: A Comparative Study.* New York: Hippocrene Books, 1990.

Shcheglova, Evgeniia. "V svoem krugu. Polemicheskie zametki o 'zhurnal'noi proze.'" *Literaturnoe obozrenie,* no. 3 (1990): 19–26.

Shneidman, N. N. *Soviet Literature in the 1970s: Artistic Diversity and Ideological Conformity.* Toronto: University of Toronto Press, 1979.

Shokhina, V., et al. "Nedoskazannoe. K itogam lit. goda." *Znamia,* no. 1 (1993): 192–204.

Showalter, Elaine. "The Feminist Critical Revolution." In *The New Feminist Criticism: Essays on Women, Literature, and Theory,* ed. Elaine Showalter, 3–17. New York: Pantheon Books, 1985.

———. *A Literature of Their Own: British Women Novelists from Brontë to Lessing.* Princeton, N.J.: Princeton University Press, 1977.

Sinyavsky, Andrei. *Soviet Civilization: A Cultural History.* Trans. Joanne Turnbull with Nikolai Formozov. New York: Arcade, 1990.

Skomp, Elizabeth. "Russian Women's Publishing at the Beginning of the 1990s: The Case of the New Amazons." In "Russian Women and Publishing," special issue, *Soviet and Post-Soviet Review* 1 (2006): 85–98.

Skvortsov, L. I. "V zhanre damskoi povesti." *Russkaia rech',* no. 1 (1968): 26–35.

Skvortsova, Galina, ed. *Zhena, kotoraia umela letat': proza russkikh i finskikh pisatel'nits.* Petrozavodsk: INKA, 1993.

Skvortsova-Akbulatova, G., ed. *Russkaia dusha. Sbornik poezii i prozy sovremennykh pisatel'nits russkoi provintsii.* Frauenliteraturgeschichte: Texte und Materialen zur russischen Frauenliteratur 3. Wilhelmshorst, Ger.: F. K. Göpfert, 1995.

Slavnikova, Ol'ga. "Petrushevskaia and Emptiness." Trans. Vladimir Talmy. *Russian Studies in Literature* 37, no. 2 (2001): 57–71.

———. "Zhenskii pocherk. A takzhe portret." *Vremia MN,* no. 124 (2000): 7.

Slezkine, Yuri. "The USSR as a Communal Apartment, or How a Socialist State Promoted Ethnic Particularism." *Slavic Review* 53, no. 2 (1994): 414–52.

Sliusareva, Irina. "Opravdanie zhiteiskogo: Irina Sliusareva predstav-
    liaet 'novuiu zhenskuiu prozu.'" *Znamia*, no. 11 (1991): 238–40.
Smith, Alexandra. "Carnivalising the Canon: The Grotesque and the
    Subversive in Contemporary Russian Women's Prose (Petrushev-
    skaia, Sadur, Tolstaia, Narbikova)." In *Russian Literature in Transition*,
    ed. Ian Lilly and Henriette Mondry, 35–58. Nottingham, Engl.: Astra,
    1999.
Smith, Karen. "Recollecting Wondrous Moments: Father Pushkin,
    Mother Russia, and Intertextual Memory in Tatyana Tolstaya's
    'Night' and 'Limpopo.'" *Studies in Twentieth and Twenty-first Century
    Literature* 28, no. 2 (2004): 478–506.
Solzhenitsyn, Aleksandr. *Cancer Ward*. Trans. Rebecca Frank. New York:
    Dial, 1968.
———. *The First Circle*. Trans. Thomas P. Whitney. New York: Harper &
    Row, 1968.
———. *Na kraiakh. Rasskazy i povest'*. Moscow: Vagrius, 2000.
Sophocles. *Oedipus Rex*. Trans. Stephen Berg and Diskin Clay. New
    York: Oxford University Press, 1978.
Sperling, Valerie. *Organizing Women in Contemporary Russia: Engender-
    ing Transition*. Cambridge: Cambridge University Press, 1999.
Spivak, P. "V sne i naiavu . . ." *Oktiabr'*, no. 2 (1988): 201–3.
Startseva, Natal'ia. "Damy s sobakami i bez." *Literaturnaia gazeta*, no. 30
    (1988): 4.
Stepanenko, L. V., and A. V. Fomenko, eds. *Zhenskaia logika*. Moscow:
    Sovremennik, 1989.
Stepanov, Vladimir. "Lzheromantika obshchikh mest." *Molodaia gvar-
    diia*, no. 11 (1973): 303–7.
Stites, Richard. *Revolutionary Dreams: Utopian Vision and Experimental
    Life in the Russian Revolution*. New York: Oxford University Press,
    1989.
Strelianyi, Anatolii. *Zhenskie pis'ma*. Moscow: Sovetskaia Rossiia, 1981.
Sutcliffe, Benjamin. "Documenting Women's Voices in Perestroika
    Gulag Narratives." *Toronto Slavic Quarterly* 3 (2003). http://www
    .utoronto.ca/tsq/03/sutcliffe.shtml.
———. "Publishing the Russian Soul? Women's Provincial Literary An-
    thologies, 1990–1995." In "Russian Women and Publishing," special
    issue, *Soviet and Post-Soviet Review* 1 (2006): 99–113.
Taiganova, Tat'iana. "Roman v rubishche: O romane Svetlany Vasi-
    lenko 'Durochka.'" *Druzhba narodov*, no. 6 (2000): 184–94.
Tarasova, Yelena. "She Who Bears No Ill." In *Half a Revolution: Contem-
    porary Fiction by Russian Women*, ed. and trans. Masha Gessen, 96–
    126. Pittsburgh, Pa.: Cleis, 1995.

Tarkhova, Lina. "Kto vernet silu sil'nomu polu?" *Sputnik,* no. 3 (1987): 122–26.

Tat'ianina, Natal'ia. "Ne tol'ko Kamenskaia." In Aleksandra Marinina, *Chernyi spisok. Posmertnyi obraz. Romany,* 5–8. Moscow: Eksmo, 2005.

Thomasy, Molly. "Rewriting Pushkin's Death: Tat'iana Tolstaia's 'Siuzhet' in Literary and Cultural Context." Paper presented at the National Convention of the American Association for the Advancement of Slavic Studies, New Orleans, November 16, 2007.

Thompson, Edward P. *The Making of the English Working Class.* New York: Vintage, 1963.

Timina, Svetlana. "Ritmy vechnosti. Roman Liudmily Ulitskoi *Medeia i ee deti.*" In *Perom i prelest'iu: Zhenshchiny v panteone russkoi literatury. Sbornik statei,* ed. Wanda Laszczak and Daria Ambroziak, 146–60. Opole, Pol.: Wydawca Dariusz Karbowiak, 1999.

Tokareva, Viktoriia. *Banketnyi zal.* Moscow: AST, 2001.

——. *Malo li chto byvaet. . . .* Moscow: AST, 1999.

——. *Vse normal'no, vse khorosho. . . .* Moscow: AST, 2002.

Toker, Leona. *Return from the Archipelago: Narratives of Gulag Survivors.* Bloomington: Indiana University Press, 2000.

Tolstaia, Tat'iana. *Den'. Lichnoe.* Moscow: Eksmo, 2004.

——. *Kys'.* Moscow: Eksmo, 2005.

——. "Miumziki i Nostradamus (Interv'iu gazete *Moskovskie novosti*)." In *Kys',* 331–37. Moscow: Eksmo, 2005.

——. "Nepal'tsy i miumziki: Interv'iu zhurnalu 'Afisha.'" In *Kys'.* Moscow: Eksmo, 2005.

——. *On the Golden Porch.* Trans. Antonina Bouis. New York: Knopf, 1989.

——. *Reka Okkervil'. Sbornik rasskazov.* Moscow: Podkova, 2004.

——. *Sleepwalker in a Fog.* Trans. Jamey Gambrell. New York: Knopf, 1992.

Tolstoi, Lev. *Anna Karenina.* Moscow: AST, 1998.

——. *War and Peace.* Trans. Rosemary Edmonds. Harmondsworth, Engl.: Penguin, 1978.

Trifonov, Iurii. *"Another Life" and "The House on the Embankment."* Trans. Michael Glenny. Evanston, Ill.: Northwestern University Press, 1999.

——. "'V kratkom—beskonechnoe.' Besedu vel A. Bocharov." *Voprosy literatury,* no. 8 (1974): 171–95.

——. "Vybirat', reshat'sia, zhertvovat'." *Voprosy literatury,* no. 2 (1972): 62–65.

Trofimova, Elena. "Elena Glinka." Trans. Jill Roese. In *Dictionary of Russian Women Writers,* ed. Marina Ledkovsky, Charlotte Rosenthal, and Mary Zirin, 215–16. Westport, Conn.: Greenwood Press, 1994.

———. "Fenomen detektivnykh romanov Aleksandry Marininoi v kul'ture sovremennoi Rossii." In *Tvorchestvo Aleksandry Marininoi kak otrazhenie sovremennoi rossiiskoi mental'nosti*, ed. Elena Trofimova, 19–35. Moscow: Institut nauchnoi informatsii po obshchestvennym naukam, 2002.

———. "Zhenskaia literatura i knigoizdanie v sovremennoi Rossii." *Obshchestvennye nauki i sovremennost'*, no. 5 (1998): 147–56.

Tsziiun, Liui. "Poetiko-filosofskoe svoebrazie rasskazov Tat'iany Tolstoi (na materiale sbornika *Noch'*)." Ph.D. diss., Tambov State Technical University, 2005.

Tynianov, Iurii. *Arkhaisty i novatory.* Munich: Wilhelm Fink, 1967.

Ulitskaia, Liudmila. *Bednye, zlye, liubimye. Povesti i rasskazy.* Moscow: Eksmo, 2002.

———. *Daniel' Shtain, perevodchik.* Moscow: Eksmo, 2006.

———. "Imenno eto propovedoval Iiusus." Interview with Vladimir Volodarskii, December 8, 2007. http://www.bigbook.ru/smi/detail.php?ID=3825 (last accessed August 3, 2008).

———. *Iskrenne Vash Shurik.* Moscow: Eksmo, 2004.

———. *Istorii pro zverei i liudei.* Moscow: Eksmo, 2006.

———. *Kazus Kukotskogo.* Moscow: Eksmo, 2002.

———. *Liudi nashego tsaria.* Moscow: Eksmo, 2005.

———. "Liudmila Ulitskaia: I Accept Everything That Is Given." Interview by Anastasiia Gosteva. *Russian Studies in Literature* 38, no. 2 (2002): 72–93.

———. "'Liudmila Ulitskaia: Ne mogli by vyzhit', esli by . . .' Besedu vel Vladimir Prikhod'ko." *Moskovskaia pravda*, no. 17 (2001): 6.

———. *Medea and Her Children.* Trans. Arch Tait. New York: Schocken Books, 2002.

———. *Medeia i ee deti. Povesti.* Moscow: Vagrius, 1997.

———. *Medeia i ee deti. Roman.* Moscow: Eksmo, 2002.

———. *Moi vnuk Veniamin.* In *Russkoe varen'e i drugoe.* Moscow: Eksmo, 2008.

———. *Skvoznaia liniia. Povest', rasskazy.* Moscow: Eksmo, 2002.

———. *Sonechka: A Novella and Stories.* Trans. Arch Tait. New York: Schocken Books, 2005.

———. "'Tvorets znal, chto on delal . . .' Besedu vela Inessa Tsiporkina." *Knizhnoe obozrenie*, no. 33 (2000): 5.

———. *Veselye pokhorony.* Moscow: Eksmo, 2006.

Ustinova, Tat'iana. *Zakon obratnogo volshebstva.* Moscow: Eksmo, 2005.

Utekhin, Il'ia. *Ocherki kommunal'nogo byta.* Moscow: OGI, 2001.

Vareikis, I., and I. Zelenskii. *Natsional'no-gosudarstvennoe razmezhevanie Srednei Azii.* Tashkent: Sredne-Aziatskoe gosudarstvennoe izdatel'stvo, 1924.

Vasilenko, Svetlana. *Durochka*. Moscow: Vagrius, 2000.

———. "'Novye amazonki.' Ob istorii pervoi literaturnoi zhenskoi pisatel'skoi gruppy. Postsovetskoe vremia." In *Zhenshchina: Svoboda slova i svoboda tvorchestva. Sbornik statei*, ed. Valentina Kizilo, comp. Svetlana Vasilenko, 80–89. Moscow: Eslan, 2001.

———. "Otvet na dva voprosa." *Znamia*, no. 5 (1995): 187–88.

———. *Shamara*. In *Shamara and Other Stories*, ed. Helena Goscilo, trans. Daria Kirjanov and Benjamin Sutcliffe, 3–58. Evanston, Ill.: Northwestern University Press, 1999.

Vasil'eva, Larisa. "Zhenshchina. Zhizn'. Literatura." *Literaturnaia gazeta*, no. 51 (1989): 7.

Vasilevskii, Andrei. "Nochi kholodny." *Druzhba narodov*, no. 7 (1988): 256–58.

Vavilon. http://www.vavilon.ru.

Vilenskii, Semen, ed. *Dodnes' tiagoteet*. Vol. 1, *Zapiski vashei sovremennitsy*. Moscow: Sovetskii pisatel', 1989.

Vishevsky, Anatoly. *Soviet Literary Culture in the 1970s: The Politics of Irony*. Gainesville: University Press of Florida, 1993.

Viren, Georgii. "Takaia liubov'." *Oktiabr'*, no. 3 (1989): 100–106.

Vladimirova, I. "Ne tol'ko byt." *Neva*, no. 8 (1981): 181–82.

———. "Svoi golos." *Neva*, no. 3 (1977): 159–66.

Voznesenskaia, Iuliia. *Zhenskii dekameron*. Tel-Aviv: Zerkalo, 1987.

———. *Zvezda Chernobyl'*. New York: Liberty, 1987.

Wolffheim, Elsbeth. "Das Frauenbild bei Viktorija Tokareva." In *Frauenbilder und Weiblichkeitsentwürfe in der russischen Frauenprosa: Materialen des wissenschaftlichen Symposiums in Erfurt*, ed. Christina Parnell, 171–82. Frankfurt: Peter Lang, 1996.

Woll, Josephine. "The Minotaur in the Maze: On Lyudmila Petrushevskaya." *World Literature Today* 67, no. 1 (1993): 125–30.

———. *Real Images: Soviet Cinema and the Thaw*. London: I. B. Tauris, 2000.

Woolf, Virginia. *A Room of One's Own*. San Diego, Calif.: Harcourt Brace Jovanovich, 1989.

Zalygin, Sergei. "Trifonov, Shukshin, i my." *Novyi mir*, no. 11 (1991): 221–30.

Žekulin, Nicholas. "Soviet Russian Women's Literature in the Early 1980s." In *Fruits of Her Plume: Essays on Contemporary Russian Women's Culture*, ed. Helena Goscilo, 33–58. Armonk, N.Y.: M. E. Sharpe, 1993.

Zhenskoe chtenie, no. 1 (1988).

Zhukhovitskii, L. "Neudachlivost'? Net—chelovechnost'." *Znamia*, no. 1 (1980): 245–46.

Zolotonosov, Mikhail. "Damskoe schast'e." *Moskovskie novosti*, January 21, 2003.

———. "'Kakotopiia': Zhanr antiutopii v sovremennoi literature."
Oktiabr', no. 7 (1990): 192–98.
———. "Mechty i fantomy." *Literaturnoe obozrenie*, no. 4 (1987): 58–61.
Zorin, Andrei. "Kruche, kruche, kruche . . . Istoriia pobedy: chernukha
v kul'ture poslednikh let." *Znamia*, no. 10 (1992): 198–204.

Index